John Benedetti

I FEEL A SONG COMING ON

MUSIC IN AMERICAN LIFE

*A list of books in the series
appears at the end of this book.*

I Feel a Song Coming On

ALYN SHIPTON

UNIVERSITY OF ILLINOIS PRESS

URBANA AND CHICAGO

THE LIFE OF

Jimmy McHugh

Library of Congress Cataloging-in-Publication Data
Shipton, Alyn.
I feel a song coming on : the life of Jimmy McHugh / Alyn Shipton.
p.   cm. — (Music in American life)
Includes bibliographical references and index.
ISBN 978-0-252-03465-7 (cloth : alk. paper)
1. McHugh, Jimmy, 1894–1969.
2. Composers—United States—Biography.
I. Title.
ML410.M4526S45   2008
782.42164092—dc22   2008047677

To John Chilton,
for his inspirational example as
a biographical researcher, and for all
his support, encouragement, and help
with this book and its predecessors.

Contents

Illustrations

ALL PHOTOGRAPHS, INCLUDING THE COVER ILLUSTRATION,
ARE REPRODUCED BY KIND PERMISSION OF
THE McHUGH FAMILY ARCHIVE.

P*reface*

IT ALL BEGAN WHEN my BBC colleague Russell Davies came down with a bad case of summer flu in July 2003. I got a panic call from his production team, Malcolm Prince and Lou Foley, asking me if I could come into London at short notice to interview somebody called Jimmy McHugh, who was visiting from Los Angeles, and who had been booked to appear on Russell's forthcoming show.

"Surely not the songwriter?" I asked, being somewhat hazy about McHugh's dates and certainly not realizing that it would actually have been the exact day of his 110th birthday. Reassured that it was his grandson, I threw a handful of CDs of various McHugh songs into the car and set off for Broadcasting House.

The interview went extremely well, and after the microphones were turned off, I found myself still talking to Jimmy McHugh III several hours later, sharing a delight in bringing alive a world that took in the Cotton Club, early Hollywood musicals, Broadway shows, and the creation of a repertoire that I knew and loved. Before long, the idea had coalesced in our minds that there ought to be a full-scale biography of this most fascinating of songwriters, and that somehow or other, I was the one to write it. This was despite the fact that

I was still working with George Shearing on finishing his autobiography, as well as writing the life of my fellow critic and jazz musician Ian Carr, whose delicate state of health made it important to finish that book briskly as well.

Soon Jim had coaxed me out to Los Angeles to see for myself the formidable archive that the McHughs had preserved, and before long, with his help and that of Lee Newman, Guy Thomas, and Julie Pavlowski, we had set up a means of digitizing key documents so that I could work on them back in Europe. In several visits to the archive, I managed to read a vast amount of material, and I have constantly found myself silently thanking McHugh himself for squirreling away so many documents. I also owe thanks to his longtime colleague the late Lucille Meyers, who did so much to organize the various papers and clippings into some kind of logical sequence of scrapbooks, albums, and files.

Biographers usually fall in or out of love with their subject as their books progress. In the case of McHugh, I have found the diversity of his life, his breadth of interests, and his achievements in so many fields from ragtime to rock and roll, from the Broadway stage to Hollywood, from aeronautics to competitive swimming, and from Harlem to Paris and London, truly fascinating. Moreover, because he grew and changed as a person, and the focus of his interests altered over time, although he may have denied us more musical hits or indeed a full-length book musical of lasting reputation, his continued achievements in every stage of his life were remarkable. I'm not sure that face to face I could have long kept up with his energy and tireless self-promotion, but I certainly found him as absorbing a character at the end of the process as I did at the beginning, for his life was truly a one-man history of twentieth-century popular music.

Alyn Shipton
OXFORD, UNITED KINGDOM
JANUARY 2009

Acknowledgments

FIRST AND FOREMOST my thanks go to Jim McHugh III for getting this project started and to Lee Newman for being such a helpful and selfless guide both to Los Angeles and to the McHugh family and its archives. I am also grateful to Guy Thomas and Julie Pavlowski for enthusiastic support and for tracking down source material and key individuals. Mark Rowles also helped to get the ball rolling on the British side of the Atlantic.

Annie Consoletti, Erik Arnesen, Izabela Berengut, and Goody B. Wiseman also helped in the preparation of sample material, images, and web information. My good friend the tireless researcher and biographer John Chilton supplied numerous press clippings in addition to those in the McHugh archive; Iain Cameron Williams and Stephen Bourne pointed me in the right direction regarding Adelaide Hall (and in Stephen's case, Ethel Waters as well); and James Lincoln Collier shared some of his Ellington research, while Danny Kennally, Brian Priestley, and Stephen Lasker assisted greatly on Cotton Club matters.

I have talked to many people who knew McHugh and his work and who have given generously in terms of both time and information. In addition to those mentioned above, they are: Anna Maria Alberghetti, Ed Ames, Army

Archerd, Jim Bacon, Buddy Bregman, Dorothy Brooks, Adele Carter, Michael Feinstein, Eddie Kafafian, Judy Kashalena, Judy McHugh, Debbie Reynolds, Mamie Van Doren, and Zeke Zarchy.

For assistance in navigating the minefield of song and lyric copyrights, thanks are due to Audrey Ashby and Linda Santiago at EMI Music Publishing, to Sam Fein at the Songwriters Guild of America, to Colleen McDonough, director of the ASCAP Foundation, to Fred Dinkins at Alfred Publishing Co. Inc., and to Jonathan Belott at the Hal Leonard Corporation.

Finally, I would like to thank those who have offered detailed comments on the manuscript as it has progressed, in particular the late Sheldon Meyer, a good friend and the doyen of editors on American music; Philip Furia; Thomas J. Riis; and my wife, Siobhan Fraser. At the University of Illinois Press, thanks are due to Judith McCulloh, Laurie Matheson, and Breanne Ertmer. I should also extend grateful thanks to Beth Gianfagna and to Barbara Hames, whose eagle-eyed attention to detail has greatly improved the book.

I FEEL A SONG COMING ON

"Home before Dark"

ON NOVEMBER 8, 1909, the curtain went up for the first time at the Boston Opera House on Huntington Avenue. Almost three thousand patrons were in the audience for Ponchielli's *La Gioconda*, in what was then the newest, brightest, state-of-the-art opera house in the United States.[1] Champagne glasses clinked, giant chandeliers twinkled, and the gilded names of the great composers shone brightly from a richly decorated proscenium arch. With its three tall Corinthian columns rising high into a classical portico that towered above the street, statues of sphinx-like figures guarding the foot of each column, and entrance lobbies leading from the sidewalk through an enormous rusticated arcade, the building planned by local entrepreneur Eben Jordan was a true temple of the arts. Its construction on a lot near Symphony Hall and the New England Conservatory of Music had been watched with passing interest by most Bostonians but with more than usual curiosity by one sixteen-year-old Irish-American boy.

As the huge classical structure emerged from shrouds of scaffolding and protective sheeting, its bas-relief terracotta panels signifying its artistic importance, James Francis McHugh vowed that once it was opened, he would work there.

On the face of it, he did not stand much of a chance. He was one of thousands of young Boston Irishmen looking for work, and he was no better qualified than any of them to look outside their usual *métier* of hard manual labor. His only previous connection with the theatrical world was his father, the plumbing maintenance engineer at another of Boston's biggest theaters, the Metropolitan, and apart from having been taught by his mother to play the piano extremely well, the boy had no special musical knowledge. He had received a conventional high school education at St. John's Preparatory School in Danvers, but his only qualifications for work were weekends and vacations spent as plumber's mate to his father and a few days selling aeronautical thrills at Squantum Aerodrome during America's first competitive air meet.

Yet, remarkably, the English director of the opera, Henry Russell, did hire the aspiring teenager within a year of that first curtain up. In due course, the daily routine of constant contact with the greatest names of the classical music world, the sound of operatic masterpieces echoing from the building's fifty rehearsal rooms, and a tough apprenticeship in the publicity department gave the young McHugh the sense of direction and purpose that was to guide his life.

To be sure, when he left the opera company, McHugh abandoned the classical world for good, turning down a place at the next-door conservatory in order to ply his trade as a song plugger—demonstrating and selling the latest popular hits—for Irving Berlin. But three seasons at the Boston Opera House taught him from the very outset of his career that hand in hand with musical success went the relentless job of marketing, of creating an event out of nothing, of making a triumph out of failure or indifference, and of putting a positive spin on every scrap of news, no matter how minor. These were to be the principles that guided one of the most fascinating lives in American music. As McHugh went on to become one of the best-selling and most popular songwriters in musical history, he made sure that he never lost an opportunity to talk up the importance of his own place in that history.

Jimmy McHugh had been born on July 10, 1893, at 64 School Street in Boston's Jamaica Plain neighborhood. This was where he spent most of his childhood, until the family moved a short distance away to 49 Bournedale Street. His parents were James A. McHugh, an Irish-born plumber, listed on the boy's birth certificate as a "foreman," and Julia McHugh, *née* Collins, whose family had lived for years among a tight-knit network of friends and relations in the Irish heartland of Boston's South End, although she had actually been born in Lynn, Massachusetts.

Jimmy was the eldest of five children who arrived over a ten-year span, and he grew up in a household where there was never quite enough money to go around. Since he was the eldest child, items were sometimes bought new for him, but once he outgrew them, everything from shoes to sweaters was passed down in turn to each of his sisters and brothers, who, in order of arrival, were May, Tommy, Helen, and Larry.

The family living room of their Victorian house, with its pot-bellied stove, was where the rough, tough Irish workingmen's world of his father met the more genteel, middle-class background of his mother. On winter evenings, McHugh senior would sit in the warmth, his shirt open at the neck, practicing boxing with his sons. As they traded blows, he frequently knocked one or another of them out cold. "As we came round," remembered Jimmy, "we found ourselves staring into father's disapproving face. 'You want to watch that,' he would say. 'Don't be a sucker for a right upper cut.'"[2] By contrast, Julie's big Chickering piano dominated the remainder of the room, below a picture of those prim and proper early American settlers, the *Mayflower* Pilgrims John Alden and Priscilla Mullins.

In the young McHugh, these contradictory elements collided. He had his mother's love for and skill at the piano, and although he was no plumber, he had his father's pugnacious determination. He also had a strong sense of his European roots, and—although he was an Irish Roman Catholic rather than a dissenting pilgrim—he shared the staunch Christian values that had arrived on the *Mayflower* and which were deeply entrenched in the New England in which he grew up.

Moreover, from his early childhood, he showed the relentless energy that characterized his entire life. He would help his mother look after his younger siblings, lining them up and dressing them for school; but even before that he would have risen at five, collected hot rolls from the nearby bakery, and delivered them to his uncle Tom Collins, who ran a bar. On his return journey home, he did a paper round, and before dressing his brothers and sisters, he swept the floors while his mother baked bread, sewed missing buttons back on, or turned torn collars. After school, he collected firewood for the stove before practicing the piano and helping to organize the family's musical evenings. "I was," he was to reflect in later life, "always a hustler."[3]

When the family let their hair down to enjoy a musical evening—Jimmy pounding the piano, Tommy blowing a bugle, Larry thumping out rhythms on the windowsill (and later on his first precious set of drums), with their father thrumming a Jew's harp—it seemed only natural to sell tickets to their friends. Jimmy recalled: "With this frightening ensemble, we executed jazzed-up versions of 'In the Gloaming,' 'When Irish Eyes Are Smiling,' and other tender Irish ballads. Neighborhood children were permitted to witness the performance for 25¢ admission. A reasonable enough price, I figured, since I was the star of the show."[4]

Yet these evenings were an exception in McHugh senior's otherwise implacable opposition to the idea that music could be anything other than a hobby. He shared the neighbors' objections to Tommy's habit of practicing bugle calls on the back porch in the evening. Only an elderly Civil War veteran living a few doors away approved, as the military calls became his signal to haul down the Union flag fluttering above his house. The elder McHugh also let it be known that in his view any man who did not have a trade was undoubtedly going to be a bum, and he emphatically did not consider that playing the piano constituted a trade.

His wife, on the other hand, who was a well-trained musician, spotted something in her eldest son's playing that stood out as unusual. He had an exceptional ear, she recalled, and the beginnings of the ability to improvise his own music: "He used to sit for hours when he was small in a chair near the piano, and he loved to hear me play. Then one day, when I had finished a piece, and had to run to the oven, he tried to play it himself. The first thing I taught him was the scale, and from there he learned fast. He sometimes invented little sonnets—cute some of them were."[5] Consequently, Mrs. McHugh devoted herself to teaching Jimmy to play as well as possible. She soon realized that almost from the outset, rather than reading the music that was put in front of him, he would instead perform exactly what he had heard her play. His ear picked up everything, and he could immediately reproduce it. As this was also the period when ragtime was in vogue, more than a little of Scott Joplin, James Scott, and Joseph Lamb, not to mention their Tin Pan Alley cousins Charles K. Harris and Harry Von Tilzer, crept into his playing. McHugh himself wrote:

> She taught me all she knew. Her dream of me as a future concert virtuoso was strained to breaking point when she would catch me playing the classics with a syncopated beat. She engaged for me a teacher by the name of Professor Kuntz.
>
> He was a portly gentleman with a high choleric content and a low boiling point. He had no hair on the top of his head and a fringe of grey fuzz sticking

out at the sides. His costume, reflecting the dignity of his calling, featured a frock coat and a wing collar. He always bustled in the door with his music case under his arm, and the expression on his face of a surprised screech owl. Our sessions began calmly. Professor Kuntz would sit down at the piano and play a composition through. Then I would sit down and play it back to him by ear. This had the effect on Professor Kuntz that a rubber hose has on hardened criminals. He became a broken man.

"Play it from the notes!" he would cry.

"Why should I play it from the notes when I know it already?" Professor Kuntz and I soon went our separate ways.[6]

The Professor was apparently even more appalled by young Jimmy's insertion of an element of syncopation into the classics than by his free and easy interpretation of the notes, but Mrs. McHugh was charmed. She actively encouraged her son to make up his own material and gently steered him away from borrowing other themes. "She rapped his knuckles when the melodies he improvised reminded her of Verdi or Puccini," ran one profile of the mother-and-son team, "and gave him a nickel if his tunes sounded original to her."[7] She often advised him on the tunes he wrote in later life, and she had an unerring ear for the hit lurking amid a pile of new ideas. It was his mother, McHugh later recalled, who persuaded him to keep working on "I'm In the Mood for Love" when he was tempted to abandon it in the mid-1930s. "That was one I had been drumming at for a long time. Mother liked it the first time I played it for her. But I put it aside. She kept asking for it. She kept after me till I got it out and finally sold it."[8]

His mother's policy of keeping after him to develop what she knew to be his rare and unusual talent was to become a vital ingredient in McHugh's decision to make his career in music, despite his father's strong disapproval. Recognizing that her eldest son was an inveterate hustler, Mrs. McHugh also instinctively knew that to reward him for his best efforts with a nickel would leave the indelible imprint in his mind that a good original tune equated to a financial reward.

With the exception of Julia McHugh's interest in music, and the way she carefully fostered her eldest son's talent, the household was like any other large Boston Irish Catholic family. The high point of the week was Sunday, when the family members began the day soon after dawn by donning their best bib and tucker for eight o'clock Mass. There would be a frantic rush for the bathroom, and only the implacable Larry, the youngest son, who later (and not altogether unsurprisingly) became a lawyer, worked out the way to defeat his father's ever more urgent calls of "How long are you going to be in there?" by taking an alarm clock in with him and setting it to exactly five minutes.

Mass was celebrated in a former car barn in Roxbury that had been converted into a church. McHugh remembered it as "a somewhat old-fashioned affair, with pews, a small altar, and a small organ, which I somehow or other found myself pumping for the services. The priest would say mass, and so on. Later I remember he contracted pneumonia and died suddenly. Being a religious type of youngster, I also remember playing ball outside. Naturally many a window was broken!"[9]

In the long, hot, New England summer days, once Mass was over, there was plenty of time for enjoyment and family fun. The greatest treat of all was when, from time to time, the McHughs would take the steamboat to Nantasket Beach, the long gently curving peninsula on the southern side of the harbor. Only richer folk traveled there by horse-drawn buggy through the suburbs of Quincy and Hull—the masses took the boat from downtown Boston to the three miles of sandy beach, with its jutting breakwaters and amusements for all the family. Even today, Hull has a flavor of that vanished past, with its carousel under the clock and the stalls selling old-fashioned sweets and other refreshments.

When they got to Nantasket, the seven McHughs were the epitome of the Victorian working family by the sea. The children capered about their father, who removed his jacket and sat on the sands, sweating profusely beneath a derby hat that remained jammed tightly on his head. His suspenders betrayed their origins by the word "Police" stenciled on them, but every other item of clothing—shoes, pants, shirt—carried the stamp of the fledgling trade union to which he proudly belonged.

In the heat of the day, Julia McHugh wore a full black silk dress with a formfitting bodice, although her severe aspect was somewhat compromised when her children discovered her sticking missing sequins back on the dress with chewing gum. Jimmy and Tommy had hair parted in the center and Buster Brown collars, and May and Helen wore cotton dresses with sashes, long black stockings, and button shoes, while young Larry was distinguished by his halo of golden curls.

McHugh remembered his family coming home on the last boat of the day, happy, worn out, and red as lobsters, with one exception: "Father's face was as red as ours, but the top of his head, sheltered by the powerful derby, always remained as white as a number one billiard ball."[10] On other Sundays, when the family remained at home, there would be visits from Tom Collins, the bar-owning uncle, on his day off. He would shout fearsomely "Where the hell's the coffee?" and then, suitably refreshed, would regale the family with tales from his bar, which stood at the corner of Northampton and Washington Streets.

This area of the South End was densely populated with Irish immigrants, the majority of them first- or second-generation Bostonians among whom Tom Collins was a striking and well-known figure. His hair had turned gray early, and he sported a snowy white crew cut. Like many a barman who spends long hours standing, he had bad feet, and the McHugh family's main memory of him was that after he had turned up on their doorstep armed with a box of chocolates for Julia, he would shout for coffee, tuck in to a huge Sunday lunch during which he recounted his latest stories, and then subside into the most comfortable armchair in the parlor to rest his aching feet. The boys took it in turns to remove his lighted cigar from his senseless hand, once he had dropped into the inevitable deep sleep that followed a hearty meal.

His bar was a gathering point for notable members of the local Irish-American community, both those who had already made their reputations, like the former world champion boxer, John L. Sullivan, and those who had yet to set foot on the larger stage, such as the cheeky young grocery delivery boys John and Jimmy Curley, the latter of whom was to become a congressman and mayor of Boston, James Michael Curley. From the age of seven or so, Jimmy McHugh saw all these characters for himself at his uncle's bar, because in addition to dropping off the morning bread, he often ran errands for Collins.

Sullivan's career in the ring and his decade as world titleholder had ended when he was knocked out after an epic twenty-one-round battle by Jim Corbett the year before McHugh was born, but he remained a celebrated personality. By the turn of the century, when young Jimmy first saw him, he was in his early forties but remained a huge and impressive figure, dominating the barroom. One journalist who was sent to interview Sullivan in those twilight years of his career described him as looking like "an unusually big Irish policeman, off duty in plain clothes. . . . He weighed, I should judge, well over 200 pounds, but having seen him walk across the room on the balls of his feet with all the lightness and gracefulness of a cat, I had trouble in convincing myself that even this was true."[11]

Speaking in a light brogue, with a fine head of dark hair just beginning to fleck with gray, a heavy mustache, a jutting jaw, and the flushed cheeks of a hardened drinker, Sullivan cut a memorable figure. McHugh's main memory of him was that the calm, peaceable man who entered the bar each evening could be a Jekyll and Hyde character: "When drunk he became the neighborhood strong boy. He would pound fiercely on the bar with his fist and roar, 'I can lick any sonofabitch in the world!'"[12]

Others who knew Sullivan remembered him regaling them with long lectures on the evils of drink. "Whiskey! There's the only fighter that ever really licked old John L.," he would begin. When ill health finally forced him to forsake his bibulous habits, he swore to use the years that remained to him to persuade young would-be sportsmen to abjure hard liquor.[13] Certainly contact with this colorful, larger-than-life figure—not to mention the living-room sparring with his father—left its mark on McHugh. He became, and remained throughout his life, an avid boxing fan. In the mid-1920s in New York, he was to spend a fortune on ringside seats at Yankee Stadium, Madison Square Garden, the Sesquicentennial Stadium, and the Polo Grounds, to watch all the great fights of the age: Greb versus Flowers, Dempsey versus Tunney, Delaney versus Risko, Dundee versus Zivic, Stribling versus Slattery, Kaplan versus Herman, McTigue versus Berlenbach, and a host more.[14] At a time when a three-course meal could be had for a few cents, McHugh was paying up to $27 for the best seats in the house, avidly following the passion ignited in him by the legendary figure of Sullivan.

The Curley boys inspired a different but no less absorbing enthusiasm in McHugh: his love of politics, particularly Irish-American politics. In later years he was to become an intimate of the Kennedy clan and a regular correspondent with several United States presidents, but it all began with his fascination for the oratorical skills of James Michael Curley.

By the time McHugh was seven years old, Curley was still employed by Logan, Johnstone and Company, the grocery business almost next door to Tom Collins's bar, but he had already launched his first assault on local politics, being elected to the Boston Common Council in 1900. He followed this success by winning seats in the Massachusetts House of Representatives, the Board of Aldermen, and Boston City Council. To McHugh he became an object of admiration—not least for the more outrageous aspects of his life, which won him the local nickname "the Rascal King." McHugh remembered:

> James Michael was so brilliant a personality, and so powerful an orator, that at the age of nineteen he won an election as alderman while doing a stretch in jail. He had run afoul of the law by passing an examination as a letter carrier for an illiterate friend. On the day of his release, he was met by a brass band, and a throng of loyal citizens escorted him in triumph to assume his duties as a public servant.

Some time later, James again felt the arm of the law when he was convicted of bribery, and served another term in the bastille. But these lapses, which would have annihilated the career of an ordinary man, seemed only to enhance his charm for the populace. He was Mayor of Boston for many years and eventually became Governor of Massachusetts.[15]

Although McHugh's grasp of the ins and outs of Curley's career in this account is a little tenuous, there was nevertheless a good degree of reciprocal admiration between the Curleys and the Collins clan, McHugh's mother's family. When Tom the barkeeper eventually died, well into his seventies, the only nonfamily mourners at his funeral were John and James Michael Curley.

In the first decade of the twentieth century, however, McHugh's interest in politics was still largely in the future. A more pressing problem loomed as the years rolled on, because as soon as Jimmy left high school, his father had plans to take him on as his apprentice. Although Jimmy was later to joke that he learned plumbing at an early age and could still fix a blocked toilet, the idea of lugging lengths of pipe around all day, soldering or welding joints, and crawling into tiny spaces to deal with recalcitrant fixtures and fittings was not his idea of a future. In desperation at his son's lack of application to the family trade, McHugh senior gave him the job of stock boy, delivering supplies from the stores to a team of plumbers. During the late summer of 1910, seventeen-year-old Jimmy dropped a length of iron pipe on his foot for the umpteenth time and walked out on his father.

He briefly walked out on his family, too, having decided to investigate a very new form of leisure pursuit. He had seen a newspaper advertisement for America's first ever competitive air meet, which was being hosted by the Harvard Aeronautical Society. The club had booked Squantum Aerodrome, an area of level if swampy ground on the edge of the tidal mudflats near Boston, from September 3 to 13 and had managed to get sponsors for some extremely large cash prizes to be awarded for various feats, such as flying at high speed in a figure of eight, covering a fixed distance, and team flying. As a result, almost all the big names in pioneer American aviation were there, and crowds of people flocked to the airfield. Indeed, there were over sixty-seven thousand paid admissions, plus hundreds of souvenir vendors, attendants, and hangers-on, which netted the organizers well over $120,000 to spend on prizes and guarantees in addition to the sponsored events.

All around Boston, there was soon plenty of excitement about the meet, because by the end of the event, the aviators Johnstone and Brookins of the American Wright Fliers team had amassed winnings of $39,250, English pilot Claude Graham-White was close behind with individual earnings of $26,900, and the Curtiss Fliers carried off a third prize of $16,500. Several European star pilots and their machines appeared, with Graham-White flying the French Farman biplane he was to land in style a few days later behind the White House and British inventor A. V. Roe demonstrating his revolutionary triplane.[16]

By today's standards this meet was a leisurely affair. Flimsy aircraft made of canvas, wood, and string staggered into the sky at what would in just a few years be regarded as very low speeds. Nor were the distances they flew anything special compared to the standards of aviation during the Great War, which followed soon after. Brookins's cross-country distance record, established a few days following the meet, was 86.5 miles, the furthest anyone in the world had flown nonstop at that time. McHugh remembered: "Tiny planes were lined up on the field like frail butterflies strung with many wires. The aviators resembled ancestors of today's comic book men from outer space in their heavy goggles, helmets and windbreaking overalls. All of the planes were open. A belt strapped the pilot into his seat, leaving his legs dangling down smartly. When one of the craft took the air, no one knew for certain if it would come down in one piece."[17]

McHugh arrived at Squantum with no clear plan. He just knew that there had to be something happening at the aerodrome that offered a young man better prospects than plumbing. And sure enough, with what would become his lifelong knack of being in the right place at the right time, almost the first person he ran into was a young Harvard student named Angie Connors.

> "Do you want to help me?" he said.
> "What do you want me to do?"
> "Come on and help me lift this thing out, it's stuck in the water."
> The tide was in and there was his "Red Devil" biplane. It was the old-fashioned kind with the motor in the back, and two seats in the front. "We're going to move it when the tide is out," he said. So we dropped off to sleep in a couple of hammocks and when we woke up the tide had gone out.
> "Let's move the thing out of here, and get it on firm ground," I said. Then I suggested to my friend that he charge 25 cents for members of the public to view the plane. "We'll put up a sign, and pick up some money." Which we did. We picked up quite a lot of money because this was one of the first ever aviation meets.[18]

In between hustling up a little loose change, McHugh and Connors went for a number of short, drafty rides in the little biplane. The sight of the "Red Devil" in the air attracted more crowds when they came back to earth. "Every time we settled down for a safe landing, I became more fearless and air-minded," wrote McHugh.[19]

In most of the accounts of this meet which he related in later life, McHugh said that it was the experience of witnessing a fatal accident soon after his final landing with Connors that put him off aviation for good and turned his mind back to a career in music. The event he would then describe in some detail concerned the harrowing deaths of the pioneer female aviator Harriet Quimby and the organizer of the meet, William Willard.

However, there is just one problem with this story. Quimby's accident happened not at the inaugural meet but at the third annual event in Squantum in 1912, by which time McHugh had already been working at the Opera House for two seasons. There is no reason why, along with many Bostonians, he might not have gone to this subsequent event and had the unfortunate experience of seeing what turned out to be a horrendous accident, but it was not Quimby's misfortune that changed his career.

Born in 1875, Harriet Quimby had been a successful journalist on *Leslie's Magazine*, for which she covered a motor racing event in 1906. This triggered her interest in fast and dangerous machinery, and she immediately learned to drive an automobile. As well as driving her own car at a time when few women had the independence of means and spirit to do so, she then enrolled in flying lessons, eventually qualifying as America's first female pilot in August 1911 at the Moisant School on Long Island. She continued to work as a photojournalist and writer for silent movies until she qualified as a pilot, but as soon as she had her license, Quimby became a full-time flier with the Moisant exhibition team.

By the time she arrived at Squantum, she had become the first woman to fly solo across the English Channel and was a celebrity. Her fee for appearing at the Boston Air Meet was rumored to be $100,000. Even if he did not leave the backstage depths of the Opera House in the summer of 1912 to join the huge crowds that turned out for her, McHugh was undoubtedly aware of her presence.

Surrounded by her adoring public, and wearing her self-designed purple satin flying suit with its unorthodox hood swept back to reveal her striking good looks (which have graced the 50¢ U.S. airmail stamp since 1991), Quimby tossed a coin high in the air to determine whether Willard or his son would accompany her into the sky in her new Bleriot two-seat monoplane. Ominously, in hindsight, this model was already proving to be somewhat unstable and unpredictable in Europe, but it was in one of these machines that she had made her successful cross-channel flight, using sandbags in the passenger seat to balance the little aircraft, so she remained loyal to Bleriot's design.

William Willard called correctly and beat his son to the spare seat in the plane at Squantum. Suggesting to the crowd that he needed a contingency plan in the unfortunate event a mishap might occur, he laughingly handed over control of the meet to Earle Ovington, another celebrity flier who had recently established the first airmail service in the United States. Then the unlikely pair—the slender Quimby and the overweight Willard—made their way to the tiny plane and took off.

Exactly what happened next is a mystery. Ovington claimed the airplane's control wires became entangled. Other observers believe the heavily built Willard leaned across to shout some comment or instruction at the pilot but lost his balance as he did so. Scrabbling to hold his seat, and causing the fragile machine to yaw violently in the air, Willard was ejected from the aircraft. Quimby fought to regain balance and control but was in turn thrown from the plane. Both occupants plunged fifteen hundred feet to their deaths over Dorchester Bay.

The plane, regaining its trim, glided serenely on until it landed, damaged but intact, on the nearby mudflats. Thousands of spectators lining the shoreline out toward the Boston Harbor lighthouse where the plane was to have turned to make its return flight witnessed the entire tragedy unfolding before their eyes.[20]

For one of the very few times in his life, McHugh was not in the right place for such an historic event to have had a direct influence on his career, but by the 1960s, when he looked back on his younger days, he was conveniently able to telescope history and intertwine his accounts of those two long-ago flying meets. Using all his Irish charm as a storyteller, he absorbed Quimby's tragic death into the McHugh legend, when he said: "One day as we stood at the edge of the field watching a small biplane [sic] come in for a landing, it crashed before our eyes, killing its two occupants. . . . The tragedy had a sobering effect on me. For a few days the thrills of aviation had provided escape from my own confusion, from mother's disappointment, and from father's disapproval of me as a piano-playing bum. But it had not provided a solution. I was no aviator. I wanted to play the piano."[21]

At the end of the 1910 meet, McHugh returned home and was enthusiastically greeted by his mother, who made him promise to give up flying and find a job. For a few weeks, his efforts consisted of sitting round the house, playing the piano, until he remembered the building on Huntington Avenue where he had dreamed of working before his apprenticeship to his father had begun. By this time, mid-September 1910, the Opera House had been open for ten months. McHugh remembered: "Boston hailed [it] as a step forward in the city's culture, but to me it was to become a glittering kindergarten where I learned the inside workings that make great careers tick. I came to understand the incredible amount of work and worry and emotional strain involved in staying on top."[22] With a mixture of sheer audacity and his gift of gab, McHugh simply talked his way into a job there.

He walked in through the rear door, climbed six flights of stairs to the administrative offices, and found himself face to face with Henry Russell, the impresario who ran the company and who had also managed Covent Garden Opera House in London a few years earlier.

> Mr. Russell was an elegant man with dark, kinky hair. He spoke with a soft English accent as he looked at me across his desk.
> "What do you want?"
> "I want to work in this building."
> Mr. Russell stared at me with mild amusement. "What can you do?"
> "I can't do anything," I said.
> "But this is an opera house. You can't do just anything here."
> I didn't answer. Mr. Russell studied me again.
> "Go home," he finally said. "If something turns up I'll let you know. What's your phone number?"
> "We haven't got a phone."
> "Your address, then."[23]

According to this account by McHugh, he immediately went home and told his mother what had happened, before going to the local church and saying some prayers. When he got back from his devotions, there was a telegram from Russell, offering him a job at the princely salary of $8 per week.

He started in the fall of 1910 as an office boy, taking messages and running errands for Russell, both during the annual fifteen-week season when a regular company presented grand opera every night, at seat prices ranging from 75¢ to $3, and during the remaining weeks of the year, when the world's great stars were presented in weekend recitals, new productions were being prepared, or a skeleton company went out on tour. McHugh literally jotted down messages on the starched cuffs of his shirt, the widespread practice of the time that gave rise to the expression "off the cuff," and he also came into daily contact with the greatest singers of the age, among them Enrico

Caruso, Amelita Galli-Curci, Nellie Melba, and Luisa Tetrazzini. Most of them were happy to give the young office boy signed pictures of themselves, and a growing collection of these was proudly hung at the McHugh family home, although Larry and Tommy's copious sporting awards threatened to overrun them as time went on.

Even before he was out of his teens, McHugh knew the value of personal contact with the stars and understood that autographed pictures, signed menus, and other ephemera linking his name with theirs were all to be treasured and hoarded. The extraordinary archive of memorabilia that he amassed during his lifetime had its origins in the earliest weeks of his first proper job.

McHugh's personal memories of the stars as they flitted in and out of the Opera House included Caruso's yellow kid gloves and dashing fedora, the petite figure of Galli-Curci, whose high birdlike voice could fill the huge auditorium, and the powerful, more thickset Tetrazzini, who was her rival for many principal roles. The Irish-born lyric tenor John McCormack was remembered mostly for his fur-trimmed lapels, Geraldine Farrar for her consistent elegance, and the tough-minded Scottish-born soprano Mary Garden—who sang in Boston during periods away from her home base in Chicago—for the way she shared executive power with Russell whenever she appeared, "bossing the show and acting out her singing roles," as McHugh put it.[24]

In the course of his work, he heard at first hand a complete cross section of the operatic repertoire of the age, from Mozart and Haydn to Verdi and Mascagni. Given McHugh's remarkable musical memory, their melodies, arias, and choruses were to stay embedded in his mind. So, too, would the visual impact of the shows. Boston productions, in keeping with the hundreds of thousands of dollars Eben D. Jordan had spent building his magnificent theater, were truly in the grand opera tradition, with a huge chorus and extras galore. In March 1911, McHugh himself was called in to ride a horse on stage in the first Boston performance of Puccini's American masterpiece *La Fanciulla del West*, which had received its world premiere at the Metropolitan Opera House in New York only ten weeks earlier. It was a glittering all-star event, although for the Boston production Amadeo Bassi sang the role of Ramirez, the bandit, that had been created in New York by Caruso.[25]

Although McHugh remembered the opera stars for their stirring performances, their on- and off-stage elegance, and their individual mannerisms, they remembered him for a quite different reason. Whenever he had a gap in his routine of running errands, he could be found sitting at one of the fifty or so pianos that were scattered around the building, in rehearsal rooms, green rooms, dressing rooms, and even restrooms. There he would be playing either the latest popular song or, more frequently, melodies from the previous night's opera, spiced up with a ragtimey syncopated beat.

"The opera singers themselves took a furtive delight in my playful assaults upon their masterpieces," McHugh recalled.[26] However, it seemed to him unlikely that Henry Russell would take a similar view, so he did his best to indulge in his rounds of the practice room pianos when Russell was likely to be safely out of earshot. Yet, as news of his talent for playing the classics with a spot of syncopation soon spread among the cast, it was only a matter of time before he was found out by his boss.

It finally happened when Mary Garden called McHugh into her dressing room as he was running past with a message for Russell. She was about to sing in a performance of Massenet's *Thaïs*.

> I found Miss Garden resplendent in a blonde wig and the flowing white Grecian gown of the opera's tragic heroine. . . . A few distinguished citizens had come to her dressing room to pay their respects. Dignity hung in the air. It shattered like a glass before a shotgun blast with my hopped-up rendition of *Aida*. At the height of festivities, I glanced up and saw Mr. Russell standing in the doorway. He had come to find out what had befallen his errant message boy and had traced the sound of revelry to its source. "Come to my office tomorrow," he said. And walked away.[27]

It always mystified McHugh that he was not fired on the spot. Instead, when he turned up for his interview with Russell the next morning, he found himself transferred to the opera's publicity department. In retrospect, it was the best thing that could have happened to him, and the marketing imperative he learned there was to remain with him all his life.

So why did Russell take his side?

The most probable reason is that—albeit unknown to McHugh—Russell's father had been a leading popular song composer, and the impresario immediately recognized in McHugh something of his own father's talent and interests. Also called Henry Russell, the older man had journeyed from England to America in 1833, and in the next eight years, before his return home, he composed some of the most enduring songs of the age. After making his New York debut as a singer in 1836, he toured constantly from coast to coast, singing his pieces to his own accompaniment. Russell wound up each show by performing his most famous hits, including "Woodman! Spare That Tree!" and "A Life on the Ocean Wave." His other best-known songs included "The Indian Hunter" and "The Old Spinning Wheel." Although Henry Russell Jr. and his brother, the conductor Sir Landon Ronald, both pursued classical careers, their family fortunes were largely founded on their father's American popular songs.

The immediate effect of Russell's decision to move McHugh to a new department was that the boy found a mentor, the Hungarian marketing manager Theodore H. Bauer.

A tense, restless man who was always planning the next publicity coup, Bauer's formidable talents inspired McHugh's lifelong admiration. The first of his masterstrokes came at around the time McHugh joined the department, when attendance had begun to flag. When it seemed that things could get no worse, John McCormack (whose wife and children had remained in New York) was discovered in an intimate situation with a woman in his dressing room. This was widely reported in the newspapers. She sued him, and the resulting headlines ensured sellout houses for the remainder of his run. Bauer never admitted his part in this episode, but McHugh and all the other press agents widely believed that it was their diminutive boss who had tipped off the press.

Soon after his arrival in the publicity office, McHugh struck up a friendship with a young Scot named Alan Cahill, and the two of them became inseparable. McHugh remembered: "Alan came down with such an acute case of the Bauer spirit, that he had cards printed for himself with the words 'Promoter of Enthusiasm' under his name. In Alan's hands, enthusiasm became a tangible commodity to be sold the way a medicine man sells snake oil."[28] Cahill specialized in undertaking seemingly impossible feats of promotion. For example, he took the old practice of "papering the house" (giving away free tickets) to new heights, by colluding with wealthy Boston men who had become enamored of a particular singer. He would suggest that the man in question buy out the entire house for certain performances, and then he would supply a crowd that cheered wildly at every appearance by the favored singer. The box-office takings were not depressed in any way, and the complete cast benefited from the imported enthusiasm of Cahill's nurses, waitresses, street sweepers, and other occupants of the "free" seats.

The only time during their friendship that McHugh saw Cahill's irrepressible spirits falter was in 1911 when the company was on a late fall tour with Mendelssohn's oratorio *Elijah*. A chorus of sixty, plus some of the main stars of the Opera House, were booked on a circuit of the northern United States and Canada by a promoter named Kronberg. Wherever they played, Cahill's usual methods of drumming up enthusiasm failed, and despite his best efforts, all they met with was apathy. From Montreal he wired McHugh to join him and try to rescue the situation, believing that it was still possible to generate excitement and interest in the tour, which featured a semi-staged and fully costumed production.

Things looked bleak when McHugh arrived in the city to find that during the time it had taken him to get there, Kronberg had disappeared, leaving the company with a string of bookings but no manager and no financial security whatsoever. Cahill decided to create some press enthusiasm by making the show look even more impressive and the production more lavish than it really was: he proposed that for the first night of the Montreal run, McHugh and other members of the backstage team should don white robes and swell the ranks of the chorus. Having arrived fresh from Boston, with no idea that the chorus performed carefully rehearsed movements on stage, McHugh struggled into a spare costume and was happily mouthing the words when he found himself moving in the opposite direction from the rest of the chorus members. As they raised their arms, he was still dropping his from the previous maneuver, and as he fell completely out of sync, he distinctly heard a voice from somewhere in the sparse audience shout, "Shoot the manager!"

When the time came to leave Montreal, the company was in even greater financial straits than it had been before McHugh arrived. There was no money to pay for transporting the copious scenery to the railroad station, so McHugh agreed to leave behind an organ as payment (conveniently omitting to mention it had actually been hired from another local concern for the duration of the show). In sub-zero temperatures, he found himself having a fistfight with one of the stagehands in a tiff over who was to unload what at the station. Eventually Cahill came to his aid, and everything was loaded onto the train to Ann Arbor, Michigan, where to nobody's surprise except Cahill's the show was met with the same indifference that had characterized its Canadian appearances.

Things went from bad to worse, and finances became more and more grim. In Reading, Pennsylvania, only a wire of funds from William R. Mac-Donald, one of the Opera House directors, provided the cast with its 1911 Thanksgiving dinner. Afterward, in the freezing November night, and with only their working suits as protection against the chill, Cahill and McHugh stole a pair of overcoats from the hotel cloakroom as they left the dinner and headed to their unheated lodgings. It was the low point of McHugh's career as a publicist for the Opera House and a lesson that not even the most energetic promotion in the world could be relied upon to transform the interest of a few into a popular entertainment.

Within a few days, MacDonald sent instructions to abandon the tour, along with further funds to bring the company home. McHugh and Cahill spent the journey engaged in an argument about religion. The devoutly Roman Catholic, eighteen-year-old McHugh found himself defending his faith to a slightly older cynic, whose main question was, "How do you know there's a God? Prove it!" But their friendship was greater than their differences, and a friend of Cahill's arranged to lend them a vacant apartment belonging to the great pianist Paderewski when they broke their journey for a night in New York, before the final long train ride to Boston. McHugh later recalled: "I played out that desperate tour on Paderewski's concert grand. By the time Alan and I had dined on delicacies from Paderewski's ice box, and crawled between the smooth sheets of his soft beds, *Elijah* seemed very far away."[29]

It took a lesson from Theodore H. Bauer himself to show them how enthusiasm could be created in the face of similar apathy back in Boston. The Opera House was to present a new production of Debussy's *Pelléas et Mélisande*, opening on January 10, 1912. There were lavish new sets by the newly fashionable superrealist Viennese designer Joseph Urban, the stars were to be Vanni-Marcoux as Golaud, Jean Riddez as Pelléas, and Mary Garden as Mélisande, and French conductor and Debussy specialist André Caplet was to conduct.

The only problem was that the Boston public had failed to buy any tickets. Even when Georgette Leblanc, the wife of the author of the *Pelléas* story, Maurice Maeterlinck, arrived in town there was little more than a minor flurry of interest. Bauer took matters in hand, calling in Cahill and McHugh: "Go down to the Somerset Hotel . . . and register as Maurice Maeterlinck and secretary. Then go up to your room, lock the door and stay there. Do not answer the telephone or speak to anyone under any circumstances."[30]

Wrapped in an all-enveloping black cloak, with a floppy black hat and a large black valise, Cahill checked into the Somerset, signing the register with a flourish as "Maurice Maeterlinck" and registering McHugh as his secretary. They shut themselves in their room and for two days endured constant attempts by the press to make contact: phone calls, pounding at the door, notes slipped through onto the carpet, and telegrams. They ignored everything, playing interminable card games to while away the hours. Eventually a more than usually thunderous hammering led them to open the door to Bauer himself, who had put out the story that Maeterlinck was in town for the performance, and that although he wished to keep his presence secret, he could be found at the Somerset. Indeed, Bauer had spiced up the story by adding a little spurious betting: "When Maurice Maeterlinck comes to this country . . . he will travel incognito. If he succeeds in eluding the American reporters, he wins a wager of $400 from Henry Russell, Manager of the Boston Opera Company."[31] The resulting flood of reporters, their interest fueled by Cahill's exotic signature in the register and the apparent determination of the great writer to remain undisturbed in order to win the generous sum of cash, created a vast amount of gossip in the papers, and the performances swiftly sold out. Bauer's tenacity and his ability to conjure a story out of nothing were both things McHugh would remember.

Sadly, Henry Russell's Boston Opera Company did not survive long into 1914, when it lost a fortune on a winter tour to France that made the *Elijah* experience pale into insignificance. The company went bankrupt and laid off all its staff, including the twenty-year-old McHugh. He would remember the thrilling sounds he had heard on Huntington Avenue for the rest of his life, and he always remained a committed opera fan, taking the best seats in New York, Paris, and London and hobnobbing with the stars when they passed through Los Angeles.

He would meet with Cahill again, from time to time, as well. They went their different ways in 1914 but many years later were reunited at McHugh's home in Beverly Hills, when opera arrived for the first time at the Greek Theatre in Griffith Park. Cahill helped the film mogul Jules Brulatour to launch the operatic career of his third wife, the former silent film actress Hope Hampton, in the late 1930s, and he stayed at McHugh's house while he promoted her cause with his usual enthusiasm. They had their religious differences as young men, but when Cahill died he apparently asked for a priest to administer the last rites, saying, "If it's good enough for McHugh, it's good enough for me!"[32]

The great classical building on Huntington Avenue closed its doors in March 1914, and the theater was "dark" until November 15, 1915, when the impresario Max Rubinoff launched his new Grand Opera Company there. *The Love of Three Kings* by Montemezzi brought the sights and sounds of opera back to the Boston public.[33] McHugh, however, did not return to the building, as his career, and his private life, were to take a completely new direction during the summer of 1914.

Before then, however, the eminent organist and tutor at the New England Conservatory, Wallace Goodrich, who had heard the young man's attempts to rag the classics, suggested that McHugh might apply for a scholarship to the conservatory, to further his talents as a pianist. However, the McHugh family's precarious finances, and the fact that McHugh was already accustomed to the independence that earning his own living had brought, led him to reject the suggestion. His future, he knew, was not to be in the world of classical music.

For a while after the opera house closed he was out of work, but as the warm weather arrived, he got a job playing the piano every evening in an ice-cream parlor at Revere Beach. Today, this stretch of shoreline a few miles north of Boston, reached from downtown via the "blue" subway line, gives only a few clues to its past as an entertainment center. The train station called "Wonderland" commemorates an early amusement park that was located there at the end of the nineteenth century and which closed for good in 1911. The park used to attract thousands of visitors, who reached it by railroad, and Wonderland's legacy, many years after its closure, made Revere a hotbed of entertainment.

Initially, the town's attractions were designed to entice visitors as they made their way back home to Boston after a day of outdoor amusement, but eventually Revere became a sought-after destination in its own right. It had restaurants, saloons, and, above all, dance halls, of which the most famous were the Ocean View, the Crescent Garden, the Hippodrome, and the Cyclone. The last of these was torn down in 1974, but in the heady days before World War I, Revere was the hottest place in the Boston area for nighttime revels: fun, feasting, and dancing.

The parlor in which McHugh played a selection of light classics and the hits of the day was on the ground floor of one of the bigger dance halls. There was bitter competition between the proprietors of the various establishments, for whom, recalled McHugh, presenting live music was little more than another way of drumming up trade. "When I played piano there, the trick was that the train would come in, and as everybody from the train came down past the big windows, I'd be playing. It got so I'd start playing and never stop until I was through at eleven o'clock. . . . There was a big rivalry, and of course when the dance halls would get out, everybody would stop by the windows again, have an ice-cream soda, and listen to more piano playing."[34]

Not everyone slipped off into the dance hall while McHugh was at work. A young girl called Bess Hornbrook was entranced by his music, and soon she was sitting from eight until eleven every evening listening to him. Her family had recently moved to the Boston area from Maine, and she had few friends. Their nightly meetings gave the couple little chance to talk, as McHugh was almost always playing, but he remembered how they gradually got to know one another as the summer progressed: "Whenever I glanced up from the piano, I would find her large, soft eyes watching me. Her face was young and appealing under a little hat with a bird on it. I was charmed with her, but we were both too young to know the meaning of love, or the larger emotion that word implies."[35] Brought up as a good Catholic boy, and without yet having arrived at the reputation he was to acquire in later life as a ladies' man, McHugh was still somewhat naive about the opposite sex. Bess Hornbrook was the first girl he ever dated.

Because of the odd hours he worked, walking out with Bess was a stroll to her door in the hot summer darkness at midnight. Soon there were goodnight kisses on the doorstep, and then, without really thinking about it, the couple decided to get married. The ceremony took place at 6:30 one evening, before his work began at the ice-cream parlor, and afterwards he walked Bess home to her own front door as usual.

McHugh lied about his age and for once in his life made himself out to be older than he really was, claiming to be twenty-one. In fact he was still twenty, a few weeks short of his twenty-first birthday; but when his mother found the license in his pocket, she did not reproach him, either for lying or for marrying, but calmly suggested that if the two of them really were married, then they ought to think about living together. For the rest of that summer, and a number of years to come, they shared a room in Bess's mother's apartment. They were an unsuitable couple with little in common and scant shared ground for conversation or friendship, and from the outset, despite McHugh's strong Catholic upbringing, the marriage was doomed to be short-lived.

With the arrival of autumn, the crowds ebbed away from Revere, and McHugh's job ebbed away as well. But this time he knew exactly what he wanted to do next. All through the long summer, he had received endless visits from Boston's indefatigable song pluggers. Each working for a different publisher, they would make the rounds of the saloons and ice-cream parlors where music was played, offering their latest songs for performance. McHugh, who was using his long hours at the keyboard not just to extemporize melodies of his own but to create complete fantasy musicals with overtures, arias, choruses, and ballads, would break off to play each new would-be hit as it was offered to him. Then the plugger would set off to a new bar or saloon, and McHugh would return to his reverie until the next plugger arrived. He said: "They would plug any place where there was a group of people. They'd walk in, go right into their song, and maybe do one other number and then out. Then another plugger from another firm would come in. . . . I would interrupt my mind only to play for them, and then, goodbye! In the winter, I joined the industrious little horde of pluggers scurrying about the city like pilgrims, dedicated to the cause of implanting popular songs upon the mind of America."[36]

McHugh had found his ideal *métier*, which was to be the foundation on which his entire subsequent career as a songwriter was built. When he was a small boy, his mother had planted the seed in his mind that creating new music brought a financial reward, and in the days before ubiquitous sound recording, or even widespread piano rolls, the sheet-music publishing industry was the major source of revenue for all kinds of popular music. Song pluggers were the army of dedicated journeymen who brought those printed songs to public attention and saw that the music was played as widely as possible.

Returning to Boston from Revere in the fall of 1914, McHugh was finally able to draw together his talent as a pianist, his instinctive ability as a hustler, and the marketing skills he had picked up from Bauer and Cahill. With a strong sense of how a show would go over with the public from his backstage experience at the Opera House, coupled with firsthand experience at playing for the pluggers who came by the ice-cream parlor, he had an intuitive grasp of which songs would work and how to maximize the impact of those that would not. The motivation of wanting to provide for his young wife and to do the best for their future was a strong driving force for success. It was also, ultimately, to be the wedge that drove them apart, because the life of a song plugger involved late hours, endless rounds of restaurants, bars, and saloons—indeed anywhere that live music was presented for the public. McHugh wrote of Bess: "She did not approve of my life in Boston. She came of a substantial family in comfortable circumstances and she did not understand show people. She thought it degrading that I hung around stage entrances, often in foul weather, waiting for some performer to emerge in order to sell him a song. I would come home late, full of enthusiasm, or depressed by the lack of it, to be met by stony silence."

Yet irrespective of Bess's disapproval, McHugh was hooked on his new way of life. He poured all his formidable energy into becoming one of Boston's most successful pluggers, working successively for several of the city's music publishers before settling at Waterson, Berlin, and Snyder, the firm whose fortunes were based on the songs of Irving Berlin.[37]

Berlin himself had started out as a plugger for the selfsame firm, but before long his talents as a performer were spotted by its founder, Ted Snyder, and soon he was supplying the majority of the company's songs for others to plug. By the time McHugh joined it in 1914, the business had established its head office at the Strand Theatre Building at Forty-seventh Street and Broadway in New York, with satellite branches in Chicago and Boston. New York had twenty teams of pluggers working the rounds, Chicago had ten, and Boston only five, but the teams worked hard and collectively pushed the sheet-music sales of the most popular items in the catalog beyond the million-copy mark.

There were two aspects to the plugger's job. The first—which in the case of Waterson, Berlin, and Snyder usually took place in their rambling offices, one flight up from the street in a network of five or six small rooms, each with a piano—was to run through the latest songs with every variety act that came through Boston, so that the music would be incorporated in their shows. The second was to be out and about, selling the sheet music and getting the songs performed.

McHugh excelled on both fronts. He could transpose by ear, so was instantly able to adapt the printed music to a key that suited any singer. He reminisced: "We used to handle all the acts. I was a punk kid, trying to rehearse them when they came in, with new songs from Berlin or somebody else in the firm."[38] This brought him into contact with a huge number of touring variety musicians, with many of whom he was to remain in touch during the years that followed, as they plied their trade all over the country. But more immediately exciting, and more suited to McHugh's energetic lifestyle, was the side of the job that took him out into the streets. For some of the time he operated alone, but at other times he was joined by two fellow members of the Boston team, Charlie Ray and Don Ramsey, who sang to his accompaniment. The three of them were known as "the Ted Snyder Trio."[39]

Over fifty years later, when McHugh set down his recollections of plugging, his excitement and enthusiasm was such that it still leaps off the page:

> We traveled on bicycles from theater to dance hall to café. We marched in parades with megaphones. Anything for a plug. We gave managers of movie houses chorus slides to four or five songs—he would flash them on the screen and the audience would sing them. . . . Backstage in the vaudeville houses we tried to get our song used as the background to an acrobatic act, to a dance, to a dog act. Saturdays I doubled at the music counters of dime stores. Everywhere we went we competed with pluggers from other firms, clamoring for the same favors. It was a desperate struggle, but it paid off.[40]

Before long McHugh was earning $8 per week, as he had done at the Opera House, and was provided with a company bicycle to pedal from one plugging engagement to the next.

For over a year the McHughs had lived with the Hornbrooks, but now there was a baby on the way. Jimmy Junior was born in their room at his grandmother's house on October 21, 1915.[41] His bassinet was improvised out of a laundry basket and trimmed with blue ribbons. With the hours McHugh kept, and the demands of a baby, it was impossible to continue living in one room, and soon the young couple and their son moved into their own apartment. For a while the tension between husband and wife eased. Her rows about his way of life gave way to a greater interest in the infant boy.

McHugh, however, was looking for ways to supplement the family income.

In the same way that Irving Berlin had started out as a plugger and then begun to write his own songs, McHugh gradually made the transition from someone who promoted other people's songs to a composer who wrote his own. His first published song, entitled "Caroline, I'm Coming Back to You," appeared in 1916. The lyricist was Jack Caddigan, who worked for the Boston branch of the Edison Company but toiled away at writing lyrics in his spare time, and the results were published by D. W. Cooper on Tremont Street. The cover featured a photogravure of a large, rheumy-eyed girl, dressed in a bonnet and surrounded by roses. But marvelous as it was for the young composer "James McHugh" to see his name in print, just to the left of the young lady's photograph, this song was not to make his fortune overnight. The would-be songwriters sold it outright to Cooper's for $15.

The impetus for McHugh to become a composer of popular songs initially came from Caddigan, who had heard him playing the piano, both as he accompanied visiting singers and also as he played solo on his daily rounds. Caddigan was convinced that with such facility at the keyboard, McHugh ought to be able to write new tunes to fit the lyrics he turned out, many of which made topical allusions to the war in Europe. Although McHugh would subsequently prefer to be given a song title around which he would craft a melody for words to be added later, his first pieces were settings of complete lyrics by Caddigan. The pair apparently finished six or seven songs, not all of which saw the light of day, but their second effort to make it to the music stores, "Keep the Love Light Shining in the Window until the Boys Come Marching Home," was again published by Cooper, appearing in 1917. This time their outright fee for the copyright doubled, to a princely $30.

At this point McHugh might have accelerated his progress as a songwriter, but the war intervened, and he was summoned into the military. Caddigan went on to work with other tunesmiths, notably James A. Brennan and Chick Story, on such songs as "The Rose of No-Man's Land," and "Salvation Lassie of Mine." Meanwhile, in August 1917, McHugh joined the newly reorganized 101st Massachusetts Regiment,[42] but before it took ship for Europe, he contracted acute appendicitis and was in the hospital recovering from an operation while his comrades set off for six successful actions on the battlefields of Flanders and northern France. McHugh stayed put in Massachusetts, and in due course he was invalided out of the service. In 1918 he returned to his former job as a plugger.

As the war ended, McHugh was torn between providing as best he could for his young family or following his instincts to develop his future career more rapidly than was possible in Boston. The city was affectionately known to Bostonians as "the Hub of the Universe," but this appellation definitely did not apply to music. McHugh knew that with the burgeoning interest in popular songs that had followed the end of the war, he ought to be in the thick of the industry in Tin Pan Alley. In addition, things were changing at his firm—Irving Berlin was in the process of severing relations with his former business partners to set up his own company, Irving Berlin Inc., which would have a markedly deleterious effect on the quality of the songs McHugh was being given to plug. But Bess would not hear of a move to New York. As a result, for the next two years, he stayed put in Boston for the sake of the family, all the while champing at the bit to get his career moving.

One early example of McHugh's instinctive ability to see the potential in a song dates from this period. As well as continuing to work for Waterson, Berlin, and Snyder, he did some additional plugging for the firm of McCarthy and Fisher. Not long after the end of the war, the latter company had released what they regarded as a sure-fire hit, by Felix Bernard and Johnny S. Black, called "Dardanella." It was first published as an instrumental and failed to sell. McHugh urged the firm to reconsider its strategy and add a lyric that would act as a hook for potential buyers. Initially the company held firm against McHugh's forceful arguments, but in due course one of the partners, Fred Fisher, added a lyric of his own, and almost overnight sales took off. "Dardanella" became one of the best-remembered songs of 1919, ultimately being recorded by a large number of artists including, many years later, Louis Armstrong.[43]

In an effort to work less antisocial hours, McHugh went back to play in the ice-cream parlor in the summer, moving his family close to the beach and living with a friend called Georgie Joy. Pleasant as this life was, he missed the hurly-burly of selling the latest songs, and he was soon back at Waterson, Berlin, and Snyder, the family meanwhile moving into a bigger apartment in West Roxbury, which he described as "half a house."[44] His hyperactivity brought a series of increases in his salary until he was earning $25 per week, a considerable income in 1919. This led to some jealousy from the firm's other, less-successful, pluggers, and after one of them repeatedly made his life difficult with barbed remarks and threatening behavior, McHugh went to the head of the Boston office with the timeworn "either he goes or I go" routine. The other man was fired, but waited behind for McHugh to leave work and then attacked him. The savage fistfight ended only when McHugh abandoned the principles of the noble art instilled in him by his father and brought the hinged flap of the office reception counter down hard on his adversary's head.

This fight was, he felt, a turning point. It underlined all his frustration at working in a second-rate publishing center and made it inevitable that he should move on. When a representative of the newly formed New York music publishing house George A. Friedman Inc. pressed a check for $500 into McHugh's hand as an advance against the salary of $100 a week he would earn in New York, he could resist no longer; and at the start of 1920 he set out for the bright lights of Broadway, leaving his wife and five-year-old son behind for good.[45]

2

"When My Sugar Walks Down the Street"

FROM THE MOMENT the Original Dixieland Jazz Band opened at Reisenweber's Restaurant at Columbus Circle on January 15, 1917, New York became the epicenter of Jazz Age America. Compared to Boston, which still had a relatively compact, low-rise urban center, New York was a teeming, crowded city; Manhattan was already stretching upward and outward, its skyline rising higher all the time, and its population spreading into the outer boroughs. Although it lacked the dense mixture of dance halls, clubs, and saloons that were crammed into the Loop area of Chicago, which had made the Windy City a magnet for dozens of small jazz ensembles, New York was the traditional home of popular song publishing, of the musical theater, and of revue. It offered a nonstop round of opportunities to a talented song plugger, and this remained the case even after the arrival of Prohibition in January 1920 drove a significant percentage of musical activities underground.

Indeed, many of the city's long-established legitimate nightclubs were forced to close because of the lack of alcohol to woo their customers. A couple of dozen famous venues survived, however, among them Reisenweber's and Shanley's, but a far greater number of new illegal speakeasies were set up; and the Jazz Age acquired a sudden frisson of impropriety as customers sought out such places, knowing that the very act of going to them was against the law. Estimates suggest that upward of five thousand speakeasies were in operation in New York by the end of 1921.[1] McHugh wrote later:

> Without knowing it, I was invading the Broadway jungle at the wildest, richest, gayest, most desperate, most fateful period in its history. The jungle was full of hunters stalking the prize of gold, and the stakes were high. The Volstead act had darkened the soft lights of Broadway's elegant restaurants, such as Reisenweber's, Delmonico's and Rector's. In their place was the lurid shaft from the speakeasy peephole. Texas Guinan, Jimmy Durante, Helen Morgan and Harry Richman opened night clubs named after themselves. Uniformed doormen were supplanted with whispered passwords and midnight raids. Society gave ground to an era of professional yeggmen, rum runners, bathtub gin and flappers.[2]

Although McHugh had been desperate to get to New York for the better part of two years after leaving the army, as it turned out he could hardly have timed things better. His arrival coincided not only with this shift in the nightclub culture of the city but with a period of unprecedented growth in the music industry.

For a start, radio broadcasting was just getting under way. Although the big networks of NBC and CBS were not set up until 1926 and 1927, respectively, several small local stations, such as WHN, which broadcast Fletcher Henderson's early efforts, were beginning to offer the plugger new opportunities as the 1920s dawned. Equally, although the first electrical recordings were not made until 1925, the record industry was growing exponentially on the basis of primitive acoustic recordings. In the wake of Mamie Smith's triumph with "Crazy Blues" in 1920, there was an explosion of blues-related material following the launch of the Okeh label's "race" record catalog in 1921. This was just the latest fad in an industry that turned out over 100 million discs a year, largely consisting of one-steps, two-steps, tangos, fox-trots, and waltzes. An amazing 1 percent of the total market was commanded by just one man, the "King of Jazz," bandleader Paul Whiteman, whose recording of "Whispering" sold over one million copies in 1920, and who went on to produce several more discs that sold in comparable quantities.[3]

The 1920s was also the final decade in which the sale of sheet music remained the major revenue earner in the industry. For sure, broadcasting and recording were growing apace, but sales of brightly colored, four-page popular song sheets still drove the business. The wholesale price was around 20¢ a copy, and once a song managed sales of more than a few thousand, it began to produce acceptable levels of revenue. The plugger's aim was always to generate sales in the hundreds of thousands, and it was perfectly possible for a successful song to sell well into the millions.

By the end of the decade, however, many sheet-music publishers went to the wall as both new media and the Depression bit, and formerly salable stock that became valueless overnight was scrapped. One high-profile publisher sold its entire stock of over seventy tons of paper for pulp, the collective inventory realizing the princely sum of $210.[4]

When McHugh arrived in Manhattan, such considerations were far in the future. Compared to the limitations of the Boston market, where he had to work with traveling variety performers and a fairly small selection of local pianists and singers in order to get songs heard, New York was a wide-open field for the inventive plugger. Within a few months of his arrival, McHugh had demonstrated that he was just such a creative talent, and by the end of 1921 he had been appointed the professional manager at Jack Mills Inc.[5] His job was to work with the show business community to ensure that as many of the company's songs got performed in as many places and in as many media as possible. Unit sales of sheet music still drove the enterprise, but McHugh was among the first pluggers to realize the benefits offered by recording and broadcasting. While the driving force of his old company, Irving Berlin, was busy building the Music Box Theatre with his colleague Sam Harris, for the explicit purpose of staging Berlin's revues, McHugh realized that there were other ways to sell music that were every bit as creative but required a lot less investment.

Yet, ironically, McHugh might not have made the move to New York had it not been for the total collapse of his marriage. In a memoir he worked on shortly before his death, he confessed to an infatuation with an actress called "Amy Royce." She is a fictitious character, who was in reality an amalgam of several of the women with whom he became involved at around the time of his move to the Big Apple. It was inevitable that being in the company of show people throughout his working life, he would come into contact with some of the most attractive women in the country—women who were infinitely more fascinating than the one he had married. McHugh also had a magnetic charm, which all those who knew him remember well. He had the gift of being able to focus his attention on a companion so that she seemed to be the only person in the world who mattered to him.

The identity of the young woman who lured him to New York (and who was responsible for introducing him to Friedman) is not clear, but it is certainly the case that his involvements soon included a young actress called Evelyn Hoey, whom he met within a short time of his arrival in New York; and in his memoir, her tragic story is intricately woven into that of "Amy Royce."

Hoey was remarkably good-looking, a blond actress and singer who was groomed by her parents to be a child star in her native Minneapolis and began a professional career in New York while still in her teens. "As soon as you gaze into Evelyn's baby-blue eyes," wrote one hard-bitten Broadway reporter, "you immediately try to figure out how much you can afford to blow in on her for flowers."[6]

She became the object of admiration for many men, and McHugh certainly had her in mind when he wrote of "Amy Royce" that

> Rich men who adored her radiance on the stage competed to escort her to the elegant little soirées that always took place after the show. They showered her with presents. I was a neophyte in the Broadway caste system. Nobody knew, least of all Amy or myself, whether I would amount to anything. I like to think she loved me. . . . I could not afford to take Amy to expensive restaurants where she would be shown off to advantage. Yet she often turned down her rich admirers to go with me to some cheap little restaurant where we talked quietly. During those evenings I came to understand her own sense of insecurity, her awareness that the time of an actress is short.[7]

Why would such an attractive and sought-after actress turn down the attentions of rich suitors for an obscure song plugger who had not yet made any kind of reputation as a composer?

What McHugh possessed, which none of Evelyn Hoey's other admirers did, was the ability to accompany her at auditions and to supply her with the latest songs. In his manuscript, he described "Amy Royce" as a "Follies" actress, and it is no coincidence that it was McHugh himself who helped Hoey become a member of that illustrious troupe. The *Morning Telegraph* reported the story as follows:

> The other day, Evelyn Hoey, looking as cute and beautiful as ever, strolled into the professional studios of Jack Mills Inc. . . . She was exhibiting a serious expression as though she had some real business up her sleeve. A reckless songwriter offered to buy her a dozen roses, but she declined gracefully. Walking up to Jimmy McHugh, composer, pianist and a member of the firm of Jack Mills Inc., Evelyn said, "Will you please come and play for me at the Amsterdam Theatre? I want to show my stuff for Gene Buck and a few others over there."

"Be with you in a minute," McHugh smiled. "Have you a chance to make the Follies?"

Evelyn nodded. Five minutes later Evelyn and McHugh were on their way to the Amsterdam Theatre. McHugh extended himself playing piano while Evelyn sang, and when she finished showing her samples, she was signed up to start with the "Follies" September 1.

Shortly after that McHugh parted with Evelyn and returned to his office and forgot the incident. Several hours later a large wreath of roses was delivered to the office—which must have cost $30 if a penny—carrying a ribbon with the inscription "Mills Forever," and a card of thanks from Evelyn Hoey. Imagine a little show girl showering roses on a rich publisher.[8]

In later life, McHugh himself was to spend a fortune sending flowers to the leading ladies in his shows, suggesting that he never forgot Hoey's kind gesture. But in his memoir he talks of how "Amy Royce" went on to do well on Broadway, eventually hooking up with a millionaire, after which her career went into decline. Later, when he and his lyricist Al Dubin were in Atlantic City, they were shocked to see headline reports of her violent death, only a decade or so after McHugh's relationship with her.

Allowing for the slight fictionalization of this memoir, which, as mentioned, appears to conflate more than one relationship into his story, the facts fit Hoey's life extremely well. At the time McHugh played for her audition, she had been starring in Ned Weyburn's revue at the Hotel Shelburne on Coney Island. She then joined the Greenwich Village Follies, ultimately leaving to join the comedian Leon Errol as his costar in the Broadway comedy *Yours Truly*. In London, in 1928, she played the lead in *Good News*, by De Sylva, Henderson, and Brown, featuring the songs "The Best Things in Life Are Free" and "Lucky in Love." That production ran for three months, following which Hoey became a nightclub singer in Paris. There, by chance, she was heard by Cole Porter, who brought her back to the United States to star in his 1929 show *Fifty Million Frenchmen* on Broadway. She introduced his songs "I'm Unlucky at Gambling," "Find Me a Primitive Man," and "The Boy Friend Back Home."

The Cole Porter musical made Hoey a star. When it ended after 254 performances, she resumed her club act, popularizing Porter's "What Is This Thing Called Love?" and Vernon Duke and E. Y. Harburg's "April in Paris," songs which she made very much her own. But just as she achieved this success in 1930, her life took a downward turn. The body of her costar in *Fifty Million Frenchmen*, Jack Thompson, was found floating in the Hudson River in suspicious circumstances, and around the same time her name began to be linked with a fast-living nightclub set. According to an Associated Press report: "She became a familiar figure in the nightlife rendezvous patronized by socialites, her blond beauty, smart clothes, and ever present corsage of green orchids making her the center of attention."[9] She attracted some notoriety in the gossip column headlines in 1932 when she sued her hairdresser for $25,000 after being accidentally burned with curling tongs, but, as she said at the time, her "honey-colored" hair was one of her greatest assets. Shortly thereafter, she became involved with Henry H. Rogers, the son and namesake of the billionaire founder of Standard Oil.[10]

Separated from his wife, Rogers lived on a farm near Downingtown, Pennsylvania, that acquired such a reputation for wild parties and unrestrained firearms practice that local residents were afraid to go near the place. On September 12, 1935, Evelyn Hoey was shot dead in a bedroom at the farm, a single bullet traveling right through her head and embedding itself in the wall.

Virtually every newspaper in the United States reported these sensational events, and McHugh, in common with readers across America, would have assumed that Hoey had, indeed, been shot dead by her paramour. More facts about the case were reported as further details emerged, but in the immediate aftermath of the killing, the weight of press opinion was that this was no suicide, as Rogers claimed, but something far more sinister. The passage of time—not to mention the first-rate legal team hired by the Rogers family—ensured that in the subsequent grand jury investigation, Hoey's death was "held to be suicide." So comprehensive was the whitewash that "except for the mention of him as the owner of the house in which Miss Hoey died, the presentment made no reference to Rogers."[11]

Press reports of Hoey's untimely demise gave her date of birth as December 15, 1910,[12] but it is likely her agent had clipped a number of years off her age, as this would have made her little more than a child when McHugh accompanied her Follies audition. She had, indeed, once been a child star in kiddie revues in Minneapolis, but although she was in all probability approximately five years older than the reports of her death suggested, there is no doubt that the beautiful golden-haired singer met her premature end by swiftly falling in with the wrong company once she reached adulthood.

McHugh—who confessed in one memoir to having been "crazy about" Hoey—was later to write: "innumerable lovers have told me that my songs played a part in bringing them together. It is my compensation for the grim little joke, repeated with such cunning variation through the years, that whenever I thought I had found love myself, it always slipped away."[13] He relates how, when he saw the headline news of his old flame's death, for a few sad moments his mind flashed back to their comparatively innocent tête-à-têtes in little cafés, away from the bright lights of Broadway, and to what might have been had their relationship been allowed to develop.

Considering the frenetic pace at which McHugh lived his life during the first half of the 1920s, it seems extraordinary that he found time for any tête-à-têtes at all. He did manage to write a relatively small number of songs at the start of the decade, but his main energies were devoted to building up the business of Jack Mills Inc. by plugging the company's new songs as hard and as creatively as possible. In due course he became a partner and stockholder in the firm. He also perfected the technique that was to serve him well throughout his life, which was to turn his plugging efforts themselves into news. By making himself and his methods for song plugging into a story, he achieved dozens of column inches in the press that would never have been given to the songs in their own right, not to mention the additional benefit of getting his own name better known in the process.

This was by no means a new tactic in the cutthroat world of promoting sheet music to the masses. Waterson, Berlin, and Snyder, where McHugh learned his craft, had long made a specialty of promoting the works of Irving Berlin in a similar way. The idea was to provoke a sense of gentle outrage that would invite curious readers to investigate the songs for themselves. Hence, a typical piece in *Collier's Magazine* that ran in early 1917 was picked up across the country by several newspapers. The *Washington Post*, for example, cited the article in asking the question: "When W. C. Brownell or Robert Underwood Johnson or some other pundit of highbrow literature bewails before the American Academy, or in a letter to the *New York Evening Post* the decadence of American taste—well, why don't they stop and consider Irving Berlin?" It goes on to deride Berlin for "never [having] had a music lesson" and to pick holes in his lyrics for the song "I'm Down in Honolulu Looking Them Over." The apparent point of the article is to lampoon Berlin's ignorance in not knowing that "Wikiwiki" translates as "Hurry up!" But Berlin's song pluggers would have been delighted, seeing most of the song's lyric and a serious piece of copy on the main editorial page of a major newspaper.[14]

McHugh's gambit of making himself the news story may not have achieved quite the same high level of editorial headlines, but it ensured that whenever news was short, the papers could be relied on to run another piece of McHugh copy. A typical example from his early years in New York runs as follows:

MIDNIGHT PLUGGING:
NEW METHOD IN TIMES SQ. TO "LAND" SONGS.

The latest song-plugging innovation is credited to Jimmy McHugh, of Jack Mills Inc. who conceived the idea of having acts rehearse new songs at the Mills offices after 11 pm at night. McHugh and his night manager George Watts have been calling for the acts at stage doors, whipping them downtown in a car, and have found the idea much more feasible than the noon appointments which so many acts find difficult to keep. Several other Times Square music publishers are reported interested in McHugh's experiment, and ready to give it a trial.[15]

Although some of these nocturnal attempts to plug songs were planned, others were simply opportunist, as the following press report from 1923 demonstrates:

Residents of the King James Hotel on West 45th Street, New York, are still talking about the unusual presence of mind exhibited by Jimmy McHugh, professional manager for Jack Mills, Inc., and Bert Grant, celebrated composer and staff writer for the House That Jack Built, at a fire which started early Monday morning at the aforementioned hostelry. No sooner did the hotel gong clang the dread fire warning than Messrs. Grant and McHugh, occupying adjoining suites, played as a four-handed duet their latest ballad, "Out Where the Blue Begins." Guests of the hotel, rushing scantily clad to the streets, stopped in their wild scramble to ascertain the source of this unceremonious harmony, and in less than half an hour, a dozen acts were assembled in Bert Grant's room, harmonizing the soft strains of "Out Where the Blue Begins." Among those bath-robed and kimonoed were the Althoffs, the Arnaut sisters, Crafts and Haley, the Amarous Brothers, etc. The incident makes Bert Grant and Jimmy McHugh the only composers to have rehearsed acts in their pajamas.[16]

The King James was at 137 West Forty-fifth Street, a few doors away from the Mills offices at number 152, and McHugh and Grant were briefly resident there. It was to be a place of refuge for McHugh, in between other lodgings, on several future occasions in the twenties. However, for most of these early years in New York, McHugh was actually living a block further uptown, at the National Vaudeville Artists' clubhouse at 249 West Forty-sixth Street. The N.V.A. doubled as a professional association and trade union for show people, and McHugh had got himself involved as the pianist for its weekly fundraising "Clown Nights" at the nearby Opry House, where "resting" actors and singers sought to raise money for any of their colleagues who had fallen on hard times. This was, of course, an excellent networking opportunity for

McHugh, who met a vast cross section of Manhattan's entertainers as he played for their various acts. It ensured they would remember him when they were working again and in need of new material of the kind Mills published.

He also found another networking opportunity when he began to play as organist at what was known as "the Actors' Church," St. Malachy's on West Forty-ninth Street, where he swiftly became good friends with the priest, Monsignor Leonard. McHugh helped to organize the weekly actors' Mass, which began at 4:00 A.M. every Sunday morning, after Broadway's theaters and clubs had closed for the night. In due course, the Mass became so popular that the Monsignor conducted two services simultaneously on different floors of the church, joking to McHugh that he was "the only man on Broadway who can pack 'em in for two shows at once!" The congregation included Marilyn Miller, Fred Allen, Frank Fay, Dorothy Jordan, and many other stars of the time, several of whom were encouraged to sing during the services. The Monsignor often sent his chosen soloists down to the Mills offices a few days in advance to rehearse their renditions of *Ave Maria* and other settings with McHugh, who thereby added further names to his voluminous address book of useful contacts.[17]

Meanwhile, he was not slow to report the charitable side of his N.V.A. activities in the press: "He was on the job every Tuesday last season and like the artists who appeared, donated his services for the entertainment of the members and the good of the organization. Jimmy is a busy man as Professional Manager for Jack Mills Inc., but nevertheless finds time to show up for Clown Nights, not to mention being on the job for the rehearsals several nights a week."[18]

Also living alongside him in the N.V.A. clubhouse at the start of the 1920s was Walter Winchell, a one-time vaudeville actor who was single-handedly inventing the job of gossip columnist and paparazzo. Winchell would lurk outside the Palace or other Broadway venues and snap the stars as they came out, reporting in the *N.V.A. News* any items of gossip he picked up during his photographic expeditions. Glenn Condon, the editor, allowed Winchell a percentage of advertising he brought in as a result of his pictures, and soon the enterprising photographer was out-earning his boss. He moved to the *Graphic* in 1924 and three years later swapped his $300 a week salary for $1,000 a week at the *Mirror*. McHugh wrote astutely that Winchell had "made Broadway conscious of itself," and of course, this experience of watching the development of a new way of reporting show business rubbed off on McHugh.[19] Having lived cheek by jowl as Winchell launched his career, the two men stayed close, and it was never difficult for McHugh to seed the ideas for stories that would later run in Winchell's column.

McHugh went further, however. He sought out his own photo opportunities, of which perhaps the most outrageous example came with the promotion of a singularly unmemorable 1923 song called "Hey, You Want Any Codfish? We Only Got Mack'rel Today!" The song was an unashamed attempt by Mills to cash in on the vogue for the British music-hall number "Yes, We Have No Bananas!," which had taken Tin Pan Alley by storm. Imitating its syllabic structure and with a tune that was not too far away from that original melody, the new song was somewhat optimistically advertised as "A Deep Sea Ditty That'll Knock 'Em Dotty—Every Line a Long, Loud Laugh, Every Chorus a Continuous Chuckle."[20]

McHugh believed that "Yes, We Have No Bananas!" was the ideal mixture of a memorable catchphrase, a snappy title, and a hummable melody, and he instinctively knew that a song that could manage the same formula effectively would be a hit. "Hey, You Want Any Codfish?" itself did not quite do the trick, but in his efforts to help it along, McHugh had himself photographed on the boardwalk at Atlantic City holding aloft a giant drumfish, with the caption reading "Jimmy McHugh, the temperamental fisherman, warbles the latest hit of popular New York song publisher Jack Mills." The picture first ran in the *Boardwalk Illustrated News* of July 16, 1923, but was soon syndicated to other papers that Mills thought might help sales of the sheet music.

When reports of McHugh's unorthodox methods ran short, then there was always the simple expedient of telling the world what a success he was: "Since Jimmie [*sic*] McHugh is associated as professional manager for Jack Mills Inc., the offices of the well-known New York publisher have been literally swamped with vaudeville acts from all over the circuits. Jimmie McHugh is considered by many one of the foremost professional managers in the music business and has a host of friends."[21] Around the same time, McHugh sent out copies of a dashing portrait photograph of himself with the caption: "Jimmy McHugh, the hustling professional manager of the Jack Mills concern, whose hard work and wide acquaintance among show people are greatly responsible for the Mills catalog going over to smashing results."[22]

As soon as McHugh acquired a financial interest in the company in 1923, he was also keen to point out both his indispensability to Mills and his growing responsibility, or as the press report on his stockholding had it, "his engaging personality, coupled with a keen sense of duty, and a desire at all times to cater to every whim and desire of his professional friends."[23] He and Mills were photographed together, smartly suited and hatted, on a visit to Bermuda, and when Mills took a trip to Europe in May 1923, McHugh was left in sole charge of the firm, which also engendered a news story.

Although McHugh played up his efforts in the press, there is little doubt that his dynamic enthusiasm and energy were indeed major factors in the success of Jack Mills's company, which went from a new start to a large and profitable concern during the years McHugh was involved with the business. The main reason for this success was that he simply loved the job. He was as inspired by plugging Broadway songs as he had been by hearing the great names in opera a decade before, and the heroes he worshipped himself were the same as those of the public who bought up the songs. Here, for example, is his account of meeting one of the legends of the era:

> It was backstage at the Winter Garden that I met Al Jolson for the first time. As a young song plugger for Mills I stood among some twenty other hardened song pluggers hanging around Jolson's dressing room one afternoon, waiting for the great man to arrive from the racetrack for his show. In my hand I clutched a song called "Dear Old Southland," based on "Deep River." Presently the door opened and Jolson strode in, a very sporty fellow in a polo coat. We closed on our quarry. Jolson gave us a brief, polite listen, a fast hello and a quick goodbye, and moved on to his dressing room leaving me in a glow. For one of the songs he had taken was mine.[24]

McHugh moved naturally through this magical world of early twenties New York. He had a professional interest in getting to know every circle of society, meeting and observing the movers and shakers who formed the city's tastes and fashions. He was a fly on the wall at Billy LaHiff's on West Forty-eighth Street, where the elegant figure of the future "people's mayor" Jimmy Walker held court. In another booth, boxers Jack Dempsey and Mickey Walker talked their way through recent fights, while the future Barbara Stanwyck, then a would-be actress named Ruby Stevens, accepted the favors of Frank Fay. Two blocks away, there was Dinty Moore's, where Sigmund Romberg launched his fight for composers' rights, and close to it, the Silver Slipper, presided over by Dan Healy, where the svelte Ruby Keeler danced. On Broadway itself was Lindy's, where the song pluggers gathered to mingle with music publishers, aspiring composers, and would-be lyricists. This was McHugh's world, and in a very short time, he knew all its highways and byways, its personalities, and its pitfalls.

However—professional, competent, ingenious, and occasionally inspired as McHugh was as a plugger—what he really aspired to do was to resume his career as a composer of songs. In later life, he recalled that "Out Where the

Blue Begins," the piece he had written with Bert Grant, was the first song of his to have been recorded. In fact he was mistaken. It was the very earliest tune he wrote in New York, "Emaline," from 1921, that first made it on to wax.

This was also virtually his only song from the early 1920s that was not published by Jack Mills. It was sold on April 29, 1921, to George A. Friedman Inc., the firm for which McHugh had moved to New York. But almost at the same time, Friedman wound up his company's publishing activities, joining Van Alstyne and Curtis and selling his catalog to Jerome H. Remick. McHugh moved to Jack Mills's firm at this point, but for years afterward there were ramifications over the royalties for "Emaline." It sold poorly in sheet-music form, notching up a mere seven thousand copies, but its ongoing life in recordings accrued a considerable amount of mechanical rights income. When McHugh's cowriter, lyricist George Little, sold his interest in it to the singer Aileen Stanley, she vigorously pursued her share of the money through the courts for several years.[25]

Within days of the release of "Emaline," the tune was recorded by the bandleader Isham Jones, and as a result, McHugh put himself ahead of many of the songwriters whose work he plugged, by having a recording of his own music issued on disc.[26] "Emaline" is not necessarily his best-known tune, but it continued to be popular for some while, until overtaken in sales by a rather better-known tune of the same name by Mitchell Parish and Frank Perkins. It is certainly the longest-lived active song in the McHugh catalog, since his previous Boston efforts quickly sank without trace.

The melody of "Emaline" and its regular but attractive chord structure demonstrated that from his very first effort as a New York songwriter, McHugh was in tune with the Jazz Age. He understood how to create pieces that stood independently as songs but that could also form a basis on which improvising musicians could jam. His day-to-day work brought him in contact with all manner of performers as he plugged the Mills catalog, but an increasing percentage of his customers were members of the burgeoning jazz scene in the city.

Not surprisingly, McHugh's next major song was a deliberate attempt to cash in on this market, and for it he collaborated with Paul Whiteman's star arranger, the composer Ferde Grofé, who had already achieved some success in writing for the rotund "King of Jazz."

The new piece was called "Stop Your Kiddin'." It was published by Jack Mills, and the third collaborator, providing the lyrics, was Jack's brother Irving, who was to be one of McHugh's closest working partners during the years that followed. By the middle of the decade it would become quite common for Mills to encourage one band to record the same song for a number of different record companies. Most famously, Duke Ellington's Washingtonians—managed by Irving Mills—made discs of the firm's most popular tunes for several disparate labels. However, some four years before Ellington started this phase of his career, "Stop Your Kiddin'" became perhaps the earliest example in the Mills catalog of a song that was promoted this way.

The Original Memphis Five, which despite its name was a New York–based band built around the circle of the trombonist Miff Mole, featuring the trumpeter Phil Napoleon and pianist Frank Signorelli, recorded it no fewer than four times. The results were issued on Pathé, Vocalion, and Arto, with all the sessions taking place in less than a month, beginning on October 19, 1922. And just in case this wasn't enough, Ladd's Black Aces (which, although its name was designed to make the unaware listener think otherwise, was a Caucasian band consisting of almost exactly the same musicians as the Original Memphis Five) made a version as well, on November 6, for the Gennett company.

There is little doubt that this frenetic burst of recording activity was due to McHugh's talents as a hustler. Plugging other people's songs was one thing, but he gave his own just a little extra push. His job as professional manager, he wrote, "meant that it was my duty to get the phonograph companies to record the songs we published. In this capacity I met the big bosses. It was my primary task to win their confidence and make them feel that I was a man of my word. Competition was murderous. But the stakes were big business. In those years with a contract from Victor you could get a bank loan. The mere fact that they took your number was assurance of a half million to a million sale."[27]

"Stop Your Kiddin'" was not bought by Victor, but the several minor labels that recorded it nevertheless ensured that sales of the sheet music were healthy. However, another of McHugh's 1922 songs did get picked up both by Victor and by its main rival, Columbia. Ironically, the piece itself was of very little merit, but it benefited from another old song-plugger's trick, namely, passing off a new song by reusing part or all of a familiar title. In this case the writers, McHugh and Harold "Jack" Frost, used the entire original title of a popular nineteenth-century music-hall song by George Washington Johnson and J. A. Butterfield and simply added a single word on the end, thereby creating the "When You and I Were Young Maggie Blues." This expedient not only lured the companies into thinking they were recording a song that was already popular but also brought the possibility that a share of royalties on the older song, which was now in the public domain, would find its way to McHugh. On December 20, 1922, The Virginians (a contingent of Paul

Whiteman's musicians, directed by McHugh's erstwhile collaborator Ferde Grofé) recorded it for Victor, followed a few days into the new year by Paul Specht's band, which cut the same piece for Columbia.

As his career went on, McHugh would occasionally fall back on this gambit of revising an earlier song or title, and in 1924 he published "What Has Become of Hinky Dinky Parlay Voo?," which was a transparent attempt to sell a new song on the back of nostalgia for the World War I favorite. In later life, when journalists suggested McHugh had written the actual wartime song itself, he seldom denied it.

An equally opportunist plugging technique was to respond to a news event with an almost instant song, and because this could lead to an enormous volume of sales, McHugh and Mills were ready to try anything that would earn them sufficient funds to move out of what McHugh described as "the neighborhood of our bare upstairs rooms on West 45th Street . . . [an area] frequented by prizefighters and their managers, prostitutes and their pimps, cheap hotels and boarding houses." To add to the unique atmosphere of the offices, the Sixth Avenue elevated railroad—now long vanished—ran past the windows, adding its clanging rumble to every conversation. Instead of this temporary refuge, they sought a suite in one of the tall buildings on Broadway where the larger publishers held sway.

In due course, they managed to move into a new building at 148–150 West Forty-sixth Street, which McHugh immediately dubbed "the house that Jack built." They did so at least in part by systematically hustling all the revenue they could out of their topical songs. The first really high-profile example of this during McHugh's time in New York was when the firm cashed in on the death of Caruso, who died on August 2, 1921. Within hours of the agency cables carrying the report arriving in the city's news offices, the songwriters Stanley and Little had come up with a ditty called "They Needed a Songbird in Heaven, So They Took Caruso Away," and Mills had the sheet music on the streets the next day. Postcards were sent to music stores in the overnight mail advertising the copies at 20¢ each wholesale and asking customers to wire in their orders. The song sold extremely well.

McHugh had the chance to turn out a similar ditty of his own, when Rudolph Valentino died on August 23, 1926. As soon as the news was out, America went into a state of national mourning for Hollywood's greatest screen lover. The papers had been running stories about his state of health for some days, and as the *Manchester Guardian* in England reported, American interest in the movie star compared to the British preoccupation with the Prince of Wales: "No monarch or war hero ever aroused more sympathetic public interest anywhere than Valentino during the illness which ended fatally today. From the day last week when he was taken to a nursing home all sources of public information were sought for news of his condition, and when the word 'relapse' spread in New York yesterday crowds gathered about the nursing home and practically besieged the telephone companies and newspapers. Women by hundreds brought flowers and prayed on the steps of the building where the patient was lying."[28]

Public interest was fueled further by the tidal wave of gossip that followed the great star's death. According to the first reports, "Death followed an unavailing blood transfusion. An X-ray examination has revealed that pleurisy affected the walls of the heart."[29] But as time went on, further reports were confusingly contradictory. It had not, after all, been pleurisy, but a perforated gastric ulcer, leading to septicemia, that brought about his death. One of his lovers, Pola Negri, then announced that the ulcer itself had been caused by a secret treatment to counter hair loss, while others suggested that he had succumbed to aluminum poisoning owing to the type of cookware preferred by his chef. Wilder rumors circulated, to the effect that the ulcer story was a cover-up for a knife attack by the jealous husband of one of Valentino's lovers. McHugh himself subscribed to this latter view, which he picked up from his parish priest, Monsignor Leonard at the Actors' Church. The Monsignor had, apparently, administered the last rites to Valentino and told McHugh conspiratorially that "he died of a stab wound he received in Atlantic City."[30]

In the world of the song plugger, the cause of death was immaterial. As soon as they found out that Valentino was lying fatally ill in a nursing home, McHugh, Irving Mills, and J. Keirn Brennan clustered around one of the pianos in the Mills offices and worked out a song called "There's a New Star in Heaven Tonight." Within hours of the news of the actor's death, the first copies had been engraved and were on the streets, complete with a suitably romantic cover photograph of the late Latin lover. Wrote McHugh: "Almost before word of [his] death flashed around the world, our song was being sung in the nation's night clubs, dance halls and from its vaudeville stages."[31]

Such fast footwork helped immeasurably to increase the fortunes of Jack Mills's firm. When it moved into its newly built Forty-sixth Street premises, on the second floor above an Italian restaurant called Luigi's, the company boasted eleven rehearsal rooms, each with its own piano, and an altogether smarter level of decor than the somewhat rough-and-ready premises it had occupied previously. The floor above held the stockrooms and business offices.

Little by little, despite his fevered pace of work as a plugger, McHugh at last began to establish himself as a songwriter. Two years after his arrival in New York, in addition to the pieces already mentioned, he wrote songs for a revue called *Spice of 1922*, including "I'll Stand beneath Your Window Tonight and Whistle." In 1923, his first published song was "Out Where the Blue Begins," although this was briefly the subject of controversy when Fred Fisher Inc. sued Jack Mills for $25,000 on the grounds that it plagiarized a 1918 composition called "Bring Back the Roses, Kathleen Mavournéen." The suit was contested by Mills, and little more was heard of this competing claim.[32] That same year, McHugh's other songs included "Immigration Rose" and "Mad," and in 1924, he produced his first significant hit, "When My Sugar Walks Down the Street."

The lyrics for this song were jointly credited to Irving Mills and the singer-songwriter Gene Austin. Having Austin's name on a song would in due course be almost a guarantee of success, because his Victor recordings were to sell, in total, a staggering eighty-six million copies between 1923 and the outbreak of World War II. It is unlikely that Austin actually contributed much, if anything, to the lyrics, and it is more probable that Mills added his name as lyricist (and gave him a cut of the royalties) as a sales device, known in the trade at the time as a "cut-in," simply in order to feature his name more prominently on the sheet music. Whether he actually wrote much of it or not, this song was to be Austin's first really big hit. Originally written for a short-lived 1924 revue called *Grab Bag*, Austin's own recording of the song was made on January 30, 1925, as a duet with the soubrette Aileen Stanley, accompanied by the dance orchestra of Nat Shilkret. Yet Austin's was just one of a host of recordings that appeared almost simultaneously and which were a tribute not only to McHugh's success as a plugger but to his knack of writing tunes which would work in every context, from musical-comedy vocals to dance-band standards, and which, like "Emaline," would be taken up by the jazz community.

Before Austin himself set foot in the studio to record it, the song had already been played on disc by the singer Fred Weaver, by the Regent Dance Orchestra, by the Chicago-style jazz group the Wolverines, by the comb and tissue paper specialist Red McKenzie, by New Orleans trumpeter Johnny DeDroit, and by the Atlanta collegiate jazz orchestra Warner's Seven Aces. In other words, within a month or two of its publication, the song had taken off in all corners of the United States and in several styles of popular music. Four months further on into 1925, its first overseas recording was made by the London-based Savoy Havana Band, while later that year ensembles as diametrically opposite in style as the Greenwich Village dance band of Billy

Wynne (featuring "hot" trumpeter Red Nichols) and the African American blues queen Clara Smith and her Jazz Band also made versions of the song.

The extraordinary success of "When My Sugar Walks Down the Street" gave McHugh his first taste of what it felt like to write a truly popular hit, a melody that was hummed on every street corner. A profusion of recorded versions took his original tune into areas he had never imagined as he sketched out the notes at his piano. He was not to collaborate with Gene Austin again, as the Texan singer rapidly went on to enjoy a highly successful solo career, recording more of his own compositions (or cut-ins) including "Lonesome Road" and "How Come You Do Me Like You Do?," not to mention selling over twelve million copies of his 1927 hit, "My Blue Heaven." Nevertheless, it was "When My Sugar Walks Down the Street" that provided both Austin and McHugh with their first significant commercial success.

One immediate effect of this was that McHugh decided to share his good fortune with his parents, by moving them into a newly built home. For a man who later became an instinctive hoarder of memorabilia, he made the somewhat surprising decision to throw out everything from their old home. "The old coal burning stove, the pictures of John and Priscilla Alden, the old black square piano—they all went!" he wrote. His mother had never even seen the new building on a corner lot in Jamaica Plain, but McHugh (with help from his brother Tommy) not only selected the site and had the house designed and built—he went to a wholesale store and bought all the furnishings, and he showed the construction team where every item was to be placed, right down to the hanging of the pictures. McHugh spared no expense, and his papers include a mortgage deed for $10,000 on the cost of the new home. "I arranged with Larry and Tommy to drive mother out to the house on Washington's Birthday. It was the first time she had stepped into a modern home of her own, with electric push-buttons inside the door, central oil-burner heating system, a sun room with a canary in it, and outside, shrubs, trees and flowers. Her delight was complete." McHugh also went on a shopping spree with his father, equipping him with smart suits and hats. His nieces attest to the fact that his generosity extended to the family of his sister Helen, and, of course, he always sent home money to his wife and son.[33]

Although his day-to-day work for Jack Mills meant that McHugh was to collaborate on several future occasions with the third cowriter of "When My Sugar Walks Down the Street," Irving Mills, he knew that to reach the next level of success as a songwriter he needed a regular lyricist of his own, with whom he could develop a joint understanding of the writing process, whose words would fit ever more closely with his music, and who would feed him a string of suitable titles and ideas to be worked up into songs.

As it turned out, he had already had a somewhat unfortunate experience with the man who ended up fulfilling this role, the Runyonesque figure of Al Dubin, when Jack Mills tried to get them together in 1923. McHugh recalled:

> One evening around seven o'clock, Jack Mills summoned me to his office. With him was a large party weighing some 330 pounds. His round body was surmounted by a smooth knob of a head set with innocent blue eyes, the thin brown hair meticulously parted on the side and slicked down. His clothes, on that first meeting, and for as long as I knew him except for a few memorable occasions when I took him to a haberdasher's and achieved a momentary splendor, looked as if he had purloined them from a beggar.
>
> When I knew Al Dubin better, I understood that nature had been lavish with him in other ways besides an oversized body. His brilliance of mind, gift of poetry, unreliability, charm, appetites and vices were all built on the grand scale.[34]

Jack Mills had discovered that the Swiss-born Alexander Dubinsky, son of Russian emigré parents, had a talent for writing lyrics that had yet to be fully developed, even though by the time of this meeting in 1923, Dubin was already thirty-two years old. He had originally fallen in love with Broadway at the age of fourteen, escaping his doctor father and science-teacher mother in Philadelphia to try and sell his first songs door-to-door in Tin Pan Alley or at theater stage doors. In an effort to persuade their son to finish his education away from such low-life distractions, his Jewish parents enrolled him—somewhat surprisingly—in the Perkiomen Catholic Seminary in Pennsburg, several miles from their Philadelphia home. For a year or two, Dubin focused his attention on school, achieving good academic results and becoming a promising athlete (he was football captain and a member of the basketball team). But then, in a pattern that was to become a familiar aspect of his life, a series of suspensions for drinking, womanizing, and leaving the seminary grounds illegally at night culminated in his expulsion shortly before graduation.

Dubin found a job working for the Witmark Music Company and eventually published his first song, "'Twas Only an Irishman's Dream," in 1916. Then the war intervened, and given the multitudinous distractions to which he was prey, he had only just begun to restart his career as a lyricist when Mills introduced him to McHugh.

Dubin had the bones of a song called "Just a Girl That Men Forget" roughed out on paper, ready for setting to music. He was quite a specialist in this type of ballad about "a good girl gone wrong," and the two men were soon huddled around a piano, finding a suitable melodic structure for the song: "We had been working less than five minutes, when a whistle came up to the window from the street below," McHugh remembered. "'Pardon me just a minute,' Dubin said. He went lumbering down the stairs. We didn't see him again for nine months."[35]

Dubin had been lured away by two other would-be songwriter friends, Fred Rath and Joe Garrey, and they ended up writing the music for his lyric but were not immediately able to sell it. A few months later, Mills bought the rights, and McHugh himself ended up plugging it, with considerable success.

As Dubin was now officially a Mills lyricist, he did actually produce one song with McHugh in 1923, another piece in his "fallen woman" vein called "It's a Man Ev'ry Time, It's a Man." Then, remarkably for someone of his size, he simply evaporated into thin air. McHugh was anxious to carry on writing with him, saying: "Any composer will tell you that a good lyricist is the rarest talent in the world—and any tunesmith lucky enough to have found one prizes him above gold. I recognized Dubin's unusual gifts, and wanted to work with him, but he had disappeared again. Dubin possessed a wife with whom he was always having much difficulty. He was usually being pursued by process servers desiring to nail him for back alimony. He had devised various methods of eluding these gentlemen and was consequently very gifted at disappearing from view."[36]

The first idea McHugh had to lure him back, knowing that Dubin always required funds to keep his wife's process servers at bay and to fuel his own bibulous lifestyle, was to offer him an account on which he could draw money against his royalties at the firm. For someone in need of ready cash, reasoned McHugh and Mills, such a scheme ought to keep him close to New York. But on this occasion, the company's generosity was to no avail. Dubin was not to be found.

As 1923 rolled into 1924, and "When My Sugar Walks Down the Street" became a hit, McHugh knew that he needed to find a lyricist as a matter of urgency. Eventually, he was tipped off that Dubin could be found working as a bartender in a particularly seedy dive back in his hometown of Philadelphia, the Blue Lantern on Ellery Street. McHugh wasted no time in taking the train to Philly. Somewhat the worse for wear, Dubin proudly announced that every bartender in the place was a college graduate, as he stood, his great girth bound in a slightly grubby white apron, polishing glasses at the bar. McHugh recalled: "I managed to tear him away from this unaccredited branch of the

Ivy League, got him dressed and pressed and sobered, and brought him back to New York."[37]

Unfortunately, Mrs. Dubin swiftly discovered that her errant husband had returned to the city, and the following day she turned up at the Mills offices with the police and had Dubin arrested for nonpayment of alimony. At this point, McHugh was living at the nearby King James Hotel, and so he stood the $600 bail to get Dubin released and checked him into an adjoining room, turning the key on his lyricist to prevent another escape. Over the next couple of years, with Dubin more or less sober and more or less prepared to work, the pair wrote several songs, of which a number became quite successful.

During World War I, Dubin had sung in an overseas entertainment troupe for U.S. soldiers, and he loved the gung-ho spirit of the wartime songs. It was he who suggested, once he and McHugh began working together, that "Hinky Dinky Parlay Voo?" could do with a makeover. The advertisements ran: "They'll get up and cheer when they hear it. Here's the king of all 'gang' songs. 'Twill put your audiences in good humor. They've never forgotten it, they'll sing it with you."[38] The resulting song did well. The sheet music included a new verse, plus one hundred additional choruses by Dubin along the lines of:

> Maybe she still is true to you,
> and true to the rest of the army too,

Or:

> Haven't you told your wife about the girls you knew?
> You must have told your wife no doubt
> But I bet you left a lot of it out.

In a specific reference to his own wartime experience, Dubin slipped in the lines:

> What has become of all the Jewish soldiers, too?
> Many a son of Abraham
> Has eaten ham for Uncle Sam.

Dubin could reel off dozens and dozens of doggerel verses of this kind, and naturally the song found a universal appeal at all levels from community sing-alongs to full-scale stage revues. According to McHugh, it was Dubin who—in similar vein—supplied many of the reams of topical lyrics that the cult-favorite vaudevillians Ed Gallagher and Al Shean sang nightly in their patter song "Mr. Gallagher and Mr. Shean" at the Ziegfeld Follies. The song's original creator, Bryan Foy, is not credited on the sheet music, nor is McHugh himself, who wrote the brief melody for the verse of the published version that Jack Mills issued in 1922, after he and McHugh witnessed the duo bring the house down on their opening night in another New York revue.

To keep the song updated with contemporary references, Gallagher and Shean paid Dubin $25 for every new chorus he penned. During the brief years of their success, until Gallagher's untimely death in the mid-1920s, they were essentially a one-song act. However, what their detractors failed to spot was that the central verses of the song constantly changed, and the topics that they discussed with a combination of naive innocence, knowing double entendres, and occasionally startling racism were as "modern as the hour" for every house at the Follies. The tall, languid Gallagher with his long cigarette holder, and the short figure of Shean, who wore a fez, finished every chorus with the refrain, "Absolutely, Mr. Gallagher?" "Positively, Mr. Shean." In between, everything from lawn tennis to loan sharks received their whimsical treatment, courtesy of the ever-inventive Al Dubin.

So successful was the song that Gallagher and Shean, having trod the provincial boards for years without success, slipped out of their existing and somewhat unfavorable contract with Shubert Theatres to join the Follies at $1,000 a week. They were promptly sued by Shubert. Their defense, which was that they were not a very good act and therefore of no value to their former contractor, collapsed in the face of their newfound success. For a while, they were forced to undertake a national tour of the company's venues but were soon starring again at the Follies. In 1924, they often played for the exclusive private parties of wealthy patrons late in the evening, after that night's Ziegfeld show had ended, and for the majority of these, McHugh was their preferred pianist. He reported—not a little impressed—that their collective fee for such private engagements was $2,000 a night.[39]

He was also their pianist during the subsequent months when Gallagher let fame go to his head and started a series of affairs with some of the best-looking actresses in town. On one occasion, his long-suffering wife gate-crashed one of the society parties at which the duo was performing on Park Avenue, with a detective named James McHugh in attendance to witness her husband's supposed infidelity. The similar names of pianist and policeman caused much amusement, but Mrs. Gallagher was less amused shortly afterward when she found her husband closely entwined with the Spanish-American Follies star Hilda Marino in McHugh's office, running through the "Farewell Blues." A former vaudeville actress herself, Mrs. Gallagher announced first, that she and a former female acrobat, Mrs. Sheehan, were about to go into business to rival her husband's act as "Mrs. Gallagher and Mrs. Sheehan," and second, that she was going to sue him for every penny he had.[40]

A positive side effect of this for McHugh was that one of Gallagher's cast-off *inamorata*, a French-Canadian girl from Montreal called Marie-Rose Lussier but known to the world as the Greenwich Village Follies singer Fifi D'Orsay, became his lover for a time. She was a striking character, slim and elegant, with a huge smile, knowing dark eyes, and a mane of black hair. He escorted her on his rounds of the clubs and theaters, which greatly enhanced his image as a man about town and successfully buried any public recollections of his Bostonian marriage, although legally that remained in force.

Lussier had launched her act by singing "Yes, We Have No Bananas!" in French and was originally billed by the Greenwich Village Follies as Mademoiselle Fifi. As she became more famous, she added the surname D'Orsay and specialized in playing the role of a nice but naughty French girl from "Gay Paree." In due course, coached in singing by McHugh during his frequent visits to the furnished room where she lived in the Upper Seventies, she landed a role in Will Rogers's 1929 movie *They Had to See Paris*. Thereafter Fifi D'Orsay went on to make a further twenty-four motion pictures. She returned to the stage in 1971 for the Broadway run of Sondheim and Goldman's *Follies*, one of the original stars of the 1920s to appear in this production about a troupe of aging actresses gathering at their former theater before it is demolished. She died at the ripe old age of 79, in Los Angeles, in 1983.

In 1924, the year that Dubin wrote his reams of lyrics for Gallagher and Shean, he and McHugh also turned out "I Don't Care What You Used to Be," "It's What You Are Today," and "My Kid," the latter written for the comedienne Belle Baker. The following year, they produced their biggest hit of the 1920s, "Lonesomest Gal in Town." However, this success immediately attracted some unwelcome negative publicity, when the jobbing lyricist Willie Raskin claimed a share of the royalties. "As a man," Raskin told *New York Morning Telegraph* correspondent E. M. Wickes, "Dubin is a wonderful fellow, but I don't think he ever took a course in business or law."

Apparently, soon after he had reestablished himself in New York, Dubin had approached Raskin and proposed that with his cash-drawing account up and running at Mills, were the two of them to write a ballad together they could "land a fat advance." Raskin suggested the title, "Wonderful Girl of Today," and a few possible ideas for lines of the verse. Dubin disappeared and returned the following morning with a full draft of "Good Little Bad Little Girl," for which McHugh then supplied a tune. But Dubin, instead of accepting the $200 that Mills offered, held out for $1,000, to be split between himself, Raskin, and McHugh, and the song lay unpublished. Later, Dubin unashamedly plundered the lyric for "Lonesomest Gal in Town," and Raskin, who was not credited, became incensed.

I asked him if I were not entitled to a share in it for having been the goat in the other number, which Dubin appeared to have forgotten. Al grabbed my hand and said, "I'll declare you in on this song, Willie." But when the declaration and signing of royalty contracts came up, I was declared out. According to law, a collaborator is entitled to a share of a song, even if he contributes nothing more than a period. And Dubin has credited me with writing one line. Personally I don't know where I stand now, so I guess I'll have to have another talk with my lawyer.[41]

Ultimately, Raskin did not get a share of the song, although he did well enough from his subsequent collaborations with Sammy Fain to become well established in his own right. But Jack Mills Inc. never let negative publicity go by unchallenged, and so—driven by McHugh's manic energy—it contrived to put the most positive spin on every mention of "Lonesomest Gal in Town." For example, a *Midweek Pictorial* feature on the art of songwriting contained the following:

Suppose a songwriter's collaborator will dash in and say, "I've got a great idea! I just got a letter from my girl back home and she says in it, 'I'm the lonesomest girl in town!' How's that for an idea?"
    The wise gentleman addressed will knit his brow and look out of the window toward Broadway. Then he will say, "That's old stuff! The country is full of lonesome girls according to songwriters. See that girl in the limousine? There's a new idea. She's wealthy, she's got diamonds, and everything, and in spite of being rich, she's lonesome. That's something new. Let's find a piano."[42]

The same feature contained photographs of McHugh with Jack and Irving Mills at work in their offices, as well as the staff who engraved and printed the sheet music. But the intended effect was to continue to reinforce the message of "Lonesomest Gal," which McHugh had successfully plugged almost from the moment it was published.

The Dubin/McHugh partnership also proved that it could react with some rapidity to a news story. Just as Jack Mills had rushed songs into print for the deaths of great celebrities, in January 1926 the songwriting duo helped the firm with an "instant" song to celebrate the wedding of Irving Berlin to socialite El-lin Mackay, the daughter of the chairman of the Postal Telegraph Commercial Cable Company, who was also a wealthy financier and art patron.

In this instance there had been a considerable degree of advance warning, because the press had got wind of the story the previous July, owing to Ellin's father's implacable opposition to his daughter's marrying an immigrant Jewish songwriter. The *New York Daily Mirror* carried the story that Clarence Mackay threatened to cut off his daughter without a cent, and Berlin's lawyer, "Cap" O'Brien, was obliged to refute the many offensive rumors that Mackay's allies had planted in the papers, claiming that Berlin was a dope fiend, a mobster, or suffering from a fatal illness.[43]

Nevertheless, it was a surprise when Berlin, on the eve of a trip to Europe, suddenly eloped with Ellin Mackay on January 4 and subsequently married her. After a short honeymoon at the Ritz Hotel in Atlantic City, they set sail at the end of the week on the SS *Leviathan* for London, occupying the presidential suite at a cost of $2,500.

Dubin had originally produced a set of lyrics for "When a Kid Who Came from the East Side Found a Sweet Society Rose" during the first flood of newspaper stories about Berlin's romance, and McHugh had come up with a melody. But because both Mills and McHugh had long-standing personal connections with Berlin, they were sympathetic when representatives of Berlin's company pointed out that it was not fair to profit from the coverage of Berlin's personal life in the daily press. Even though the song had been announced, and orders were coming in for it, Mills decided to keep it off the market.

However, when the wedding itself took place, Berlin's firm rushed into print with his own song, "Always," claiming it was his wedding present to his bride. McHugh and Mills both knew that he had written the song "long before Berlin ever met her."[44] With such plain evidence of Berlin himself capitalizing on his personal life, Mills's scruples vanished, and the Dubin–McHugh song, beginning "The story I'm tellin' / 'Bout Irving and Ellin . . . ," was rushed into print. It was, as the *Morning Telegraph* observed, "just a flash, good for the hour . . . and may sell one hundred thousand copies."[45]

Yet, despite his experience of and love for the music industry, Dubin was never able to see the importance of plugging his latest work with the same clear, energetic vision as McHugh, who reflected later: "Dubin was really a bard. He loved the poems of Robert Service, Poe, Shelley and Byron. My trouble with him was that he was always getting drunk and disappearing on me. Or else he would come from a night in some sporting house wanting to write more lyrics about prostitutes."[46]

Dubin's indifference to selling their work sufficiently enthusiastically was one of the factors that finally caused the pair to go their separate ways, despite the success of "Lonesomest Gal." Ultimately, McHugh and Dubin were to work together again in the 1940s, before Dubin's life of excess sent him to an early grave, but their last major collaboration in the twenties was a song designed to promote a silent movie, *The Big Parade.* The idea was to corral nostalgic sentiment for the Great War into a compelling reason for going to see the movie. The patriotically red, white, and blue cover of the sheet music features a victory parade of American soldiers against a background of troopships and the trenches, but in this brave company even the maimed and the limbless are strutting along with their chins up. The horror of war is subsumed into the rosy glow of national pride and military pomp. According to McHugh:

One day I was waiting for [Dubin] to bring me a recitation on our song "My Dream of the Big Parade." We used to give it out to the acts because it was a sure-fire number. Blossom Sealey had broken it in at the Palace, where Benny Fields was the first entertainer to sing through a megaphone on the stage. I waited and waited but Dubin did not appear. Finally I left the office. Walking down Ninth Avenue I suddenly saw him carrying furniture into an apartment. While I had been waiting impatiently all day, Dubin had been helping some no-good bum move.[47]

At this, McHugh's irritation with his lyricist's lack of commercial instincts reached boiling point, but there was another equally important factor in the split. In addition to his already frenetic life as a partner at Jack Mills, a plugger, and a composer, McHugh had been attempting to keep pace with Dubin's hyperactive social life. For a period of eighteen months, from late 1924 until a few months before their association ended in 1926, composer and lyricist kept up a frantic social whirl. They ate, drank, and smoked to excess, tumbling into bed at dawn; but while the rotund Dubin generally snored the daylight hours away, McHugh was up within an hour or two, bathed, shaved, and immaculately dressed, to begin his day's work at the office, rehearsing acts, schmoozing with record company executives, and promoting the latest wares of Jack Mills Inc.

In the evenings, after looking in on shows at which their newest songs were being sung, Dubin and McHugh would eat the 65¢ six-course dinner at the L&W Restaurant on West Forty-fifth Street. The voracious Dubin often worked his way through two full dinners before they ventured off into the night. Many evenings the twosome wound up opposite the Pierpont Morgan mansion at the apartment of Sammy Chapman, *bon viveur* and future husband of the dressmaker Ceil Chapman. There they would be joined by other songwriters, such as Sammy Fain and Irving Kahal, and by numerous showgirls who were enticed to join the party with the promise of meeting Cole Porter, Irving Berlin, or other equally illustrious composers (who, of course, never showed up).

For a month or two in midsummer 1925, these activities decamped into the West Fifty-seventh Street duplex of a well-known socialite, who lent McHugh her apartment while she vacationed in Europe. There was more booze, further partying, and in the midst of it all, McHugh briefly took up with an attractive young woman who became his constant companion for some weeks. As their guests whiled away the nights in this borrowed apartment, Dubin pretended to be the butler, continuously serving alternate rounds of drinks: one to the guests and a second to himself.

The young woman whom McHugh encountered during his stay in the duplex was called Marietta (no reference to her surname survives), and his dalliance with her lasted from July to September 1925. The girl had been introduced to McHugh by the owner of the place the night before she left for Europe, during a farewell party that doubled as a reception for Eddie Quinn, the mayor of Cambridge, Massachusetts, who was an old friend of McHugh's from his Boston days. The apartment itself was quite spectacular, described by McHugh as having: "a large living room . . . two storeys high. The furniture was Spanish antique. The chairs, walls and drapes were cardinal red. The magnificent proportions of the room were set off by a tremendous stone fireplace, beautiful panelling, and a grand piano enthroned upon a dais, rising a foot off the floor. The bedroom rejoiced in silken coverings, silken drapes and silken sheets."[48]

As McHugh, seated at the piano on the dais, played a selection of his recent songs for Quinn's reception, a young lady timidly approached him and asked if he knew where she could find a piano. Assuring her he was just the man to help, he suggested she call by his office the next day. Thinking that her inquiry was idle party chatter, he was somewhat nonplussed when she duly arrived the next evening, in a head-turning scarlet outfit, and even more so when she offered to buy one of the beat-up pianos in the Mills practice rooms. McHugh was scheduled to take a number of record company executives to dinner and then on to a boxing match that evening, so he lightly suggested that if she wanted to pursue the question of the piano further, she could meet him after the bout at the Fifty-seventh Street apartment (into which he was moving that night), and he gave her the key.

When he arrived at the apartment, she was waiting for him, along with a large bunch of roses on the piano. He remembered: "The lady herself was sitting in one of the cardinal red chairs. She wore a stunning low-cut evening gown. As I served the first drinks, I realized that at that moment I couldn't recall her name. But after a few hours' conversation, we left arm in arm for Atlantic City."[49] The affair prospered briefly, and it is possible to chart its progress, because just as lovers today might communicate by email, Marietta and McHugh sent one another cables, several of which survive. Indeed, for the next twenty-five years, much of McHugh's life was to be reflected in his voluminous collection of Western Union telegrams.

From a flying visit to Chicago, Marietta sends McHugh "ALL MY LOVE, A BIG HUG AND KISS." A few days later (although a week in advance of the actual day he was thirty-two years old), she sends him an early-morning cable to the duplex at 205 West Fifty-seventh Street, saying, "WAKE UP! IT'S YOUR BIRTHDAY. LOTS OF LOVE, MARIETTA."[50] And so the affair continued, wound into McHugh's hectic schedule and hedonistic lifestyle. Yet, throughout the parties, the late nights, the cigarettes, and the booze, something about Marietta failed to ring true. Although she was well-bred and talked of her finishing school, she appeared to have no family, no friends. Finally McHugh questioned her, and she confessed that she was the kept woman of a Californian millionaire.

McHugh immediately realized that her lover had sent her East as a tactful way of breaking off his relationship, and he did not want to be the one to pick up the pieces. He ended the affair the same week that he moved out of his temporary luxury quarters. "Everything had to go," he wrote. "The beautiful apartment, the high times, the lady."[51]

He retreated from his luxurious surroundings to the first of a series of small boardinghouse rooms, and as he moved from minor hotel to hotel, her cables followed him. When she could no longer track him down, she tried the office. "NO WORD FROM YOU. FROM NOW ON, I AM BUSY. ALSO, GOODBYE FOREVER," read one from September 14, but just three days later she was both defiant and resentful: "PHONED YOU MONDAY AT LUXOR, BUT OPERATOR SAID YOU WERE NOT REGISTERED. . . . AM LONESOME AND BLUE FOR YOU TOOK ALL MY LOVE, MARIETTA." It was the last he heard from her.[52]

Back in Dubin's exuberant company, McHugh's high life continued, but just in time, common sense caught up with him. He later wrote:

> Since I never slept, my creative powers dwindled. I was burning the candle at both ends, writing nothing, getting nowhere. Keeping pace in my headlong plunge toward self-destruction was Dubin. . . . His weaknesses were food, liquor and houses of prostitution.

Actually we were going through a phase common to show people. Most of us pass through a period of wildly sampling human experiences, in defiance of the laws of common health, on the grounds that it makes better artists of us. Some of us become tangled in the tentacles of dissipation and disappear forever into the wretched twilight of futility, failure and death. Others pull out of it—a few of the lucky ones who hear the warning voice in time.[53]

One day McHugh collapsed in the office. Coming round, stretched out on a strange bed at the King James Hotel, he found Dubin ready to whisk him off to Lakewood to recuperate. This New Jersey country club was a favorite destination for wealthy New Yorkers who wished to detoxify and relax. A day or two later they were back in the social whirl, but McHugh now started to pace himself. He drank only milk but still had the shakes, hallucinations, and night terrors. He became a hypochondriac for several weeks, seeing fatal symptoms in even the tiniest pimple on his chin, and moved from hotel to hotel trying to find some rest. Once he was pulled over by two plainclothes cops as he walked along Broadway with a well-known heroin sniffer called Little Maxie, who financed his habit by selling song titles to composers at $5 apiece. McHugh was petrified that the police, seeing his hollow-eyed appearance, would discover the copious needle marks on his rear end, the result of visiting a succession of doctors for vitamin shots, and jump to the wrong conclusions. Fortunately, after examining his nostrils and checking his arm for tracks, they let him go. Maxie was not so lucky and was marched away to the precinct headquarters.

The solution to his near nervous breakdown was rooted deep in McHugh's past. He went back to church. He and Dubin (who had recently converted to Catholicism following the indoctrination of his schooldays) rang the bell at the Church of the Holy Innocents on Thirty-seventh and Broadway and asked for a priest. McHugh went to confession, and his recovery began. He became a regular attendee at the church for months afterward and moved into a small room in Carnegie Hall to start to sort out his life.

By contrast, Dubin did not keep up his church attendance. The two men worked together sporadically for the first months of 1926 and once or twice again the following year, but in the aftermath of "The Big Parade" incident, Dubin drifted out of McHugh's life for the better part of a decade. He became Harry Warren's lyricist, and between them the pair turned out over sixty hit songs between 1929 and 1938, including all of the *Gold Diggers* revues.

3

"Everything Is Hotsy Totsy Now"

A SEQUENCE OF HIT SONGS

IN THE AFTERMATH OF his breakdown, McHugh briefly turned into a popular radio star, as a member of the Hotsy Totsy Boys. Remarkably, this double act had achieved its first success during the height of McHugh's months of dissipation with Dubin. Although McHugh regarded Dubin as "his" lyricist from 1924 to 1926, part of his job at Mills was to supply tunes at the drop of a hat for any of the firm's wordsmiths, and high on that list came Jack Mills's younger brother Irving, who was also McHugh's fellow Hotsy Totsy Boy.

In many ways, Irving, born in January 1894, is the more fascinating of the two Mills brothers. They, like Dubin, were the sons of Russian Jewish immigrants and grew up on the Lower East Side of New York City. Their father died when Irving was eleven, and both boys went to work to keep the family in funds. After a succession of jobs as a hotel page boy and theater usher, Irving became a song plugger. When the family moved to Philadelphia, he demonstrated songs for Snellenberg's Department Store, plugging only their own brand of sheet music, singing by day in the store and by night in various theaters and clubs. He then went to work as a plugger for Leo Feist, until he and Jack set up their own firm in 1919.

Whereas Jack, two years his senior, focused on building up the publishing business, finding writers and plugging songs, Irving assumed a much wider role in shaping twentieth-century popular music. He had a relatively prolific recording career himself as a vocalist with, for the most part, medium-sized jazz groups comprised of New York session players, variously including Red Nichols, the Dorsey Brothers, or Joe Venuti and Eddie Lang. He would record the same song for the in-house record labels of all the main store chains, so that, for example, Sears Roebuck, Montgomery Ward, and McCrory's could each have its own version, performed by a slightly different Mills combination, such as his Music Masters, his Modernists, his Musical Clowns, or his Hotsy Totsy Gang.

He subsequently became the manager for Duke Ellington, Cab Calloway, Lucky Millinder, and a host of other African American artists. As Ellington's manager, he applied considerable skill to promoting the artistic side of Duke's work, getting his compositions and recordings assessed on completely different critical criteria from the rest of the acts he handled. He combined his continuing work as a publisher with running Mills Artists' Booking Agency and, in the years prior to World War II, also became head of the American Recording Company, which was later subsumed into Columbia.[1]

Yet, throughout the 1920s, despite a limited formal education that might well have inhibited a lesser man from attempting to write concise couplets, Irving Mills provided lyrics for scores of his brother's publications. Sometimes these were cynical exercises in adding additional verses to extant songs in exchange for a cut of the royalties, but more often than not, he provided all the lyrics himself for completely new tunes, as he had done as early as 1922 for Grofé and McHugh's "Stop Your Kiddin'."

One of the first songs that he and Jimmy McHugh knocked together in the normal run of business at the beginning of 1925 was a simple little number called "Everything Is Hotsy Totsy Now," taking its title from a catchphrase coined by the cartoonist Billy DeBeck, whose popular characters Barney Google and Snuffy Smith were given to describe anything that turned out for the best as "hotsy totsy."

The lyric has a knowing mixture of innocence and experience that is exactly in tune with the risqué era of the speakeasy, with its frivolous language putting a lightweight gloss on more serious matters, just as P. G. Wodehouse's novels use the superficial banter of Bertie Wooster and his circle to satirize the double standards of the age. In an era when Victorian social mores still appeared to be the backdrop to American society, when drinking alcohol was officially illegal, and young girls were chaperoned and counseled not to "get into trouble," the idea of a free-spirited woman who was going to make her own decisions about "spooning" with her young man and how far she was prepared to go gently mocked the hypocrisy of a society that was collectively turning a blind eye to the Volstead Act.

> 'Cause I got myself a brand new hotsy,
> I'm her totsy and she's my hotsy,
> Everything is hotsy totsy now.
> And when we spoon she don't say stop-sy,
> Don't call Mom-sy or her Pop-sy
> Everything is Hotsy Totsy now.

Mills's simple wordplay was ideal fodder for his fellow pluggers to spawn a host of ingenious marketing ideas, and these fueled the success of what was otherwise a pretty flimsy song. Within a short time of its release, Jack Mills was sending out a flyer in the form of a marriage license, dated the 26th day of March 1925, which solemnized the union of "Hotsy, of anywhere, U.S.A." and "Totsy of the same place . . . in the presence of Irving Mills and Jimmy McHugh as witnesses." Embossed over the city clerk's signature in red was "'Everything is Hotsy Totsy Now,' Jack Mills latest and greatest song hit."

Quite a few wags decided to reply to this missive, and McHugh kept one letter sent in the following August from the Fawn Club near Lake Placid in the Adirondacks, in which the bandleader Frank Roberts wrote: "Received your letter giving proof that 'Hotsy' and 'Totsy' are legally one. This is a great relief to me because these same two have been staying here together all summer, and you know how sensitive we musicians are about such things!"[2]

With copious storefront window displays of the sheet music that showed the songwriters Mills and McHugh side by side, and press photos that had them shaking hands over the piano, the piece was swiftly "taking first place as the plug song of Jack Mills."[3] The firm did its best to turn Hotsy Totsy into a brand, or as its display placards put it, "The big fox-trot sensation of today." In the precious time he spent out of Dubin's hedonistic company with Fifi D'Orsay, with whom he had resumed his affair following his fling with Marietta, McHugh was still so obsessed with the song that he taught her the lyrics and was charmed by her French accent as she sang "'Otsy Totsee." Soon he was finding opportunities to accompany her in public, as she incorporated the song into her act.[4] There was even, at the height of the song's popularity, a short-lived Hotsy Totsy Club located on the rear ground floor of 754 Seventh Avenue.

Early in the life of the song, Mills and McHugh began to appear together as "The Hotsy Totsy Boys." This started in March 1925, the month the sheet music was released, with the two of them singing around New York and then undertaking a plugging trip to Chicago.[5] McHugh remembered that visit well, because, as he later recalled, they "invaded with such eager ferocity that I . . . succeeded in setting some song of ours with a singer in every theater in town. This still stands I believe, as something of a feat."[6] The Chicago trip was followed by a two-week plugging visit to Boston, to exploit this and other Mills songs, and resulted in a "sheaf of orders."

In much the same way as "Yes, We Have No Bananas!" had captured the public imagination, "Everything Is Hotsy Totsy Now" did the same, and, largely owing to its simple catchphrase, the song was eagerly recorded by the California Ramblers, the Coon-Sanders Nighthawks, and the Indiana Five. Indeed, Mills and McHugh recorded the song themselves on May 14, 1925, as the Hotsy Totsy Boys, but the Gennett Company was not happy with the results, and it lay unissued until 1979. Although the masters were destroyed soon after the recording session, a test pressing survived in the Mills offices and was taped by the collector Jerry Valburn shortly before the test disc itself was thrown out. When Valburn's tape was released on LP, jazz experts mistakenly identified the pianist who accompanied Mills's vocals and kazoo as Duke Ellington, owing both to Mills's subsequent involvement with the bandleader, and the clear affinities with Duke's playing evident in McHugh's accomplished syncopated style.[7]

Recording was one thing, but the publication of this song coincided with a huge growth in the possibilities of using radio as a means to plug the sheet music, which was not without its concerns for some of McHugh's colleagues. He recalled:

> Radio was just coming in. The undreamed-of potential of the new radio audience appalled everybody. John McCormack received 20,000 letters after his first broadcast and issued a statement in favor of the new medium. WOR had a station over in Newark. In order to get a broadcast plug, all the song pluggers would go over to Newark to get on it. Later the Loew Theaters started a broadcasting station in Loew's State Theater. It was almost next door to our office and very convenient.
>
> The increased facilities of communication only increased the frenzied competition among the song pluggers. We became a crowd of dedicated pushers who almost never slept and endeavored to be in as many places as possible at the same time. In the course of an average day, Irving Mills and I would appear on broadcasts as often as twenty times with our songs. These were the days of

crystal sets and makeshift equipment. We used to call it the "block-to-block hook-up." All of the big stars, Harry Richman, Al Jolson and the rest would run in now and then for a guest slot. The studio was a small bare room with a piano and a mike.[8]

Irving Mills's son Bob confirms the frantic pace at which his father and McHugh worked: "Once radio blossomed, Irving was singing at six radio stations seven days a week plugging Mills tunes."[9]

The publicity photos of Mills and McHugh called them "Radio's Favorite Songsters," and for a while it seemed as if—in addition to his high-pressure lifestyle, his management responsibilities at Mills, and his career as a composer—McHugh was going to make the transition into a performer. He even took the precaution of insuring his hands for $25,000 at Bazzell and Sons.[10] But while Irving Mills continued to balance his life between his business activities and singing on records or at the broadcasting microphone, McHugh made the decision to pull back from performing. He was never afraid to roll up his sleeves and play, and his subsequent career included some extremely high-profile engagements, from the opening of Radio City Music Hall to playing for the future Queen of England in London, but he knew his main forte was to be writing songs and hustling up a market for them. One factor in his decision may have been the arrival of press reports stating that other singers were making a better job of his current song than he and Mills did. A review of Hilda White Kay's broadcast over the WAAM network noted that "her singing of 'Everything Is Hotsy Totsy Now' is the first time we have waked to the realization that this particular piece of modern ingenuity has a wealth of melody in it."[11]

One significant event that outweighed his career as a performer was that in November 1925 McHugh entered the rankings of the annual songwriters' popularity contest for the first time. The *Morning Telegraph* reported that he had come in sixth with 1,969 votes. First was L. Wolfe Gilbert with 22,650, and third was Irving Mills with 8,415.[12] The ever-competitive McHugh took this as a challenge. Nothing better than first place would do for him in the future, and as he gradually extricated himself from the excesses of Dubin's lifestyle, and—surrounded by the bohemian atmosphere of Carnegie Hall—focused once more on composing, his achievements in 1926 were to be his best yet.

In addition to the Caruso memorial song and "The Big Parade," the year produced McHugh's second major hit, a piece on a par with "When My Sugar Walks Down the Street." This was the endlessly catchy "I Can't Believe That You're in Love with Me," with lyrics by Clarence Gaskill, who had been responsible for the songs in that year's *Earl Carroll Vanities* (a show whose titillating seminudity meant that, despite the excellent songs featured in the production, music was the last thing on the minds of its patrons). Like a lot of McHugh's most enduring melodies, this one took a while to grow to its full potential, but it went on to become one of the most-recorded songs of all time. It was first put on disc, as so many of McHugh's 1920s tunes were, by a New York session band with the trombonist Miff Mole and his circle, this time under the leadership of Roger Wolfe Kahn. But it was the musicians who picked it up in the following decade who ensured its longevity and continued popularity.

Most significant of all was Louis Armstrong, who made his famous trumpet and vocal version in April 1930, and this had the effect of turning the tune into a jazz standard. Not only were versions subsequently made by musicians who closely followed Armstrong's template, such as his fellow trumpeters Cootie Williams and Nat Gonella, but the piece found its way into the repertoire of Teddy Wilson, Earl Hines, Billie Holiday, Artie Shaw, Count Basie, and, in due course, almost all the big names of the swing era. Later it was to become one of the most requested songs in Frank Sinatra's repertoire.

At the core of the song was the clean match between the contour of McHugh's melody and Gaskill's words. More often than not, a popular song succeeds because its tune is hummable. We may remember the title and a line or two of the lyrics, but it is generally the tune that sticks in the mind to be whistled or hummed. Thanks to Armstrong, Holiday, Sinatra, and other singers from Peggy Lee and Dean Martin to Dinah Washington and Mel Tormé who have recorded it, we remember this song for both music and lyrics:

> Your eyes of blue
> Your kisses too,
> I never knew what they could do,
> I can't believe that you're in love with me.
> You're telling everyone I know,
> I'm on your mind each place you go,
> They can't believe that you're in love with me.

McHugh's ability to produce neat musical phrasing, which caught the nuance of the lyrics, was to be one of his greatest attributes as a song composer, and, as he subsequently reflected, he was well aware of the progress he was making toward regularly producing more substantial hits than he had hitherto managed:

I began to make headway as a composer, [because] I became impatient to get away from the crappy ballads about loose women so dear to Dubin's heart. I had learned a good deal about the demands which the popular song imposes upon the writer. The more I learned, the more I wanted to deal with bigger themes. Conversely, it is the very limitation of the popular song that is the key to its greatness. The simple tune is the great tune. In the construction of commercial ballads you try to limit the range to eight, or at most nine, notes, and to maintain an overall simplicity of theme so it will be easy to sing.[13]

Later that year, it was again Gaskill, with a little help from Irving Mills, who provided the words for McHugh's follow-up song, "I Don't Mind Being All Alone, When I'm All Alone with You." This never caught on with the same degree of success as "I Can't Believe That You're in Love with Me," despite being promoted by Jack Mills as "the melody hit of the year."[14]

McHugh's other songs of 1926 included "After I Took You into My Heart," which was plugged with a romantic story that had him meeting "a sad-hearted girl sitting all alone in a corner of a nightclub. . . . In the course of conversation she told this popular songwriter a little story of her life which gave him the inspiration to write his latest song."[15] The result of this increased output and its successful promotion from Mills was that during September, McHugh was honored at a banquet held at the Monte Carlo Night Club, "in recognition of his splendid achievements in the field of popular songwriting during the past two years."[16]

Early in 1927, again anxious to be "making headway," McHugh attempted to produce a dance tune that would have the same impact on the public as the "Black Bottom" had since its introduction in 1923.[17] The result, "Baltimore," introduced to the public by the exotic Follies dancer Gilda Gray (who had made her name by belly dancing in New York a year or two earlier), never burgeoned into a popular fad, but, like a lot of McHugh's songs, it quickly caught on with both white and African American performers. During the launch of her film *The Devil Dancer* at the Rivoli Theatre, Gray used "Baltimore" as the cornerstone of her stage act, which included a team of twelve dancers, and reportedly "created a sensation."[18]

The first recording of the piece was actually made in April 1927 by the black bandleader Clarence Williams and his Blue Five, who conjoined the two dance fads of the day by recording "Take Your Black Bottom Dance Outside" for the flip side of the same record. Shortly afterward, the white trumpeter Red Nichols cut the song with his Redheads, which paved the way for the mercurial Bix Beiderbecke to make a version with Frankie Trumbauer a little later in the year, at almost the same time as his African American counterpart

Fletcher Henderson made his. McHugh had the knack, it seemed, of writing tunes that would convert into convincing jazz in a variety of styles.

What is noticeable and unusual about the recording history of this tune, however, is that it spawned a large number of recordings in Britain, by, among others, Fred Spinelly and his Lido Club Band, Birt Firman's Dance Orchestra, and the Filipino pianist Fred Elizalde, whose Cambridge University group was one of Britain's most accomplished jazz ensembles. The reason for this sudden spate of recordings was that McHugh made his first visit to Europe in June of 1927, and needless to say, he found plenty of opportunities to plug his wares.

Why McHugh chose this particular time to visit Lawrence Wright, the British agent for Jack Mills Inc., is unclear, but it may well have had something to do with another of his romantic entanglements coming to an end. In his files is a note dated "Easter Afternoon" from a lady called Bérenice. She writes: "I've been doing a lot of thinking and have come to the conclusion I can't see you, for a while anyway. I can't be in the routine you want. It is impossible for me. I am more sorry than I can say things are turning out this way. . . . I don't want you to feel the reason for this is another man—there is none. I'm very fond of you, but regardless of that, I can't go on."[19] In 1927, Easter fell on Sunday, April 17, and it would appear that McHugh booked his first-class passage to England within days of receiving that note. He sailed for Southampton on the SS *Leviathan* on Saturday, June 11.

For the six years he had been in New York, he had maintained a somewhat formal, distant contact with his wife and son. He had been diligent about sending half his salary home to provide for his family, and undoubtedly his regular attendance at confession and the generous donations he made to Catholic causes eased his conscience as he dallied with a succession of actresses, singers, and dancers.[20] He received terse updates from Bess about their son's progress along the lines of "Jimmie [*sic*] doing well," and occasionally he was the recipient of rather distant letters from his son.

Dear Daddy
   The weather is very good hear. I hope so their. I am going to play football this afternoon. That little boy you met that time came around and played with me yesterday. Don't forget Holycross and Boston C. game.
   Your sun
   James McHugh [21]

Until Jimmy Jr. reached high school age, he saw his father only fleetingly, and these mannered letters were their main point of contact. Yet every woman whom McHugh dated would soon become aware that he remained a married man, and that as a practicing if somewhat morally lax Catholic, he conscientiously supported his absent family, sending flowers or telegrams with his usual diligence for birthdays, high days, and holidays. This duality was no doubt the "routine" that Bérenice found insupportable. It suited McHugh to be seen around town with the likes of Fifi D'Orsay on his arm and to carry on clandestine affairs with other women. But to put them first? To make a proper commitment? Love them, even? Forget it.

Setting sail from the United States, McHugh left his tangled love life behind, and he docked in Southampton with only work on his mind. He immediately caught the boat train to London and settled in at the Piccadilly Hotel for the princely sum of £1; 2s; 6d. per night.

> I got into town around 11 p.m. at night, and by 12 o'clock, after checking in . . . I was on my way out with orchestrations under my arm to start my New York routine of contacting the singers and bandleaders at the numerous cafés and hotels in London. Everywhere I went I ran into musicians from Boston, like Carroll Gibbons at the Savoy, who was the orchestra leader there. It seemed within a short time they were all giving parties for me. Of course, I had taken two special songs over there to try and get started, and they were "I Can't Believe That You're in Love with Me," and "I Don't Mind Being All Alone, When I'm All Alone with You." Because I kept plugging away at them, before long I found that they were becoming big hits. Word had reached Lawrence Wright down at Blackpool, and he called me by telephone and said, "Jimmy, what are you doing to my business? You're disrupting it!" I replied, "Lawrence, I've got two big hits for you, which are well on their way."[22]

As it was the middle of the British summer holiday season, Wright had decamped from his London offices in Denmark Street to the Lancashire seaside resort of Blackpool in the northwest of England. This town, with its miles of beach, its famous donkey rides along the sand, not to mention its dance halls, tower, pier, and theaters, served the huge industrial conurbations of Liverpool and Manchester, and it was second only to London as an entertainment center in the 1920s. Then, as now, it had a certain faded charm, and McHugh—who was summoned there for a meeting with Wright—described it as "fifty years behind our own Coney Island." It was a magnet for the English working class, and during the annual summer breaks or "wakes weeks" at the factories of the northwest, which were staggered throughout the months of June, July, and August, the town filled with laborers and their families, taking time away from their dark, satanic mills to flock in profusion to its entertainments and attractions.

The equivalent of today's electronic amusement arcades at Blackpool were booths where song pluggers would display huge placards of the lyrics to the newest hits and impart them to the passing crowds with the aid of a long white pointer. McHugh reported: "Naturally, in this way they were able to teach the songs to thousands of people. It was really a very elementary way, but it was thrilling to walk around the streets and hear all these voices, singing the songs of the day. Not only that, but when these people would return to the city they always bought the sheet music of the numbers, so it was certain to sell a million copies easily."[23]

McHugh was fascinated by Blackpool, which in many ways was perhaps more like Atlantic City than Coney Island, albeit with a more bracing climate. He wrote: "It was just like a great big circus. They had a tremendous restaurant, a theatre, a circus and just everything in one large building, called the Hippodrome. It was just huge, covering acres and acres of ground. They also had a dance hall in the place with five tiers of balconies . . . just a fabulous spot." It was a song-plugger's paradise, and McHugh went to work with all the skill and charm he could muster. Many years later, Lawrence Wright was to write a friendly note to McHugh from his summer home at Carlin Gate in Blackpool, saying: "The donkeys on the sands still remember the happy times we had together. Hope you are still full of pep with your famous smile full of happiness."[24]

In Blackpool he also met the bandleader and publisher Herman Darewski, who had the seventy-five-piece band at the Tower Ballroom, and thus added another influential name to his list of contacts in the UK. But perhaps the most significant contact, in terms of its impact on McHugh's future career, was his meeting on the same night, June 28, with the producer Lew Leslie, whose revue *Blackbirds of 1926* was also featured at the Tower Ballroom. This African American show was still running in Britain after its launch in New York the previous year. It had notched up 279 performances at the London Pavilion, and its Blackpool appearances marked the final stages of a year-long international tour.

It was a huge hit, as the N.E.A. press agency's London correspondent Milton Broxner reported that same week, largely because of its star singer and dancer Florence Mills: "The show . . . promises to run on all through the summer and on and on indefinitely. The Prince of Wales has been to see the performance over and over again. Society has followed in his wake."[25] So all-pervading was its impact, according to Broxner, that in every part of the country women buying tan stockings had begun asking for "the Florence Mills shade."

McHugh, who already knew the trumpeter Johnny Dunn, leader of the show's lively pit band, the Plantation Orchestra, went backstage to locate Leslie, and, as he recalled, after finally tracking him down, "I told him I wanted to do a show for him."[26] This was the initial contact between the two men that eventually led the following year to their work together on *Blackbirds of 1928*, the show that launched McHugh's most accomplished songs of the 1920s.

Returning to London, McHugh prepared for a short trip to Paris. Before he crossed the channel, he encountered the singer Helen Morgan, who was to become known to the American public later in the year as the star of *Show Boat* but who had just launched her recording career in Britain with "Hutch" (bandleader Leslie Hutchinson) accompanying her. She was about to open in cabaret at London's Café Anglaise. Turning up for her opening night, McHugh, who knew Morgan through her appearances at "The House of Morgan" in New York, where she sat atop the piano, sipping brandy and singing sultry songs, found her sitting disconsolately on a curbstone on the edge of Hyde Park, some distance from the club. "Before the opening she was so nervous, she was afraid to go on," he wrote. "She'd had a little to drink." McHugh gently coaxed her into returning to the club and going on stage, where she became the star of the show.[27]

McHugh's long-term impact on Britain continued to be felt for months to come. Not only did the bands mentioned earlier record his current hit, "I Can't Believe That You're in Love with Me," but he started the ball rolling in popularizing his new dance, the "Baltimore." It took a while, but by the end of the year, the Baltimore, with steps devised by "the World's Champion Charleston dancer" Beryl Evells and her partner Barrie Oliver, was being touted as "The New Dance For Crowded Ballrooms," and its principal steps—"the essence of gracefulness, easy to learn and pleasing to watch"—were illustrated in the *Westminster Gazette*.[28]

For the last two weeks of his European sojourn, McHugh stayed in Paris, aiming to rejoin the *Leviathan* at Cherbourg on July 12. If Florence Mills was the toast of London that July, then her fellow African American, Josephine Baker, was an even bigger star in Paris. One contemporary account ran as follows:

The lithe Josephine came to Paris almost unheralded. She first appeared at the swell Champs Elysées theater in a show called simply *Revue Négre—Negro Revue*. It was a singing and dancing show, such as we have been familiar with for donkey's years. But soon all the Parisian cognoscenti were flocking to the house. And then suddenly, the show disappeared from the swell Elysée district. The reason was not a failure. It was a success. The Folies Bergères claimed Josephine at a huge salary. She's been packing the house ever since. Her form has been done by French sculptors. Her face has been painted by French artists. She has opened a cabaret of her own. Her vogue goes on undiminished.[29]

Surprisingly, McHugh did not descend on Josephine with his usual armful of arrangements. Almost as soon as he arrived in the city, he found an all-consuming distraction, as he later recalled: "My first night there, I took a bus to see the sights of Paris. Returning to the hotel later, I saw this beautiful creature in the lobby. I tried the old gag: 'I'm sorry but I don't speak French . . .' 'If you'll ask me in English,' she replied, 'I'm sure I can help you.'"[30] McHugh somewhat delicately wanted to know if the "beautiful creature" was a prostitute. "I happen to be a very nice respectable lady," she told him, and from then on his twelve days in Paris were spent almost entirely in her company, apart from an evening or two when he met with an old friend, Jack Donohoe, to drink in one of the tougher neighborhoods. McHugh gave the woman a recording of "I Can't Believe That You're in Love with Me," and it echoed around the courtyard behind the Hotel Ambassador, where they were staying, in the evenings.

The couple spent their days hand in hand, taking in the sights and sounds of Paris. She no doubt accompanied him when he bought an expensive collection of thirty neckties at the Ritz Cravat Company. After visiting the Opéra Comique and dining at several out-of-the-way cafés, on McHugh's thirty-fourth birthday they wound up in a smart restaurant in St. Germain where there was a large fish tank from which one could select one's dinner. McHugh wrote: "Feeling sentimental about my birthday and seeing the fish, I began to think about the family in Boston, and I became rather sad. I told [her] how wonderful she was, and what a great thrill it was meeting her. I noticed a strangeness in her manner. 'Of course,' she said, 'You know I'm married?' The melancholy of the day was complete."[31] Two days later, the woman took the train to Cherbourg with McHugh, and she filled his pockets, even his socks, with little notes saying, "I love you!" "I'll always remember you!" "Don't forget me!"

Soon after McHugh embarked on the SS *Leviathan* he sent his erstwhile companion a cable: "MISS YOU VERY MUCH. CAN'T SLEEP NIGHTS. LOVE KISSES." There is no clue to her real name or identity in McHugh's files, except a cable she sent a few months later from Paris, warning him not to betray their affair. It reads: "FAMILY ARRIVING NEW YORK WEDNESDAY. CAREFUL PICTURE AND TALK. LOVE OLGA."[32]

Back on board ship, McHugh was soon distracted from his love life. The SS *Leviathan* was awash with celebrities, and having used his charms on the steward to get upgraded to A-deck, he was soon mingling with the great and the good. His fellow first-class passengers included, on the one hand, the film actress Hope Hampton and her husband, the aging Jules Brulatour, whom she sent to bed while she partied the nights away, and, on the other, a collection of famous American aviators who had all just narrowly failed in their bids to win the Orteig prize for the first nonstop flight from New York to continental Europe. McHugh's old passion for flying was briefly rekindled in the presence of such aeronautical pioneers.

Charles Lindbergh had in principle already won the $25,000 award for his solo flight in the *Spirit of St. Louis*, which landed in Paris on May 20. But he had ridden roughshod over the rules by not allowing the requisite sixty days between his registration and his take-off, so there was an outside chance that the trustees of Orteig's donation would still award the money to another contender. Therefore, the two rival attempts that had also been preparing both took off, and the crews of Commander Byrd's *America* and Chamberlain's *Columbia* were now making their way home. During early June, the *America* had reached the French coastline and the *Columbia* flew to Berlin, but neither team was ultimately successful in claiming the prize, as the trustees decided to reward Lindbergh's solo feat by waiving the rules regarding his registration.

Nonetheless, Byrd's and Chamberlain's teams had achieved something remarkable for the time. As Senator Thomas J. Walsh of Montana said during his onboard speech in recognition of their efforts: "Aviation's triumph proved that heroes can be recognized in peace better than in times of war, because their deeds were constructive events. . . . Time would prove that what had been so recently done was a genuine contribution for the peace of the world."[33] The liner held a special "Heroes of the Air" night, for which Jimmy McHugh produced a new song, sung for the occasion by Hope Hampton to his own accompaniment. When the *Leviathan* docked, McHugh skillfully maneuvered himself into position next to the fliers for the photographs that appeared on the nation's front pages. Yet within just a few months he was to be making front-page news of his own, with a new lyricist, and a new job, in the unlikely setting of Harlem.

"I Can't Give You Anything but Love (Baby)"

MEETING DOROTHY FIELDS

IN THE PHOTOGRAPH of the returning fliers on the front page of the *New York Times* on July 24, 1927, a dapper Jimmy McHugh appeared to be at the very zenith of fashionable society, standing close to Commander Richard E. Byrd as the SS *Leviathan* docked. Yet, within days of his return, he was to find himself at the heart of a very different element of life in Manhattan, the violent gangster mobs who not only managed the city's elaborate network of organized crime but who were gaining an almost complete stranglehold on its places of entertainment.

During the same week as his voyage home, a much talked-about new show opened in Harlem, at the Cotton Club, which stood at the junction of Lenox Avenue and 142nd Street. *Breezy Moments in Harlem* started its run on July 13 and was soon being billed as "The hottest show around at the coolest place in town."[1] Throughout the years that McHugh had been in New York, the uptown district of Harlem had little by little become more noticeable on the city's social radar. Although his main efforts as a song plugger had been focused in and around the Broadway theater district, McHugh, in common with all music publishers, could hardly have failed to notice that a ready market for his wares was establishing itself in the newly fashionable Harlem clubs, where, for the most part, well-heeled white audiences from downtown went in search of black entertainment. Yet it was not until after his trip to London and Paris that McHugh got seriously involved in what was going on there, and when he did so, it was the result of an accidental meeting.

His time away from the United States had given him the chance to reflect on his recent career. In six and a half years, he had not only become one of the most successful pluggers in New York but had written a couple of major hit songs and several others that had sold almost as well. He had become a member of ASCAP (the American Society of Composers, Authors, and Publishers) but only at the lowest level, and he was anxious to move up its rankings alongside some of the other composers who were also part of the Mills stable, such as Egbert Van Alstyne ("In the Shade of the Old Apple Tree"), Ted Fiorito ("Toot Toot Tootsie, Goodbye"), Gus Kahn ("It Had to Be You"), and the virtuoso saxophonist Rudy Wiedtoeft.

However, being McHugh, he aspired to a higher level than all of them. He aimed to become as well known as Irving Berlin, Victor Herbert (who had died in 1924), George Gershwin, and Jerome Kern, and he realized that to achieve the same level of impact as these most successful fellow songwriters, he needed to write an entire Broadway show. He wrote: "My efforts to get on Broadway had culminated in a resounding zero. Broadway was a haughty young wench with no apparent inclination to bestow her favors on me, a brash young Irishman. She played her favorites. No crass outsiders were being considered to elbow them aside. But I was enamored. The less Broadway wanted me, the more I wanted Broadway. Like a sulky suitor, frustration settled down on me like a London fog."[2] Bustling about Manhattan as he resumed his day-to-day work for Jack Mills, McHugh nurtured his dream to write for Broadway, and so he made a point of stopping to talk to any show producers he happened to run into, just in case they could give him a helping hand to break into what increasingly seemed to be a closed world.

Not long after his return, he spotted one such producer in the street, Walter Brooks, the man who had presented the highly successful African American musical *Shuffle Along*, which had run for over five hundred performances on Broadway back in 1921–22. The show had made a star of Florence Mills—whom McHugh had only recently heard in Blackpool—when she replaced its original leading lady, Gertrude Saunders. Huge crowds had packed Daly's 63rd Street Theatre during much of McHugh's first two years in New York to witness Mills's remarkable skills as a dancer and singer, particularly in the show's hit song "I'm Just Wild about Harry."

Hoping that Brooks might be just the man to help him, McHugh stopped him for a chat.

> "What are you doing, Jimmy?" Walter asked me.
> "This and that," I told him.
> "How would you like to write some songs for me? Think you could?"
> "Sure. What do you want me to write?"
> "I'm putting on a new show at the Cotton Club," Walter said. "I need some new numbers for it."[3]

And so it was that McHugh found himself swept away from Broadway, for the time being at least, and immersed in the new, vibrant experience of 1920s Harlem. Outwardly, this northern district of Manhattan looked much like any other part of the city. Its main boulevards, Lenox and Seventh Avenues, were both broad, tree-lined thoroughfares, with two carriageways. Much of the area close to the 125th and 129th Street railroad stations consisted of spacious buildings constructed around the dawn of the twentieth century to accommodate people who wanted to live outside the downtown business areas but have easy transportation to and fro via the elevated railroad.

Inwardly, Harlem was different. Between 1904, when there was a real-estate slump, and the start of the 1920s, there had been a massive influx of African Americans. White realtors, desperate to shift their overpriced inventory, encouraged the newcomers first to buy and then to rent the available property, which was soon settled at a density never envisaged by those who had originally planned the area. Estimates suggest that as many as three hundred thousand people were living in housing designed to support only sixty thousand.

With such a substantial population crammed into a relatively small area, Harlem became a microcosm of inner-city problems. There was poverty, there was crime, there was overcrowding, there was barely adequate sanitation. On the other hand, at the time McHugh arrived in Harlem, the close-knit African American community had plenty of positive things going for it. There was a staunch churchgoing core of the population whose Christian values were reflected in everything from storefront places of worship to the huge Abyssinian Baptist Church; and with their Sunday-best clothes and innate decency came an underlying civic pride, a new political hope inspired by the likes of Marcus Garvey and W. E. B. Du Bois, and—at the same time—the movement of writers, artists, and intellectuals that became known as the Harlem Renaissance. The writings of Claude McKay, Langston Hughes, and James Weldon Johnson and the paintings of Aaron Douglas encompassed a remarkably self-aware movement in which the nuances of jazz and blues were powerful ingredients.

However, exceptional as these positive cultural elements were, nothing was more remarkable about Harlem than its depth of talent in entertainment. At the most domestic level, there were rent parties, where a pianist such as James P. Johnson, Willie "The Lion" Smith, or Luckey Roberts would entertain in someone's home with their ragtimey "stride" specialties. The hard-up tenant would charge admission for those who wished to hear the music in order to raise money for the rent. The same pianists, and their colleagues like Fats Waller, Lippy Boyette, and Joe Turner, also played for several of the smaller clubs and cabarets in Harlem, in particular Leroy's on 135th Street, a proving ground for pianists who tried to outdo each other in spectacular displays of skill known as "cutting contests." Waller was also the organist at the Lafayette Theatre in July 1927, having earlier entertained at the Lincoln (a theater catering mainly to a black audience).

Other clubs and speakeasies had little bands, and the most prosperous of them even mounted floor shows. Only a few such venues catered exclusively for the local black clientele, and of these, Smalls' Paradise at Seventh Avenue and 125th Street was the best known. But the majority of the big venues, notably Connie's Inn and the Cotton Club, presented black musicians, singers, and dancers for a white audience that came uptown to savor this exotic and dangerously erotic entertainment. The Cotton Club, seating an audience of close to seven hundred, with a small dance floor, a stage at the end of its horseshoe-shaped auditorium, and an elegant decor fitted out with artificial palm trees to create a "jungle" ambience, was the biggest and most high profile.

Walter Brooks, with a track record as a successful producer of African American musical entertainment behind him, was nominally the manager of the Cotton Club. In reality, his job was a thinly disguised front for some of the most unpleasant mobsters on the planet, who had initially been drawn to the club as a means of promoting bootleg liquor but who also used it to control numerous other nefarious activities. When McHugh first accepted Brooks's invitation, he was still new to Harlem, and although he might have suspected who really ran the place, he had no initial contact with any gangsters.

That was soon to change. To pep up the existing show, and without writing any new material, McHugh, acting on his plugger's instincts, simply squeezed the songs he had been selling in England into the program. On the first night that his existing hits, "I Can't Believe That You're in Love with Me" and "Baltimore,"[4] were performed in a revue called *Dan Healy's Blushing Browns*,

McHugh's table was plied with champagne, apparently sent by the management. McHugh recalled:

> I hadn't ordered the stuff. In fact at that time I was a teetotaller. Nevertheless I was presented with a check for $240. I told the waiter, "Take this to the bosses and tell them what they can do with it." The waiter departed. A few moments later, he was back. "The bosses want to see you," he said.
>
> Little did I know that in those days it was the custom for big shot gangsters from outlying areas, such as Jersey City, Brooklyn and the Bronx to run up a large bill, then send the check back and challenge the management to come out and try to collect.
>
> The office was not large. As I walked in I was greeted by a group of expressionless faces. Among them was Owney Madden, whose record as a leader of the old Gopher gang of Hell's Kitchen had earned him the nickname of "Owney the Killer." Physically he was a lean, hard, quiet man with black hair, piercing blue eyes and a rather cute Irish face. Mentally he had a steel bear-trap mind, the cold judgement and the flintlike executive ability that was to enable him to become the most powerful personage in Manhattan's underworld. Another man facing me in the office was Big Bill Duffy. Duffy also had a record. Along with several partners, Duffy ran the Silver Slipper on West 48th Street. Next to Bill Duffy sat Ben Marden and Jack Arken, two gentlemen who, in addition to their flourishing night club, rum-running, horse-racing, fights and other assorted business activities, also owned a cemetery. Among the other immobile faces in the Cotton Club that night were Mike Best, known to the nefarious society of the underworld as the "Baron of Yorkville," and also Frenchy [DeMange], who was later kidnapped by the Cole gang and held for ransom, and Harry Block, alias "The Thin Man."
>
> They were the lawless hierarchy of the most lurid decade of professional triggermen. All were killers. The big time rackets of New York were divided among them like the pieces of a pie. In his realm, the power of each was absolute; he controlled breweries, laundries, florist shops, and any other business you can name. I won't say how they came by this control. This was the era of the twenties when anything went and lawlessness was the rule.[5]

McHugh accused the mobsters of being "a bunch of cheap bums," shocking them into silence, until Ben Marden asked him what the problem was. McHugh complained that they were charging him for champagne he hadn't ordered. Within a few minutes it became clear that although Walter Brooks was being paid a $1 per head cover charge levied on each customer, out of which he should have been paying McHugh, he had actually handed over nothing. After a short conference, the hoods decided to pay McHugh $250 per week. "'Is that all right with you?' Marden asked. I had been making $100 a week at the publishing house. From that moment on, Marden and I became good friends. I think he would have killed for me, although I never put his devotion to the test."[6]

For the time being, McHugh did not give up his position at Jack Mills Inc. He added the salary from the Cotton Club to his income as professional manager at Mills and, in his inexhaustible way, combined his existing publishing, plugging, and songwriting commitments with nightly visits to the club and the planning of new shows there.

He arrived at precisely the right time for a change. The bandleader Andy Preer, frontman of the "Cotton Club Orchestra" since 1925, had died suddenly in late May. Although the band was leaderless, it was continuing to play at the club until Brooks and his bosses could find a suitable replacement. Brooks himself had recently handed over the day-to-day direction of the shows to the singer and dancer Dan Healy, and Healy was on the hunt for writers who would bring hit songs to his entertainments. McHugh knew he was the man to do this, but in late 1927, still picking up his songwriting career after the trip to Europe, he was once more in need of a lyricist.

Over the closing months of the year, everything came together. Duke Ellington's band took up residence at the club, becoming the centerpiece of a new revue conceived by Healy, and the band played songs written by McHugh and a new young lyricist, the former schoolteacher Dorothy Fields.

It is unlikely that McHugh would have become central to this renaissance of the Cotton Club if he had not struck up a working relationship with the gangsters who ran the place. Marden was won over after McHugh challenged the cost of the champagne on his opening night, but the key to his long-term success there was the way he handled the rest of the stony-faced crew who had greeted him in the office.

Chief among them was Owney Madden, whose dominant role in New York's underworld was comparable to Al Capone's in Chicago. His Irish family had moved to England to avoid the famines in the 1840s, just as an earlier generation of McHughs had fled from the Emerald Isle to Boston. Like many a gangster, Madden was good at covering his tracks, and for many years the general view—based on his own account—was that his family moved to Wigan and then Liverpool, from whence they migrated to the United States when he was a small boy. Recent research indicates that on leaving County Mayo in Ireland, Madden's family had actually settled on the other side of Britain altogether, in Leeds, in the Kirkgate slum area of that city. One forbear, Mary Madden, died there of famine fever in 1847, but the rest of the family survived, and Owen (Owney) Madden was born on December 18, 1891, at 25 Somerset Street. He was still a small boy when his mother and father, Mary and Francis, put their children into St. James' Orphanage while they went to America, sending for Owen when he was nine years old.[7]

Madden therefore came straight to Ellis Island from a Leeds orphanage, and even after he became a gangster and convicted killer, spending several years in the state prison at Sing Sing, the two great passions of his working-class Yorkshire childhood never left him: boxing and pigeons. He had his Irish background and love of boxing in common with McHugh, and this undoubtedly helped them get along, although McHugh was surprised to find that Madden also continued to keep pigeons, even in the urban fastness of Harlem.

> One day Owney Madden took my arm. "Come on upstairs," he said, "I'll show you around." We climbed the stairs to the Cotton Club roof. Never will I forget the sight that confronted us. The entire roof was covered with cages of pigeons. There were nearly 200 of them. The pigeons were all pedigreed and registered, each with its own leg tag. Owney warned me: "Don't touch any part of the railing—these birds are well protected." The wire round the railing carried more voltage than the Sing Sing electric chair. The pigeons were Owney's pride and joy, perhaps partly because they were the bearers of good tidings. When one came fluttering home with its leg message attached, Owney knew that the latest load of alcohol had gotten through.[8]

The other major partners in the Cotton Club were Frenchy DeMange and Harry Block. Weighing in at 240 pounds, and standing well over six feet tall, DeMange did not smoke or drink, but he had plenty of experience at bootlegging and safecracking. The epitome of the tight-suited, muscle-bound gangster, and nominally secretary of the corporation that ran the club, he was often around as the floor show was being rehearsed or revised. When, in one of his business deals, he acquired a laundry, he motioned McHugh over and asked him to include a song about it in the revue. Puzzled by how to comply with this somewhat unusual request, McHugh hit upon the idea of integrating Hoagy Carmichael's "Washboard Blues" into the program. "Each chorus girl had a washboard about two feet long. In the blue diamond, where the soap usually goes, we had the name of Frenchy's laundry. It was one of the hit numbers of the show."[9] Such quick-thinking song-plugger's instincts obviously played well with DeMange. (This would have gone down well with Jack and Irving Mills, too, as they were the publishers of Carmichael's song.)

Block was the member of the entourage who took a day-to-day interest in running the club. He saw to it that although the club's printed menu only offered soft drinks, champagne was available at around $30 a bottle, and a fifth of Scotch could be had for just over half that price. Setting these costs so high did not discourage the big spenders from downtown, but they kept the local African American population away, something which was Block's underlying aim. Reported the *New York Age:* "The Cotton Club, located at the heart of Harlem at 142nd Street and Lenox Avenue, does not cater to colored patrons and will not admit them when they come in mixed parties."[10] Block and his deputy, a former machine gunner named Herman Stark, rigidly enforced their policy and employed a one-time boxer, Kid Griffin, as floor manager to guarantee it was adhered to.

Nevertheless, Block also ensured that all the club's wait staff and entertainers were African American, importing most of them from Chicago as that city's nightlife gradually waned in the late 1920s. Indeed, he also tried to bring in the great New Orleans trumpeter King Oliver, who had been one of Chicago's most popular jazz bandleaders, to replace Preer, but Oliver turned him down on the grounds that the fee was too low. It became one of the great ironies of the swing era that Oliver's career declined rapidly from that point, but the band that arrived in his place—for a mere $800 per week—went on to become one of the great successes in jazz history.

It was Jimmy McHugh who suggested that Block should hire Duke Ellington, whose band had played for much of the previous three years at the Kentucky Club at 203 West Forty-ninth Street, a short distance from Times Square. McHugh said: "I heard Duke and I wanted him. For one thing he and his boys could read. The band I had to let go couldn't. I had to sit down at the piano and play every tune for them until they learned it. Not only could Duke read, he promptly went to work writing the orchestrations—at $50 each—for the show."[11]

For his part, Ellington always gave McHugh credit for this introduction, although it has puzzled some of Ellington's biographers as to why a white Bostonian songwriter would go out of his way to bring Ellington's band to the club. However, the reason becomes more obvious when one realizes that Ellington had been managed since late 1926 by Irving Mills. To Irving and Jack Mills, having their publishing firm's general manager take up an extra job as a songwriter for a gangster-run club might not have looked like a particularly attractive idea. But if, by doing so, he could use his gangland contacts to land Mills's protégé a regular job, help create a new repertoire for the band (to be published by Mills), and make money for all the partners at Jack Mills through Ellington's broadcasts and recordings, then this would sweeten the pill. If (as eventually happened) McHugh ultimately left song plugging to focus on writing, he would have given the brothers something far more valuable in return.

In late 1927 Edward Kennedy Ellington was twenty-eight years old, and although he had begun to make records under his own name at the end of 1926, he had yet to make his mark as one of the most original composers and bandleaders in jazz. On the other hand, he was already notable for his personal sense of elegance and style and for the corresponding panache with which he presented his band. Growing up in Washington, D.C., he had become a passable ragtime and stride pianist, and he settled in New York in 1923 with a collection of musicians from his hometown, who gradually made a name for themselves at the Kentucky Club. In their early days, they played the generic, small-group Dixieland attempted by most early 1920s jazz bands, but Ellington gradually enlarged his lineup from the original six men, adding some very distinctive soloists such as trumpeter Bubber Miley and trombonist Tricky Sam Nanton, and he began to tailor a repertoire of original material.

It was Ellington's potential as a songwriter that led Irving Mills to take an interest in him, although as Ellington explained, his earliest contact with his future publisher and manager was a cynical exercise in moneymaking:

> My initial encounter with Irving Mills occurred during my first six months in New York. He was known as the last resort for getting money by those who had been peddling songs all day without success. I first heard of him second-hand, and one day I joined a group of five or six songwriters. The personnel varied, but they would get together, each with a lead sheet of what they considered rather ordinary blues under his arm, and head for Mills Music. The procedure, they explained, was to sell those blues outright to Irving Mills for fifteen or twenty dollars. It was very simple—no hassle. Just give him the lead sheet, sign the outright release, pick up the money and go.[12]

We know from McHugh's account of his work for Mills that this constant uncritical acquisition of songs was an everyday part of the business. Some were published; some were given new lyrics, tweaked into life and pushed into the hands of artists who might promote them; and others sank without trace. In Ellington's work, Mills saw the chance not only to tap into a creative stream of extremely high-quality compositions but to use Duke's own band to promote the songs, both on records and, if the chance arose, on the radio. By the time Ellington arrived at the Cotton Club, Mills had published several of his pieces, namely "The Creeper," "Creole Love Call," "Birmingham Breakdown," "Black and Tan Fantasy," "Down in Our Alley Blues," "East St. Louis Toodle-Oo," "Hop Head," and "Immigration Blues."[13]

Although Ellington's talent was only beginning to be recognized by the wider world, this body of work was sufficiently distinctive, and its composer so prolific, that it set him apart from the crowd of other songwriters whose work Mills routinely published. What is more, just as he had done a few years earlier with McHugh's song "Stop Your Kiddin'," Mills ensured that these pieces were recorded, and in the case of several of them, recorded more than once, principally by Ellington and his band, using different names for different labels.

Under his contract with Ellington, Mills effectively owned 45 percent of the band, which gave him a share of recording revenue; and in addition to publishing Duke's music through his Gotham Music subsidiary, just as he had frequently done with other songwriters in the early 1920s, he concocted lyrics for the instrumentals or made subtle alterations to the music in order to claim a lyricist's or co-composer's credit. Indeed, he saw his instinctive publisher's input as essential, saying, "Whatever they did, I thinned out. His music was always too heavy."[14] Just as McHugh worked with would-be songwriters to develop their work for publication, Irving Mills did the same with Ellington, urging him to try a particular sort of tune, or proposing titles and suggesting images that might inspire a melody.

Some commentators have seen this as the ruthless exploitation of a black composer by his white publisher. At the time, Ellington himself saw Mills as an essential component of his business. Mills pushed him to write, published the results, and plugged them remorselessly. He also helped Ellington record for hitherto whites-only record labels and in due course promoted his cause both with ASCAP and the movie industry. He took a sizable share of the revenue for this, but he also cannily fed Duke's desire to do everything "first class," from Pullman-car travel to exquisitely tailored band uniforms, and for this he gained—for the next decade or so—Ellington's trust.

In the early fall of 1927, Ellington left the Kentucky Club and in an effort to keep his band together (pared down to just eight men from his usual ten), he agreed to go on the road, touring the Keith-Albee theater circuit as the pit band for a revue by Clarence Robinson called *Dance Mania*. It played the Lafayette Theater in New York in mid-November 1927, before leaving to open on November 21 at the Standard Theater in Philadelphia. At precisely the time Ellington was appearing at the Lafayette, McHugh and Dan Healy were putting together the new winter revue for the Cotton Club.

Consequently, McHugh persuaded Stark and Healy to hear the band at the Lafayette, suggesting that it was exactly what the show needed, not least because it was backing a variety cast similar to the one that they planned to present at the Cotton Club. According to Ellington's banjoist, Fred Guy, at a tavern near the Lafayette, Stark and Healy signed the band to appear in their forthcoming show. According to Ellington himself, the group also auditioned for Harry Block at the Cotton Club, along with one or two other bands. As it turned out, Ellington, hustling round town to bring his depleted ranks back up to the ten men required by the club, was very late to the audition. So, too, was Block, with the result that Ellington's was the only band he heard. He concurred with his colleagues that they should be hired as the new resident orchestra.

When the opening date for the Cotton Club show was set for December 4, however, there was a problem. Ellington's Philadelphia run in *Dance Mania* overlapped it by a week. On Saturday the 3rd, according to McHugh, Owney Madden got hold of Duke on the telephone.

> "Ellington," Owney said. "You open in New York tomorrow."
> "What about my contract?" asked Duke.
> "Forget it."
> "I can't do that," Duke said. "The theater manager won't forget it, even if I do."
> The Cotton Club boys then proceeded to handle the situation in their own characteristic fashion. They called Boo Boo Hoff, a pal and power in Philadelphia's underworld. Boo Boo sent a certain party known as Yankee Schwartz to call upon the theater manager. Yankee opened the conversation on a conciliatory note.
> "Be big," he said reasonably, "or you'll be dead."
> Duke Ellington opened at the Cotton Club.[15]

This show, *Dan Healy's New Winter Revue,* was the first of seven in which Ellington's orchestra appeared as resident band at the club between December 1927 and September 1930. At first, not everyone was enamored with McHugh's choice. Ned E. Williams, who had been press agent for Bill Duffy's nightclub, the Silver Slipper, came along as Dan Healy's guest. "I can't say that I was too much impressed with the Ellington crew on that visit," he wrote. "It definitely didn't have the form and polish that it acquired later." Meanwhile, Block—used to the altogether less challenging sounds of Preer's band— complained that Duke's was "jangling and dissonant," and Big Bill Duffy, like Madden and McHugh, a man of Irish stock, so disliked what he heard that he issued a stony-faced instruction for something "melodic," as a result of which McHugh found himself pleading with Ellington to include *Mother Machree* in his program.[16] Yet when the first reviews came out, McHugh's judgment was spectacularly vindicated. Despite the fact that Ellington's normal lineup had one or two makeweight musicians added, such as the violinist Ellsworth Reynolds, the critic Abel Green could hardly have been more enthusiastic in *Variety*: "In Duke Ellington's dance band, Harlem has reclaimed its own after Times Square accepted them for several seasons at the Club Kentucky. Ellington's jazzique is just too bad. . . . The fifteen numbers take more than an hour to unloose, but it's a type of entertainment that defies lackadaiscal [*sic*] interest. It compels attention and any overlength is only the result of audience demand."[17]

A combination of word of mouth and other equally positive press reviews helped to keep Ellington at the club. As the months went by, he added further distinctive soloists to his lineup, notably the clarinetist Barney Bigard and alto saxophonist Johnny Hodges, and began creating a repertoire that played to their musical personalities and gave his band a truly individual sound. Ellington also broadcast frequently from the club, and just as Irving Mills had hoped, his popularity began to climb.

For the sections of the show when it played for dancing, Ellington's band performed mainly its own music. To accompany the floor show, however, it played the fresh music written for the revue by McHugh and his new lyricist, Dorothy Fields. There were at least two of their songs in the revue that opened on December 4, namely, "Doin' the Frog," and "Harlem River Quiver."[18] The latter song was recorded by Ellington's ten-piece band just fifteen days after opening night, and it is a perfect example of his "jungle" style, with a roaring statement of the opening theme from trombonist Tricky Sam Nanton, who brays out the tune before Ellington takes a suave piano solo and ushers in the nimble baritone saxophone of Harry Carney. Exciting, slightly raw, but at the same time sophisticated, this disc gives us an opportunity to eavesdrop on how the band was playing the piece each night in the club as the accompaniment to a solo dancer: "a boyish bobbed hoyden, said to be specially imported from Chicago for her Annapolis proclivities, [who] does the 'Harlem River Quiver' like no self-respecting body of water. The teasin'est torso tossing yet, and how!"[19]

This and "Doin' the Frog" mark the official debut of what would become one of the major songwriting duos of the era, which also developed into the most consistently creative partnership of McHugh's life. His brash Irish personality helped Fields come out of her shell and develop the confidence to write lyrics that captured the flavor of the time, and she gave him an entrée into the theatrical establishment way beyond his experience as a plugger.

All of Dorothy Fields's immediate family were in the audience for the first night at the Cotton Club, and they were somewhat scandalized by the explicit songs delivered in other parts of the program by the singers Aida Ward and Lethia Hill. The lyrics left little or nothing to the imagination: Ellington's drummer, Sonny Greer, would shout, "What do you want, Mama?" and Hill would roar back, "Jelly roll, jelly roll, nice and brown / If you want *my* jelly roll, you've gotta come to town." Then Ward would sing, "Don't monkey with my Monkey" and "I've got a flat tire papa / Don't you try to re-tire me."

They were, recalled Fields, "three of the most shocking, ribald, bawdy, dirtiest songs anyone had ever heard in the 1920s."[20] Her father, the well-known Jewish comedian and actor Lew Fields, had to be reassured that Dorothy had not written *those* lyrics, and he apparently sought out Block to have an announcement made to the audience that Miss Fields was not responsible for such ribald songs.

Born in 1905, Dorothy Fields had show business in her blood. Her elder brother Herbert wrote the books for a number of Rodgers and Hart musicals, and another brother, Joseph, was a playwright; but their father was keen for his youngest child to make a life for herself outside the theater. Despite her wish to go onstage, Dorothy's parents intercepted and rebuffed letters of engagement from theater companies, and the closest she came to an acting career was teaching Spanish and drama at her alma mater, the Benjamin School for Girls on Manhattan's Upper West Side.

One weekend she was staying with a cousin at Woodmere, Long Island, and came in from what she described as "a strenuous day on the tennis courts" to be introduced to a young composer called J. Fred Coots. He played some of his recent work and, knowing that she had written a handful of published poems for various literary magazines, suggested that she come up with lyrics for his tunes. After a few false starts, she did exactly that, and by the end of the day, Coots was equipped with four potentially publishable songs.

Fields later discovered that her father immediately sent word to his contacts in the industry that he would be much obliged if they did not encourage his daughter by publishing her work. Consequently, Coots drew a blank with most of the Tin Pan Alley companies he approached, but Lew Fields had reckoned without the fact that Coots had worked as a plugger for Jack Mills and that his old firm would be happy to consider his new songs. Naturally, Coots and Dorothy were received by the firm's general manager, Jimmy McHugh. In an interview with *Metronome*, Fields recalled: "There were at least twenty people in Jimmy's quarters. They were singers, musicians, authors and composers. Outside was a buzzing of voices, playing of pianos, and the practicing of new numbers on the professional floor. Swell chance for a potential songwriter to meet with any success here, but I reasoned that I might as well dally round until McHugh would dispose of my efforts—negatively. I was just preparing to leave when Mr. McHugh halted me and offered me the comment that my lyrics missed fire, but . . ."

At this point in her recollections, Fields was interrupted by McHugh himself, who pointed out: "If you remember, Miss Fields, I didn't exactly say that, but what I did say was that you were trying to write *up* to the people, and I told you to write *down*, give them that which they understood, something that should not tax their intelligence."[21]

This meeting took place in early October 1927. That same month, the film actress and would-be aviatrix Ruth Elder announced her plans to become the first woman to fly across the Atlantic. With the same instinct for a timely song that had prompted their efforts to commemorate Caruso and Valentino, McHugh and Jack Mills decided the moment was ripe for a celebratory ditty named after Elder's monoplane, the *American Girl*. Consequently, to see how she responded to McHugh's advice, they offered Dorothy Fields $50 to come up with a lyric, for which Mills had already drafted the opening lines: "You took a notion to fly 'cross the ocean, 'Our American Girl.'" Despite remonstrating with Mills that "you don't just take a notion to fly across the ocean," Fields duly delivered her verses next day.

However, fate took a hand in postponing her first efforts at becoming a published songwriter. Although Elder's celebratory telegrams were all ready to be sent, and ticker-tape parades duly organized, on October 13 her plane crash-landed into the ocean, some three hundred miles short of the French coast, after it developed an oil leak.[22] As a result, although the song "Our American Girl" was published, it was never distributed. Dorothy Fields nevertheless collected her $50, having proven to McHugh that she could come up with apt and witty lyrics under pressure of a deadline. She was not the only one to benefit: when Elder and her copilot George Haldeman finally arrived back in New York in November, they were greeted by a ticker-tape parade celebrating their magnificent failure.

McHugh quickly became besotted with the demure, somewhat shy Fields, describing her as "a vivacious charming creature, with a beautiful face and big eyes."[23] He suggested that the two of them might try writing a song or two together, and before long they had produced their first successful piece, "Collegiana." It was written in direct response to the "Varsity Drag," by De Sylva, Brown, and Henderson, which had been published in the late summer and widely recorded during August and September, notably by the popular dance bands of Sam Lanin and George Olson. "Collegiana" is the epitome of a "roaring twenties" song, in which college students abandon their studies for "a new degree [in] dancing." Flappers, endless campus parties, and college hops are all conjured up in Fields's lyrics; and as well as echoing the kind of internal rhyme scheme she so admired in Lorenz Hart's work (in this case "pedagogue" and "go to bed agog"), her words show the easy, relaxed vernacular style she was to make her own for the next forty-five years as a professional lyricist.

McHugh was impressed. He immediately asked her if she would collaborate with him on the forthcoming Cotton Club revue. She replied that she would have to ask her parents. "Somewhat dubiously, they agreed to let Dorothy work with me. I paid her $100 a week. From that day on we were inseparable. We lunched, went shopping, attended football games, because of our work."[24] In spite of their contrasting temperaments, there were good reasons for Fields and McHugh to spend plenty of time together socially. They were both in failed marriages, living separately from their respective partners, and, once Fields had launched herself as a lyricist, they both became totally immersed in their work and the helter-skelter lifestyle that surrounded it.

Back in 1924, Fields had married Dr. Jack Wiener, a chest specialist from the Montefiore Hospital with a private practice on Fifty-eighth Street, and the couple lived in style on Central Park South. Although they occasionally appeared together in public for big social and family occasions, Fields returned to her family's apartment on West End Avenue not long after her honeymoon was over. Yet because she and McHugh were each technically married to someone else, she could join him on his nightly rounds of clubs and theaters, and the two could dine out or attend launch parties or first nights while retaining an acceptable measure of propriety. For Fields this was the passport to a show-business life that she had long hoped for but which had been blocked by her father. For McHugh, she was the perfect companion as much as she was the perfect lyricist: witty, urbane, biddable, and totally without the foibles and failings that had made working with Al Dubin so unpredictable.

From late October 1927 onward, McHugh and Fields began writing together in earnest. The song that was to become their first great hit, "I Can't Give You Anything but Love, Baby," was among the earliest they produced and was aired in public—albeit for one night only—even before the Cotton Club show opened. McHugh remembered: "One day as Dorothy Fields and I were walking along Fifth Avenue, we stopped to glance in Tiffany's window. A boy and girl walked up to us as we stood there, and we heard the young man remark to his girl, 'Gee, I wish I could give you everything, Baby, but I'm afraid all I can give you is plenty of love.' Needless to say, this was real inspiration, so Dorothy and I hurried home to put it down in music and words."[25]

They persuaded the impresario Harry Delmar to include the resulting song in his forthcoming variety show, *Delmar's Revels*, which was to open at the Shubert Theatre on November 28, 1927. Most of the show's songs had been composed by Jimmy Moncao, Jesse Green, and Lester Lee, with lyrics by Billy Rose and Ballard McDonald, but it was an accepted practice of the time for a producer to add an extra number or two, particularly if these were potential hits and might bring some zest to an otherwise workaday score. The revue was the New York debut of Bert Lahr and the comedienne Patsy Kelly, and Delmar had them dressed as a penniless couple, sitting on the stoop of a tenement, singing Fields and McHugh's verses to one another. For whatever reason, the number was a disaster, and Delmar pulled it from the program after one performance.[26]

If it had not surfaced again a month or two later in another production entirely, that might have been all that was ever heard of the song. But when it did reappear, as we shall see, in a most successful guise, rumors began that it was not the work of Fields and McHugh at all but a song by Andy Razaf and Fats Waller that McHugh had bought (along with a bunch of others) on behalf of Jack Mills the previous year and then altered slightly to claim as his own. Razaf's biographer, Barry Singer, speculates that it was this song to which Waller referred in a *New York Post* interview: "The average rate for such a song, he says, was $250. Among the songs thus disposed of was one [that] knocked about for three seasons until it was finally inserted in a musical comedy. Featured in that show, it became the best seller of its season and netted $17,500 to its 'composer' who paid 'Fatts' [*sic*] $500 for it."[27]

Not least because Waller made some particularly attractive recordings of this tune, enthusiasts for his music, including his son Maurice in a biography written many years after his father's death, have consistently claimed it as his composition. Waller's regular lyricist, Andy Razaf, was also to make similar claims in later life. Yet despite Maurice Waller's account that his father would not hear the song played in the house, so aggrieved was he by McHugh's "theft" of the piece, the evidence for Waller and Razaf having composed it is so slight as to be unconvincing.

From his very earliest work, McHugh had shown himself naturally able to write the kind of melody on which jazz musicians could improvise and which fitted well into the aesthetics of the Jazz Age. At the very outset of their collaboration, Fields's lyrics had all the elegance and memorable qualities that were to surface in her work over the next few months. Furthermore, in the verse to "I Can't Give You Anything but Love, Baby" she uses the rhyme "gotten/rotten," borrowed not from Razaf but from a song by her brother's collaborators Rodgers and Hart called "Where's That Rainbow?," much as she had recently used a Hart-style internal rhyme scheme in "Collegiana."

It is true that as professional manager at Mills, McHugh bought songs for cash from a range of would-be songwriters, black or white; but by 1927–28 Waller was already known as a marketable name, and there would be no reason for McHugh not to publish the song as Waller's own, had he bought it. Indeed, Jack Mills Inc. made plenty of money from publishing hit songs by other African American composers, just as the firm was beginning to do with Ellington and would soon do for Waller himself, with his *Connie's Hot Chocolates* show of 1929. Waller was frequently cavalier with his work, and he undoubtedly did part with certain songs for a few dollars—Andy Razaf reported that the two of them would "grind out" several songs in the latest style and "take them up to Mills or some Broadway office and get a nice sum for them." (Most famously, according to the bandleader Fletcher Henderson, money was not even part of the equation, as the outsize pianist swapped several numbers for the price of a hamburger.) However, it is likely that this is not one of the many Waller works that he sold so cheaply, a view further backed up by a contemporary press report that an entirely different songwriter was a claimant. From the *Sunday News:*

> Lew Brown, partner in the immensely successful publishing firm De Sylva, Brown and Henderson, claimed that he suggested the title and outline of the number of Miss Fields and Jimmy McHugh while dining with them one night. They then went ahead with the song and failed to credit him. Accordingly, Brown felt he was entitled to compensation. He consulted his attorney and determined to sue. When it came time to make an affidavit, however, Lew did not show up at the lawyer's office. He probably forgot to get up on time, and that was the end of the lawsuit.[28]

Credited to its rightful composers, "I Can't Give You Anything but Love, Baby" was to surface again as the hit song in Fields and McHugh's next venture together, Lew Leslie's revue *Blackbirds of 1928.*

After his return from England with Florence Mills, Leslie had been planning a follow-up revue for her, in the wake of their highly successful tour with *Blackbirds of 1926.* However, not long after she came back from Europe, Mills became ill and died suddenly. Her funeral on November 6, 1927, brought Harlem to a standstill, according to the press of the time: "Fifty thousand negroes, exclusive of those who blackened surrounding roofs, hung out of the windows and clung to fire escapes, contributed to the spectacular splendor with which Harlem buried its greatest negro actress."

Mills's $10,000 hammered-bronze casket, covered in floral tributes (including, it was rumored, one from the Prince of Wales), was carried at the head of a two-mile motorcade. Her fellow entertainers Ethel Waters, Gertrude Saunders,

Aida Ward, Cora Green, and Edith Wilson marched in the procession, dressed in somber gray, with downcast eyes. Five thousand people crammed into the Mother Zion church, and "the strains of *Deep River* flowed from the church and mingled with the shouts of police in the street, the sudden hysterical disturbances, and the drone of a movie airplane overhead."[29]

A day or two before the burial, Lew Leslie called McHugh to see if he wanted to visit the funeral parlor to pay his last respects. In this unlikely setting, Leslie proposed that McHugh and Fields might like to write the next show for him. "I thought to myself, 'How can he start talking business at a time like this?'" said McHugh, "but being practical-minded I told him, 'sure, I'd like to do a show.'"[30]

Once the new Cotton Club revue was up and running, Leslie came to Harlem to see it and resume his discussions with McHugh. Not long after the opening night, Ellington had persuaded the powers that be to allow him to add an extra ingredient to his band, the singer Adelaide Hall, whose eerie wordless singing was featured on Duke's disc of "Creole Love Call." The song, recorded on October 26 and recently released, was becoming an extremely popular record. It was the diminutive, charming figure of Adelaide Hall whom Leslie had in mind as the successor to Florence Mills in his own productions, and seeing how she had become a highly successful addition to the Cotton Club cast convinced him he was right.

However, Leslie's single-minded conviction soon brought him into conflict with the gangsters who ran the club. He had worked for them some years before, preceding Brooks and Healy as producer of the Cotton Club floor shows, and maybe he thought this gave him carte blanche to behave as he wished. To mount his new revue, Leslie took over a West Fifty-seventh Street nightclub called Le Perroquet, which had been run for the previous year at a colossal loss by the teenage musical prodigy Roger Wolfe Kahn. The venue had originally been named Giro's, and Kahn, partially financed by his banker father and partially by the numerous dance bands that he led or managed, imported French chef René Racover from Le Perroquet Restaurant in Paris and refurbished it as a Parisian-style club. It had a raised stage, a glass dance floor lit from below, and high-quality cuisine for five hundred diners.[31] When Kahn decided to cut his losses to focus on composing and his new passion for aviation, Leslie swooped in and took over the venue as a going concern, renaming it Les Ambassadeurs. He saw its potential for hosting a Harlem-style revue in the heart of the Broadway theater district while at the same time creating an intimate club atmosphere in what was actually a very sizable establishment. McHugh recalled:

I wasn't aware of the fact that Leslie was contacting the artists at the Cotton Club and putting them in the show. This was brought to my attention one day when the boys from the Cotton Club called and told me to get Leslie up there right away and straighten himself out. He went, but continued to take people from there. We were going through a lot of strenuous rehearsing and had the entire show laid out. The night before the opening the boys called me again, and said, "Tell that no-good Leslie to come right up here, because if he doesn't, we'll sprinkle a little kerosene in the lobby!" . . . Whatever deal he made I'll never know, but he certainly straightened them out, and they let the show go on.[32]

To create the songs for *Blackbirds*, McHugh had put in place a writing regime with Dorothy Fields that, he later noted, was tough even by his energetic standards.

After an evening out, I'd leave her and go and work on tunes at night to have them ready for the next morning. I worked every night in the Mills offices from midnight to three or four a.m., banging out tunes for [the] new project. The heat was off in the building and I wore my overcoat. As a general rule I like to write a title first and work from that. Dorothy would come over early in the morning, at seven a.m. I'd play the tune I'd written to a title we'd gotten the night before, and she'd often have the lyric finished in one or two hours. She was a brilliant, fast writer. By noon we often had the song finished. We worked closely in perfect synchronization.[33]

Apart from a selection of "high yellow" (the term then used to describe light-skinned African Americans) chorus girls, the main artist whom Leslie had lured from uptown to perform this newly written score was—as he had planned—the Cotton Club's most recent recruit, Adelaide Hall. Although *The Blackbird Revue* was originally announced for a late December 1927 opening, his spot of bother with "the boys," explained to the world at large as "an electrical fault," meant that the show actually started its life on January 4, 1928.

To modern eyes, the show might appear to have been an exercise in racial stereotyping. Set "Way Down South" and opening in "Dixie," it mingled caricatures of rural African Americans with "bad men from Harlem." It was racy and raucous, its dances fast paced and spectacular, and it offered Hall a chance to show her all-round entertainment skills as opposed to her wordless scat singing with Ellington. Press reviews suggested that she was, indeed, the ideal heir to Leslie's previous star: "Saw Adelaide Hall, the understudy of the late Florence Mills, who has suddenly been catapulted into Broadway to take the place of the 'little blackberry' who could sing the blues like nobody else in the world. . . . But you'll see Miss Hall's name plastered in lights yet."[34]

Dorothy Fields's father had been scandalized only a month earlier by what he heard at the Cotton Club, but Adelaide Hall's scantily-clad performance of "Diga Diga Doo" in *Blackbirds* was directly in the same tradition of sexual innuendo and double entendre that he had so disliked. Dorothy Fields was, it seems, a quick learner, as her lyrics used the title of the song as a thinly veiled metaphor for sexual intercourse.

With this *frisson* of naughtiness, delivered with what one reviewer called a "wiggle dance," and with Miss Hall's shapeliness apparent because "there are few garments to prevent accurate estimates on the latter score," the show exemplified what the historian Kathy J. Ogren calls a "contrived tradition . . . the persistence among whites of stereotypes about black entertainment [that] have trapped both blacks and whites in roles that were not 'authentic' but staged."[35]

Yet, at the time, the publicity for the show made no pretense about its origins. McHugh's old friend Walter Winchell, writing in the *New York Evening Graphic*, drew attention to the image it projected compared to the reality behind its creation:

> Those hot tunes and those weird sonorities are the work of James (or as he is more familiarly known, Jimmy) McHugh, who is an Irishman, or at least of Irish descent, and he was brought up in the fashionable and conservative Back Bay section of Boston. He has never made an extensive study of the black race, or of the old Spirituals. The knack of rhythm and melody just comes naturally to him, and if the performers were white instead of sepia-shaded, no-one would ever go into the origin or background of the type of tunes he writes, when he composes the score for a colored revue. Well, maybe it's the way the numbers are staged by the colored producer and the dances staged by the colored dancing master? Wrong again. All that is the work of Lew Leslie, who is Jewish, and besides he is his own backer, and owns the whole shooting match. Then besides this, the lyrics which blend with Mr. McHugh's melodies perfectly, and the titles of the numbers, which sound as if they could only be the brain children of some Afro-American librettist are the creations of one of New York's most popular debs.[36]

Leslie knew that the time was right for another full-scale African American musical on Broadway. His show was up and running as a cabaret at Les Ambassadeurs in January 1928, but it already had rivals. Con Conrad's *Keep Shufflin'*, with a score by Fats Waller and James P. Johnson and starring the black comedians Miller and Lyles, was undergoing tryouts in Philadelphia, and it was booked to open at Daly's 63rd Street Theatre on Broadway in late February. Johnson himself was also hard at work on *Messin' Around*, a revue which he was cowriting with the pianist and pioneer record producer Perry Bradford (although this show was delayed in coming to New York and did not open at the Hudson Theatre until the following year). In addition, Dorothy and DuBose Heyward's play *Porgy*, which featured a predominantly African American cast, was well settled into what was to be a 367–night run at the Republic Theatre. *Porgy* was based on DuBose Heyward's 1924 novel, and the popularity of both book and play explains why Leslie included both a skit based on it and McHugh's song of the same name in *Blackbirds*.

Leslie aimed not only to challenge these competitors but to outdo them, and the progress of *Blackbirds of 1928* from restaurant revue to full-scale Broadway show took four months. A vast amount of work by Leslie and his team reshaped the original production, trimming out the dead wood and hugely expanding the cast. *Blackbirds* went from being a single one-act entertainment with a cast of forty to a full-scale, two-part variety show with over one hundred performers; and instead of featuring just one star it now had several, of whom the first to be added to the cast was Aida Ward, another refugee from the Cotton Club.

Leslie's first reviews in the press were lukewarm, and he set about revising the show a few weeks after opening, with a complete relaunch of the piece as *Blackbirds of 1928* at midnight on February 21 (exactly one week before *Keep Shufflin'* arrived in town). The audience was liberally packed with Broadway stars, not to mention the film actresses Fannie Ward and Patsy Ruth Miller and the celebrity journalist Finley Peter Dunne, creator of the satirical Irish bartender Mr. Dooley.[37]

At this point, "I Can't Give You Anything but Love, Baby" was not included in the revue's running order. New songs by Fields and McHugh written for this early version of the show were Adelaide Hall's features, "Shuffle Your Feet," "Diga Diga Doo," and "Baby," plus Aida Ward's songs "Dixie" and "Porgy," the latter a reworked version of McHugh and Jack Frost's earlier number. Hall and Ward together romped through "Bandanna Babies," and the entire cast closed the show with a riotous "Magnolia's Wedding Day." The lyrics to "Bandanna Babies" introduced the words "Doin' the New Low-Down," an idea Fields and McHugh subsequently worked into a completely new song that was later added to the show.

On what was effectively *Blackbirds'* second opening night on February 21, McHugh got his first taste of the Broadway lifestyle. There were telegrams of congratulation from Mr. and Mrs. Lew Leslie, from Lew Fields, and—

especially important to him—from Jack and Irving Mills: "YOU DID A GREAT JOB, JIMMY OLD BOY, LOTS OF LUCK!" Western Union also delivered a short line of complaint from McHugh's writing partner, who obviously felt a bit left out of things: "WHERE IS THAT TELEGRAM YOU PROMISED ME? DOT."

Buoyed by some slightly brighter press notices, the revue continued to run at Les Ambassadeurs for a few more weeks, but financially it was in trouble, and so Leslie conceded to the inevitable and closed the club. In mid-April he began to reshape the show with the idea of presenting it in a Broadway theater, and he took the traditional route for such a production by taking this new, third version of the show out on the road. It opened in April at Nixon's Apollo Theatre in Atlantic City, enlarged to two acts but with only comedian Tim Moore added to the star lineup. The male dancer U.S. Thompson (husband of the late Florence Mills), who had led the company in a couple of comic dance routines, was dropped from the cast, and Blue McAllister was promoted from the male chorus to lead the new dance "Doin' the New Low-Down."

To extend the length of the show, Leslie added a number of comic sketches and playlets, which—even though he had offered a $100 prize for the best skit—somewhat weighed down the production and detracted from the pace and gaiety of the singing and dancing. The main addition to the musical part of the show was "I Can't Give You Anything but Love, Baby," revived from its ignominious failure in *Delmar's Revels* and tucked into the first half of the program between two skits, "Bearcat Jones' Last Fight" and "Getting Married in Harlem." At this point, so as not to conflict with the song "Baby," the lyrics of the new song were changed to "I Can't Give You Anything but Love, Lindy," an allusion to a character mentioned in one of the revue sketches. Adelaide Hall and Aida Ward shared the song, with a further contribution from Willard McLean.

After previews in Atlantic City and Philadelphia, Leslie was ready to bring *Blackbirds* to Broadway, and it duly opened at the Liberty Theatre on May 9. Dancer Bill "Bojangles" Robinson was a last-minute addition to the New York cast, and this proved to be an inspired idea; he featured his celebrated routine of tap dancing up and down stairs in "Doin' the New Low-Down" before joining Adelaide Hall and Aida Ward in place of McLean for "I Can't Give You Anything but Love." The *Daily News* reported: "For a quarter hour last night, the show was absolutely his and his alone. Then he generously passed a bit of it back to his partner, Miss Hall."[38] The song they shared with Aida Ward now took on its original title, since the other major revision that Leslie put in place for Broadway was to cut the song "Baby." Again, there was a flood of telegrams, and amid the usual congratulations from friends and family, Herbert Fields and his songwriting partners Rodgers and Hart sent the most prophetic message: "MAY BROADWAY GET THE LOW DOWN FOR A LONG TIME TO COME!"

The reviews, when they came next day, were a mixed bunch, but on the whole moderately favorable. The *Daily News* pronounced it the best of the current crop of "Colored Revues," the *New York Times* praised its "knack of finding the right stuff of entertainment in simplicities," the *Broadway Guide* welcomed Dorothy Fields to the "top-notchers of the rhyming profession," and the *Brooklyn Eagle* found it "vivid, bright and rhythmical." But the heavy-weight critics did not like what they saw. Gilbert Gabriel and Wilfred J. Riley dismissed it, Percy Hammond in the *Herald Tribune* found the whole thing too slow, and Alexander Woollcott, doyen of the Algonquin circle of writers and author of the *Stage* column for the *World*, found it a "third-rate Broadway musical tinted brown."[39]

Such reviews from this handful of powerful voices outweighed all the other more positive notices, and similar condemnation had been known to close a production within days. Leslie's revue came perilously close to such failure, but what saved it was his own iron-willed determination to succeed. He ruthlessly trimmed and reshaped the show, removing two comedy sketches and auditioning five more before settling on livelier replacements. He repositioned the tableau built around "Porgy" from the opening of the second half to the end of the first, thus bringing down the curtain with a large dose of pathos instead of introducing a gloomy note as soon as patrons had retaken their seats after the intermission. Above all, he worked on the pace and speed of McHugh's musical numbers, "realizing," as one subsequent press report put it, "that the success of a colored show depends on its pep, zip and dash. He ordered daily rehearsals and kept the chorus girls going at a pace that was reflected in all future performances."[40]

For five weeks Leslie hemorrhaged money at the box office, having cut his ticket prices to the bone. The show played to sizable houses but at well below breakeven. The press report continued: "Word of mouth advertising worked at a snail's pace. Playgoers, what there were of them, liked the show and broadcast the good news in 'raves,' but business remained only so-so. The most encouraging sign, however, soon reared its welcome head in the form of a song, 'I Can't Give You Anything but Love, Baby,' which was beginning to be sung everywhere. The tide turned. Business grew, and when the tenth week was reached it had leaped to capacity."[41]

By following Walter Brooks to Harlem and writing for the Cotton Club, McHugh had believed he was turning his back on Broadway. Within less than a year, capitalizing on that uptown experience, he was the composer of the year's second most successful Broadway musical and cowriter of a song whose record sales eventually exceeded three million.[42]

He was also, for the first time in his life, a wealthy man. His contract with Leslie's Blackbirds Productions Inc., signed when the show went on the road in April, had given him 1 percent of the box office gross. From September onwards, that gross figure generally exceeded $20,000 at the Liberty and often came in at well above $34,000. In addition, Leslie launched a touring company starring Gertrude Saunders and Harriet Calloway to take the show on the road; and soon McHugh was also receiving a similar percentage from "The sensation of two continents: the fastest, funniest, most tuneful revue in America" as it played in Boston and Philadelphia, before a third troupe began playing the major theaters on the Pacific Coast. Even after the New York show moved to the Eltinge Theatre on West Forty-second Street in early 1929, McHugh was still taking home his 1 percent share of weekly box office receipts totaling well in excess of $18,000.[43]

So, in addition to his combined salaries from Mills and the Cotton Club of $350, McHugh was generally collecting around $500 a week from the three simultaneous productions of *Blackbirds*. His further income from sheet music and recordings was also substantial—even though for the songs written specifically for the show, his contract with Leslie obliged him to pay 30 percent of that money over to Blackbirds Productions.

Before the year was out, "I Can't Give You Anything but Love, Baby" had been recorded by Rube Bloom, Mary Dixon, Duke Ellington, Seger Ellis, the Goofus Five, Bill Haid, Annette Hanshaw, Ukulele Ike (Cliff Edwards), Nat Shilkret, Lee Sims, Marek Weber, and Paul Whiteman in the United States and by the Rhythmic Eight, Carroll Gibbons, and Sid Roy in England. Within the first few months of 1929, further recordings were made, including Louis Armstrong's immortal version. Overseas, Sam Wooding's band in Barcelona, Lud Gluskin's in Berlin, and Weiner and Doucet's in Paris were at the forefront of numerous foreign groups recording the song. Ultimately, as late as 1932, the show's continuing popularity was such that a set of six 78-rpm discs were made of highlights of *Blackbirds of 1928*, with the twelve sides including performances by Ellington, Adelaide Hall, Bill Robinson, Ethel Waters, the Cecil Mack Choir, the Mills Brothers, Cab Calloway, and Don Redman's band.

Hall's recording of "I Must Have That Man" gives a good aural impression of the way she performed the song in the show, although she is accompanied on the record by Ellington's band rather than the Will Vodery house band that played for *Blackbirds*. She takes liberties with the written melody line, smoothing it into a form of sung conversation and drawing the audience into her confidence, helped by some neatly accomplished internal rhythms from Fields, such as "awful" and "lawful" or "Hades" and "ladies." There are changes of tempo, and the second verse is accompanied by some manic, high-speed piano from Ellington, suggesting that Hall was frantically dancing as she sang, before she moves into a wailing lament, backed by Ellington's moaning brass, with Barney Bigard's sinuous clarinet weaving around her voice like gossamer. After a scatted break, she finishes with one of her trademark high, soaring, wordless vocals, which finally gives way to a gasp of "I mu-uust have that man!" Her relaxed, confident artistry opens a window into the long-vanished world of *Blackbirds*, as does her assured, swinging performance of "Baby," backed by such splendid playing from Ellington's brass section that it seems incredible that the song was cut from the show.

By the late summer of 1928, Jimmy McHugh was no longer just a song plugger with a few hits to his name. With "I Must Have That Man," "Diga Diga Doo," "Doin' the New Low-Down," and above all, "I Can't Give You Anything but Love, Baby," he and Dorothy Fields had established themselves on the same level as the most successful songwriters of the age.

The McHugh family, circa 1905: (*left to right*) James A.
McHugh, Helen, Larry, Jimmy, May, Julia McHugh,
Tommy

McHugh (*extreme right*) as office boy at the Boston Opera, circa 1910, with Henry Russell (*foreground*)

McHugh in Boston during his song-plugging years

Bess Hornbrook at the
time of her marriage to
McHugh in 1914

McHugh's office at
Jack Mills

McHugh and Irving Mills—The Hotsy Totsy Boys

McHugh (*right*) with
Lawrence Wright, the
British agent for Jack
Mills, in Blackpool, Eng-
land, 1927

McHugh with Dorothy
Fields, Hollywood, 1930

McHugh with Tommy Dorsey: their friendship endured long after the Dorsey Brothers' band premiered "Lost in a Fog" at the Riviera Club

...oduction and enunciation, but either a

James McHugh and Dorothy Fields, song writers. They have written some of the theme songs you've been singing.

McHugh and Fields: more than musical partners

McHugh with Jimmy Jr.
in Beverly Hills

McHugh and Fields in
Hollywood

McHugh at the piano as Shirley Temple and Bill Robinson rehearse steps for *Dimples*

Carmen Miranda

Jimmy McHugh and Harold Adamson

Frank Sinatra lunches with McHugh and Adamson during filming of *Higher and Higher*

Jimmy McHugh and Feliza Pablos

McHugh and
his mother

McHugh and Bing Crosby with poolside bathing beauties, at the
time of the swimming galas in the late 1940s

Doing the social rounds with Louella Parsons and meeting Marilyn Monroe

Weekend poolside party at McHugh's house, with Clark Gable holding forth at the table

Mr. First-Nighter—
McHugh prominent
in the audience
for Judy Garland,
alongside Frank
Sinatra and Debbie
Reynolds

McHugh's Indian summer as a performer with his "Singing Stars"

McHugh at the piano given to him by George Gershwin

5

"Livin' in a Great Big Way"

FIELDS AND McHUGH

ON BROADWAY AND IN HOLLYWOOD

WITH *BLACKBIRDS OF 1928* playing successfully on Broadway, and its touring productions out on the road, Fields and McHugh were nevertheless continuing to supply new songs to the Cotton Club. The floor show there changed every six months or so, and with each revision of the program, new numbers were required, as well as revivals of previous successes. Also, when a star such as Aida Ward returned to the cast at the Harlem venue—as she did in September 1928, shuttling between *Blackbirds* on Broadway and the late-night Cotton Club show—she not only brought her favorite songs back with her but required a few new ones to revivify her act.

Their work having been included in the club's *Show Boat Revue* (which opened in spring 1928 and was still running when Ward returned), several other Fields and McHugh songs then became the mainstay of Dan Healy's next Cotton Club venture, *Hot Chocolate*, which opened on October 7, 1928. It included a song they had written a little earlier, "Harlemania," as well as the new compositions "Japanese Dream," "Misty Morning," and the title song, "Chocolate Hot-Cha." The team was also to supply several numbers for the subsequent March 1929 show *Springbirds*, including "Hot Feet," "Arabian Lover," plus a revival of another slightly older song, "Hottentot Tot."[1]

Hot Chocolate, in particular, traded on the success of *Blackbirds*, one reviewer saying: "The Cotton Club revue is a classic of *Blackbirds*, with the finest array of delightful original costumes and artists ever seen in Harlem at any club catering to the best people in and out of town." The review singled out Adelaide Hall's namesake, Josephine Hall, as the leading entertainer but added:

> Lethia Hill, a prima donna with a pleasing voice and Danny Small's Five Dancing Juveniles, sure step off some real hot dancing. This Japanese number is worth going a long way to see. Another team of girls who are a treat for the eyes and sing and dance marvelously are Beckett and Theret. One girl wearing a tuxedo looks well in it, and sure knows what the well-dressed colored youth should wear. Her partner is also gifted with a fine personality. Miss Beckett is especially clever, leading the hot number of this show called "Chocolate Hot-Cha." This will probably be as big a song hit as Mr. McHugh and Miss Fields' "Diga Diga Do" [*sic*] in *Blackbirds*. What a number "Chocolate Hot-Cha" is! And those costumes and a chorus of creoles is "Just too bad"![2]

Praising Duke Ellington's orchestra as the finest African American band of the time, the reviewer goes on to suggest that those who want to experience the equivalent of a Broadway show every bit as good as *Blackbirds* could do no better than travel "15 minutes in a taxi through Central Park" to the Cotton Club.

Meanwhile, in a direct contrast to working for the hoodlums of Harlem, Fields and McHugh found themselves invited to write the songs for a real live Broadway show, a full-scale book musical called *Hello Daddy*. This title was ironic in more ways than one. Not only did it refer to the plot, adapted from the German farce *The High Cost of Living*, about three respectable business-men, each of whom is conned into supporting what he supposes is his own illegitimate son, all having had a love affair many years ago with the same actress, but the show also marked what was to be the final appearance on stage of Lew Fields, Dorothy's father. The book was by her brother Herbert, and she and McHugh supplied several musical numbers, including "I Want Plenty of You," "In a Great Big Way," "As Long as We're in Love," "Futuristic Rhythm," and "Let's Sit and Talk about You." The show opened at Lew Fields's own Mansfield Theatre on the day after Christmas 1928.

Over thirty years previously, Fields had made his name as a knockabout comic with his partner Joe Weber; and though they had ceased working as a double act in 1904, so that Lew could focus on production and theatrical management, there were periodic reunions. Despite his spry image as an immaculately turned-out gentleman of the theater, as one of the reviews of *Hello Daddy* described him, once Fields got in front of the footlights, his old comic demeanor, stage business, and shtick came to the fore. "Lew Fields is very funny in this play, and does a back fall that many a younger man would hesitate doing for fear of a severe injury. The reception afforded this lovable veteran actor, comedian and producer when he came on the stage had the earmarks of sincerity."[3]

Described by the theater critic Robert Coleman as a "tuneful, diverting, amusing extravaganza," in which "McHugh's tunes alone make it worth the price of admission,"[4] *Hello Daddy* was really kept running for almost six months not by Lew Fields's old-style knockabout comedy but by the ensemble singing and dancing brilliantly staged by Busby Berkeley. Like Lew Leslie, Berkeley had his chorus girls dance in high-energy style, but he was already exhibiting a flair for the synchronized large-scale routines that would make him a household name in later life. Those numbers stopped the show, and the dancers' efforts were aided by the band of Ben Pollack, one of the city's finest medium-sized jazz groups, featuring such luminaries as the young Benny Goodman on clarinet, Jack Teagarden on trombone, and the tough-toned Chicagoan cornetist Jimmy McPartland.

It was McHugh who had insisted that the musical director, Max Steiner, hire Pollack's group, and with his usual song-plugger's flair, he then ensured that Pollack recorded the best songs from the show, not once, but—just as Ellington was wont to do for Irving Mills—several times under various different names. "Let's Sit and Talk about You" and "Futuristic Rhythm" were recorded by Ben Pollack's Park Central Band for Victor on December 24, 1928, but within days, slightly varied versions of the same lineup recorded "Let's Sit and Talk" for Harmony (as Jimmy McHugh's Bostonians), for Okeh (as the Louisville Rhythm Kings), and for Victor again (as Pollack's Park Central Orchestra). No doubt this frenzied recording activity and Mills's attempts to plug the songs in the usual way helped to keep the show running, as it transferred first to the George M. Cohan Theatre and then, in May, to Erlanger's Theatre.

"Then," recalled McHugh, "we got a call from Ziegfeld to do the midnight roof show."[5]

This was, in many ways, a greater measure of Fields and McHugh's success in the eyes of their white Tin Pan Alley contemporaries than *Blackbirds*. To the songwriting community, providing songs for African American revues—however successful—was not as significant an achievement as writing for the doyen of New York impresarios.

Unquestionably, Florenz Ziegfeld was by 1929 the best-known and most successful producer of revues on Broadway. At the suggestion of his common-law wife, the Polish-French actress Anna Held, he had initiated his *Follies* shows in New York in 1907, in imitation of the *Folies Bergères* in Paris. Ziegfeld's *Follies* ran more or less without interruption until his death in 1932, and their hallmark was his personal selection of beautiful chorus girls who sang and danced to music by the finest show composers of the age, including Berlin, Gershwin, and Kern.

In 1927 he had taken the gamble of putting on Oscar Hammerstein II and Jerome Kern's *Show Boat*, a hugely costly production and one which Ziegfeld was initially concerned might not succeed because of its dramatic and racially controversial storyline. He opened the newly built Ziegfeld Theatre that same year with the musical *Rio Rita*, before mounting the premiere of *Show Boat*. When McHugh visited him to discuss working on his new late-night revue in 1929, Ziegfeld was firmly ensconced in a spacious office on the second floor of his Fifty-fourth Street building, his desk surrounded by model elephants, which he believed were lucky, especially if their trunks were held aloft. He favored pictures of elephants in the decor of his theaters as well, but the main feature of his office was a small window looking down into the auditorium, from which he could see every detail of a performance.

Ziegfeld's *Midnite Frolic* shows were slightly smaller-scale revues than the full-scale *Follies*. They were meant to run late at night for the "after-theater crowd" but were nonetheless adorned by some of the best-looking actresses and dancers in show business and featured songs of the same quality as those in his main revues, provided as usual by the best songwriters of the age. The 1929 *Midnite Frolic* was not presented at Ziegfeld's own auditorium but was set in the newly refurbished cabaret venue above the New Amsterdam Theatre, which McHugh described as "a fabulous nightclub." With his extravagant flair for decoration, Ziegfeld had hung the ceiling with hundreds of balloons, and the chorus girls wore strings of exotic orchids.

For the opening on February 6, 1929, he had not only assembled a particularly stunning collection of his "glorified girls" but hired the entire Paul Whiteman Orchestra; the singer and star of *Show Boat*, Helen Morgan; the Duncan Sisters, one of whom played a demure white girl named Eva and the other her "half-nude" blackface counterpart, Topsy; Tamara Geva, the Russian ballerina and ex-wife of George Balanchine; and *Follies* stars Charlotte Ayres, Lillian Roth, Eileen Healey, and Paul Gregory. Two weeks into the run, the cast was joined by the "idol of Paris and London, [the] newest Paramount star," Maurice Chevalier, for his first ever appearance on American soil.[6]

Ziegfeld took a close personal interest in rehearsing every detail of the show. McHugh was particularly impressed when Whiteman's lead trumpeter, Henry Busse, was reprimanded for playing too loudly during a parade of showgirls. "Never allow anything brassy to be played when a beautiful girl is showing off her body, Jimmy," Ziegfeld explained, telling him that music for the girls should be "soft, lush and melodious."[7]

Fields and McHugh contributed several songs to the *Midnite Frolic*, including "Raisin' the Roof," "I'm Looking for Love," and "Squeaky Shoes." Far from having to wait for their work to become recognized by word of mouth, as had been the case with *Blackbirds*, the songwriters discovered that everyone who was anyone was there for the first night. A cartoon of the premiere shows the slinky figure of Helen Morgan in her characteristic pose atop the piano, with Paul Whiteman merrily conducting the band, in front of Mayor Walker and his crowd and such show-business luminaries as Gertrude Lawrence, Noël Coward, Beatrice Lillie, Will Rogers, Eddie Cantor, Lillian Gish, and Lew Fields, not to mention a host of writers and critics headed by Robert Benchley. Waiting for McHugh when he arrived at the venue, among the many cables, was a telegram from his cowriter: "ALL THE LUCK IN THE WORLD FROM US TO US DOT."

Any appearance by the Ziegfeld girls was, according to McHugh, a magnet for the richest men on Wall Street, who showered their favorite dancers with gifts. Consequently, McHugh had very particular memories of the first night, starting with the powerful mix of political, financial, and show-business personalities in the audience: "All these guys sitting around there just started hustling. Then a girl friend of Ziegfeld's, Lillian Lorraine, invited him to have an ice-cream soda with her. He had a white Palm Beach suit on, and they went together and had their soda. She ordered chocolate, and before he knew what was happening, she had thrown the full soda right over his suit. She was absolutely beautiful, but a real toughie, yet so charming that he was crazy about her."[8]

Once its director and entrepreneur had escaped the ire of Miss Lorraine, his former mistress, and changed into a dessert-free suit, the opening night of the show was a success, and it settled in for a comfortable run. As 1929 went on, it was revised into a second edition with new songs added, including "Because I Love Nice Things." The *Midnite Frolic*'s main contribution to posterity is the March 1929 recording of the show's signature number, "Raisin' the Roof," by Frank Trumbauer's band, a contingent from Paul Whiteman's Orchestra that featured the mercurial cornetist Bix Beiderbecke in a couple of cameo vignettes in the arrangement. From a broad historical perspective, this recording is significant because Fields and McHugh were simultaneously contributing to the repertoires of the two most high-profile bands at the height of the Jazz Age, and those bands reflected both sides of the country's racial divide: the African American Ellington orchestra, which performed nightly at the Cotton Club, and Paul Whiteman's big band, which included many of the stellar names in the white jazz world.

At the time, however, the show's principal outcome was seen as the successful musical partnership between Maurice Chevalier and Lilian Roth, who went on to star together in the movie *The Love Parade*.

By mid-February 1929, Fields and McHugh had three shows running simultaneously on Broadway. As a result, they were even better-off than they had been once *Blackbirds of 1928* struck lucky. Their good fortunes continued when on the first anniversary of the opening of the full version of the show, Lew Leslie put a replacement team into the Eltinge Theatre and took the original *Blackbirds* cast to Europe from June to September 1929, adding yet another touring version of the revue to those that were already on the road. In an extravagant gesture typical of his fondness for sending flowers to his leading ladies and telegrams to all and sundry, McHugh celebrated by dedicating a novelty piano solo to his successful lyricist. In mid-1929, "Dorothy," co-written by McHugh and the specialist pianist Frank Banta, was published by Mills Music (the new name of Jack Mills Inc., as of earlier that year). In return, Dorothy signed McHugh's autograph book: "I Can't Give You Anything But Love, Dorothy."

Then, McHugh recalled, "Because the money was rolling in, both of us decided to do a little investing."[9]

He and Fields dined one night with Charles Marcus, who was married to her sister Frances. Marcus was a director of the Bank of the United States, which had been founded by his father and had by then established almost sixty branches. Although a year or two previously Marcus had handed overall control to his brother Bernard, who was now running the bank, he encouraged Dorothy and McHugh to invest in it. The bank was regarded as a rock-solid prospect and was trading at $220 per share.

"Like a good many other people who were making money, I decided to buy some of this Bank of United States stock," said McHugh.[10] He went to a friend who worked at another New York bank, the Irving Trust, to discuss his plans; and the friend, who probably had some inkling that Bernard Marcus was not running the business with due propriety—he was later jailed for his part in the biggest banking collapse in U.S. history—tried hard to dissuade McHugh. The friend even pointed out that the assets of McHugh's old firm

Waterson, Berlin, and Snyder, which had gone into receivership, could be bought for a few thousand dollars (a purchase that would have included all of Irving Berlin's early copyrights) and encouraged McHugh to buy into a business he really understood.

But McHugh was not to be moved and invested the majority of his savings and earnings in the Bank of the United States. He then began trading shares on the margin, buying on credit and selling for a paper profit before his debts were called in. On some days he would make as much as $5,000. He wrote: "I would just reconvert it again for more stock. Had I been wise, I might have cashed some of that in, and just kept the ready cash, but I didn't know better. When I was doing all this on the stock market, not a day would pass by that I didn't send four dozen roses to St. Malachy's church for the altar."[11]

In his immediate circle, it was not only McHugh but Herbert and Dorothy Fields who were to lose almost everything when Wall Street started its dramatic fall on Black Thursday, October 24, 1929. The Fields siblings had set even more store by Charles Marcus's recommendation to invest in the Bank of the United States than McHugh had done, not least because Marcus had bailed Lew Fields out of near bankruptcy more than once, and so they trusted what they saw as his wise financial instincts.

As the slide on the New York Stock Exchange began, McHugh was tipped off that he ought to withdraw any cash he had in his various New York bank accounts. He remembered:

I immediately started making the rounds of the banks. My first stop was the Manufacturer's Trust. When I got to the door there was a big sign: "Closed." This is the place where many people lost fortunes, among them Eddie Cantor. I dashed over to the Irving Trust company and said to my friend, "I don't know how much money I need, but I need a lot of it now, on account of my stock!" He said, "Jimmy, we can give you $3,000 today and maybe $3,000 tomorrow, but that's the best we can do." So, I took the $3,000 and went to Wall Street to turn it in. I was looking forward to tomorrow when I thought I would be able to pick up another $3,000, but when tomorrow came along, all the banks in the United States were closed.[12]

The last two months of 1929 produced a kind of suspended animation among those whose fortunes had been wiped out in just a few days. They walked through the city stunned by what had happened, as if on the outside of reality, unable to comprehend that even though things appeared to be normal, they would never be the same again. There was talk of recovery, and indeed the markets did rally in early 1930, only to plunge downward again later that year and continue falling until 1932. It seemed almost impossible to those who had counted their wealth in hundreds of thousands of dollars that they were effectively penniless. McHugh himself had at least got cash squirreled away in various accounts, and with royalties coming in from his shows and more commissions underway, he was somewhat insulated against the scale of the disaster—until the second slide of the markets late in 1930, when he had his jewelry (tie pins, cufflinks, signet rings, and such) valued at $1,500, and his bank books show him desperately drawing on the last of his savings.[13] But, in 1929, others were not so lucky, and for a time a siege mentality took over until everybody had adjusted to their new status.

McHugh remembered with vivid clarity that a day or two after the crash, he and Dorothy Fields were walking along West Fifty-seventh Street, when she recalled she had an appointment at the hairdresser. He insisted on hailing a cab, but she fixed him with her large mournful eyes and said, "No, Jimmy, no cabs, we'll walk."

While she was having her hair done, he spotted a one-hundred-dollar bill lying on the sidewalk outside the National City Bank. He changed it at the Park Central Hotel and returned to the hair salon to pay for Dorothy's cut. "She didn't have any money either," he remembered. "She had lost everything along with her family and relatives. It was quite a deal in those days to loan someone even as little as two dollars."[14]

McHugh decided to move out of his well-appointed apartment in the Des Artistes building on West Sixty-third Street, where he had lived since the start of his successful Cotton Club career. He found a small room with no heat and no private bathroom on the fourth floor of a walk-up on Riverside Drive. It was, however, very cheap, and he reckoned that he would be able to continue to send adequate money back to his wife and son in Boston by making such economies in his own life.

Being McHugh, he also decided to throw himself into work as never before, to regain some measure of financial security. And the place where he decided he and Fields could reestablish their fortunes was Hollywood. This was to be a prescient move, because in the 1929–30 season that followed the crash, seventeen Broadway theaters closed and several were converted into movie houses, putting dozens of actors out of work and signaling a permanent change in the theatrical landscape in New York.[15] In contrast to the costly business of going to see a live stage show, Depression audiences flocked to the comparatively inexpensive escapism of the cinema, and several studios announced a major increase in output and investment.[16] It was also perfect timing in terms of the technical development of the talking picture, as most companies were beginning to attempt to bring musicals to the screen in the wake not only of Al Jolson's pioneering *Jazz Singer* of 1927 but a more important role model, the 1929 Oscar-winning film *The Broadway Melody*, made by Metro-Goldwyn-Mayer (MGM).

By late 1929, the main studios were only just starting to lure major song-writing talent away from Broadway. In the space of the next twelve months, numerous songwriters made the move, including Sigmund Romberg (*Viennese Nights*), De Sylva, Brown, and Henderson (*Just Imagine*), and Irving Berlin (*The Cocoanuts*). By April 1930, Gene Buck, the president of ASCAP, was advertising in the press to commend all those members who had "answered the call 'On To Hollywood!,'" and these panel advertisements listed several notable members by studio, among them the reprobate Al Dubin at Warner Brothers.[17]

Early in 1929, before the Wall Street crash, Fields and McHugh's first song, "Collegiana," had appeared in the movie *The Time, the Place and the Girl*, and on the back of this minor success, McHugh was convinced that they could emulate their other former Broadway colleagues and enter the Hollywood studios to work on full-length musical films.

At the end of 1929, newspapers announced that he and Dorothy Fields had signed with MGM to write songs for the movies, striking a deal that would certainly provide them with short-term insulation against the effects of the country's financial crisis: "Jimmy McHugh and Dorothy Fields as a writing team have gone with Metro for three months with an option, they will receive $2,000 weekly. Of this amount $500 will be looked upon as salary, and the other $1,500 weekly charged against future song royalties. McHugh has a piece of the Mills publishing house. Whether he is under contract to it as a writer isn't stated. Mills is not mentioned in connection with the Metro-writers transaction."[18]

Before they left for California, however, there was the little matter of providing the music for another Lew Leslie revue, on which Leslie had been working since his return from France with the *Blackbirds* company in the sum-mer of 1929. Slated to open at the Majestic Theatre on February 25, 1930, it was to be his first all-white production. The *International Revue* boasted a cast of twenty-four, plus a chorus directed by Busby Berkeley, and it starred Gertrude Lawrence and Harry Richman. It was also to feature the dancer La Argentinita, who was secured at great expense, but—overweight and some-what ungainly—she proved such a flop with preview audiences that Leslie was forced to pay her off.

McHugh and Fields created a complete collection of new songs for the show, although overall these lacked the consistency and flair of their *Blackbirds* score. Consequently, today nobody much remembers their number about the Wall Street Crash called "The Margineers," however acutely felt its sentiments were at the time, and the same goes for "I'm Feelin' Blue," "International Rhythm," "A Gipsy in Love," "I've Got a Bug in My Head," and "Cinderella Brown." Nevertheless, the two songs they wrote for the principal stars were to be among their most enduring creations: "On the Sunny Side of the Street" was written for Richman, and "Exactly like You" for Lawrence.

The former song caught the mood of the times precisely. Its cheerily optimistic lyric counterbalanced the gloom of the Depression, and given what Fields and McHugh themselves had lost in the crash, it was not without a deep-seated irony. As far as the general public was concerned, "On the Sunny Side of the Street" was an archetypal feel-good number, and within a few weeks of the opening of the revue, an "original cast" record by Harry Richman was on sale. A veteran of *George White's Scandals* and the *Ziegfeld Follies*, Richman was a somewhat larger-than-life stage personality. This comes across in his version of this song, which was heavily modeled on Al Jolson's mannered style of delivery and does not really draw out the frothy optimism of the lyrics. Better by far, and ultimately more enduring, was Jack Richmond's recording, made the following month with the Casa Loma Orchestra and soon heard all over the United States. In the decade that followed, the tune was recorded by several big stars, with Peggy Lee's version with Benny Goodman and the numerous recordings by Louis Armstrong among the best.

"Exactly like You," by contrast, was to become famous not only in its own right but for providing the basis for many other songs. Just as he had done in several pieces since the beginning of his songwriting career, McHugh had created a perfect chord sequence for jazz musicians to improvise over and to use as the basis for alternative melodies. Plenty of contrafact tunes now exist based on these chords, including the more or less contemporary "Swing Out, in the Groove," by the New Orleans trumpeter Wingy Manone, and such songs from subsequent decades as Al Cohn's "Bright," Babs Gonzales's "Gettin' Together," and Todd and Kenny's "Laughing at Life."

Both these hit songs from the *International Revue* followed a similar trajectory to "I Can't Give You Anything but Love, Baby," becoming widely recorded and achieving excellent sheet-music sales. Breaking with their established practice of publishing with Mills Music, Fields and McHugh allowed all their songs from the show to be published under a blanket agreement with Shapiro, Bernstein and Co., and that company must have been very gratified to see the entire collection swiftly included in the "top ten" in *Zit's Weekly*, the Tin Pan Alley magazine. It is significant that several of the other best sellers were also songs designed to purvey a cheerful optimism to listeners in the early months of the Depression—for example, slightly higher up the list was "Happy Days Are Here Again."[19]

Fields and McHugh expected to earn handsomely from these new hits, but their publishing deal for the show channeled all the royalties through Lew Leslie. They trusted him after his exceptional success with *Blackbirds*, but this time Leslie had overreached himself. The self-belief and confidence that had seen him through the troubled early days of *Blackbirds* did not achieve the same turnaround of fortunes for his *International Revue*, although early opinion in the press was that he would somehow manage magically to rescue the show after La Argentinita's dismissal. The papers reported in April that the recovery was well in hand: "They are talking along Broadway about Lew Leslie. For the second time he has lifted a flop show off the floor and put it more or less steadily on its feet. The first time it was *Blackbirds*, a Negro revue. This time it is the *International Revue*."[20]

When he finally admitted defeat, closing the show on May 17 after only ninety-five performances, Leslie had lost around $300,000.[21] Fields and McHugh issued a writ for their unpaid royalties, money they could ill afford to be without, but Leslie was unable to pay them; and although he took immediate steps to rebuild his career by returning to the African American shows that had made his reputation, there was a distinct coolness for the best part of a year between the producer and his songwriting team. This was further exacerbated later in 1930 when Fields was compelled once again to sue Leslie for unpaid royalties on the hitherto gilt-edged *Blackbirds*.[22]

For the time being, however, McHugh and Fields were in Hollywood, working together on their first picture, *Love in the Rough*. In a new city, away from Fields's estranged husband and with few people, if any, aware of McHugh's married past, they were effectively a couple. McHugh later wrote: "Dorothy and I became very close—too close. I prayed to God to break it up. I was always praying to God to break it up. There was always something that made me know it was wrong, that it could not end well. . . . Let us say merely that Dorothy Fields was the love of my life, musically speaking. Something happened to us both when we worked together. We outdid ourselves. Some merging of temperament and personality that allowed us to reach up and grab off a few great ones. I have not worked quite as well with anyone else."[23]

Years later, when his acting and singing protégée Mamie Van Doren asked

McHugh the secret of this instinctive, almost telepathic, communication with Fields and how it created such perfectly matched melodies and lyrics, he looked her in the eye and said frankly, "We were going together." To the outside world, they were a close pair of professional songwriters, each married to someone else, but at the heart of their working relationship was a discreet love affair that was to last until the mid-1930s.[24]

Love in the Rough was not an unqualified success, being described by even its most enthusiastic critic as "slight, spotty and none too entertaining,"[25] but it provided a swift learning curve for its songwriting team. McHugh and Fields produced seven songs, including "I'm Learning a Lot from You," "Go Home and Tell Your Mother," "One More Waltz like Kelly Can," and "Doin' That Thing" (a tune that was at one time considered for the movie's title). It starred the up-and-coming actor Robert Montgomery, who had recently played opposite Joan Crawford in *Untamed*, and Dorothy Jordan, whose stage experience stood her in good stead for the musical numbers. In other respects the film was most unlike a stage musical, as it was partly filmed outside, on fashionable golf courses with "beautiful scenic links." By and large it also avoided the rather wooden "chorus style" of theatrical musical comedy transferred to celluloid, although in an effort to explain to viewers how music came out of nowhere on the golf course, one scene was accompanied by a squadron of caddies playing harmonicas.

For Fields and McHugh, besides the excitement of being in a city that seemed almost untouched by the Depression, where they could indulge publicly in their attraction for each other by attending a constant round of receptions and parties together, there was a significant change to the way they worked. Unlike the theater, where McHugh was used to laying out the entire scheme of a show with its producer and taking a hand in casting and musical direction, he and Fields became small cogs in a larger mechanism. They were simply writers supplying "work made for hire," and although they benefited from royalties on their songs, the pieces they wrote were merely those required by the producers, as was clear from the organizational chart for the Music Department at MGM:

> When a song or dance number is contemplated for a picture, the Producer will confer, if possible during preparation of the script, with the Head of the Music Department, who will review the requirements and make the necessary assignments of personnel. After song and dance numbers have been written and APPROVED by the Producer, the Producer will arrange a meeting of the following people to plan, prepare and execute the number.

TITLE	FUNCTION
a) Producer	Final decision
b) Picture Director	Tying in the number with remainder of story
c) Unit art director	Design of background and set
d) Head of Music Department	Execution of musical end
e) Prod. Mgr. of Music Department	Physical preparation of musical end
f) Song Writers	Collaboration
g) Dance director	Development of number
h) Cutter	Determination of cuts

The result of this conference will be reduced to a CUTTING CONTINUITY which will be a guide for the director and enable a budget to be made.[26]

As "collaborative" cogs in such an unwieldy mechanism, McHugh and Fields faced the constant risk that their most creative efforts, musically speaking, would end up on the cutting-room floor. In addition, they spent much more time on their contribution to each production than they would for a stage show, given the complexity of the studio system, the number of people who had powers of approval, and the process of actually filming and recording each song.

Furthermore, instead of being published by Mills Music, their output was now to be distributed by the Robbins Music Corporation, part of the Loews Theatres conglomerate that distributed the MGM movies. Indeed, just before their first film was released in August 1930, Louis K. Sidney, in the distributor's central production department in New York, became almost apoplectic in his instructions to theaters to plug only Robbins products: "Our money is invested in Robbins Music Corporation, and since this is a fact, we expect our theaters, our musicians, leaders and organists to adhere to my letter of last week, by playing only Robbins tunes. There will be positively no excuse for your playing any other songs in organ solos, overtures and recessionals."[27]

In the movie world, plugging was not left to chance or to the efforts of men such as McHugh had been before his move to Hollywood and the de facto end of his plugging career at Mills. Central marketing decided what the hit songs from each film would be and ruthlessly publicized them. Louis K. Sidney left his managers in no doubt of what was expected of them:

There is a forthcoming Metro-Goldwyn-Mayer Picture entitled LOVE IN THE ROUGH which will be released early in September. The picture has four (4) songs that are potential hits. The name of these four songs are

GO HOME AND TELL YOUR MOTHER
I'M DOIN' THAT THING
I'M LEARNING A LOT FROM YOU
ONE MORE WALTZ.

These numbers are our own property, published by our music company, the Robbins Music Corporation. When you play the picture LOVE IN THE ROUGH, I want you to begin boosting those four songs, two to three weeks prior to the playing of this picture. Go to it extra heavy. . . . Where you have an orchestra, let the orchestra use them as an overture, using slides, calling attention to the fact that these four numbers are from your last [*sic*] week's picture.

As well as dictating what songs were to be plugged, the studios and distributors undertook test screenings to see how rough cuts of the movie played to various audiences. After one such early showing of *Love in the Rough*, under its original theatrical title of *Spring Fever*, Fields and McHugh received a telegram from the agency that had helped secure their MGM contract, saying: "SAW PREVIEW. . . . SPRING FEVER EXCELLENT COMEDY PICTURE REGISTERED STRONGLY WITH AUDIENCE STOP YOUR NUMBERS GOT OVER VERY STOP [*sic*] GO HOME AND TELL YOUR MOTHER WILL BE POSITIVE HIT."[28]

By the time *Love in the Rough* came out, Fields and McHugh were back in New York, working on another Broadway revue at the Vanderbilt Theatre. Their first MGM contract had given them six months' work, with a guaranteed minimum of $50,000, and during 1930 they elected to spend two periods each of about three months in Hollywood, returning to New York in between to keep their theatrical career alive. During the next four years or so, they shuttled quite regularly from coast to coast. They provided songs for such stage shows as *Shoot the Works* and *Singin' the Blues* (both in 1931) and Lew Leslie's revues *Clowns in Clover*, *Rhapsody in Black*, and *Dixie to Broadway* (all 1932), while their prolific movie career saw them contribute songs to *Cuban Love Song* and *Flying High* (both 1931), as well as *Dinner at Eight*, *Meet the Baron*, *My Dancing Lady*, and *The Prizefighter and the Lady* (all 1933).

Although not all these shows and movies yielded hit songs, there was generally at least one number in each that broke through to a wider public. Indeed, that is about all that can be said for the *Vanderbilt Revue*, which was produced by Lew Fields. Inspired by his success with *Hello Daddy* to put on a revue featuring yet more original music by his daughter and McHugh, Fields recruited a sizable cast for what he envisaged as a two-act show. Although there was additional music by Mario Braggiotti, Jacques Fray, and E. Y. Harburg, the bulk of the score, with such songs as "Blue Again," "Button Up Your Heart," "Cut In," and "You're the Better Half of Me," was by Fields and McHugh.

In a cast of thirty that featured several radio comedy stars, with the additional voices of a complete Russian choir, the main musical contribution was from McHugh's old flame, Evelyn Hoey. According to one critic, despite Hoey's ravishing looks, there was one aspect of her delivery that the audience found irritating rather than attractive: "the show has several pleasant songs by Dorothy Fields and Jimmy McHugh, interpreted by Evelyn Hoey in a croon that is agreeable enough, if only she wouldn't sing baby talk."[29] The "baby talk" seems to have been just one of a number of unsuccessful features that sealed the show's fate. Following the fanfare of its grand opening on November 5, the revue closed after only thirteen performances, and with it, the curtain came down on Lew Fields's theatrical career. He was never to venture into stage production again, after failure on such a grand scale.

Two years later, when he and Joe Weber celebrated their partnership's golden anniversary with a grand dinner at the Hotel Astor, for the first time in his life Fields looked only back and not forward toward his next venture. The dinner was a wallow in nostalgia, with the sumptuous printed program featuring exquisite photos of the pair's heyday at the Weber and Fields Music Hall, performing in such antiquated song and dance shows as *Twirly Whirly*.

While the *Vanderbilt Revue* was opening and closing in such short order, Fields and McHugh had already gone back to Hollywood. The Los Angeles press noted that the "songwriting team are expected from New York to start their second Metro period November 1. . . . It's now a question of what Fields and McHugh will do on arrival."[30] Their return to California also meant that they missed the opening of that fall's Cotton Club show, Walter Brooks's *Brown Skin Vamps*, which began its run in Harlem on November 22. The club was still closely allied to Irving and Jack Mills, who retained their strong links with its gangland owners as well as with the resident bands of Duke Ellington and the newly arrived Cab Calloway. However, because the move to Hollywood had involved changing their publisher, for the first time since December 1927 Fields and McHugh's newest songs would not be featured at the club, where Irving Mills still ruled the roost. Instead, as the Duke Ellington band set off on a short tour to promote its new movie *Check and Double Check*, a new Mills aggregation called the Cotton Club Jazz Fiends arrived, playing a program that revived the much earlier songs of McHugh and Al Dubin. Once again, old numbers such as "My Kid" got an airing in public.

Before Fields and McHugh settled back into their West Coast routine at the studios, they could at least take some comfort from the fact that one of their new songs, "Blue Again," had survived the *Vanderbilt* disaster and with the help of their new publisher, Jack Robbins, was becoming something of a hit. Recordings of the piece by the Yale Collegians, Red Nichols, and Duke Ellington were all finding their way into the shops ahead of Christmas. The following April, Louis Armstrong also recorded a version that used its simple, accessible tune as the basis for some stunning trumpet improvisation, plus a characteristic Satchmo vocal that very clearly displays the inventive harmonies that McHugh employed in the middle eight bars, while at the same time showing a certain disdain for one of Fields's weaker lyrics (including rhyming "blue again" with "half past two again").

Back on the MGM lot, following a brief visit to Los Angeles by McHugh's parents and his son Jimmy Jr., the pair started work on two features for the 1931 season, *Cuban Love Song* and *Flying High*.

The former of these was set in a highly fictionalized version of Cuba; indeed, it was more Californian-Mexican than Cuban in terms of everything from the visual street settings to the accents of the cast, and in subsequent years this dashed its chances in Latin America, where both Cuban and Mexican diplomats attempted to persuade MGM to suppress it.[31] Its plot—which owed more than a little to *Madame Butterfly*—centered on a U.S. marine who falls in love with a Cuban girl and fathers an illegitimate son, whom he later returns to the island to collect: a plotline which in itself was controversial for 1930–31, with its overtones of moral turpitude among the armed forces. It was to star a rather oddly assorted cast, including Jimmy Durante, Ernest Torrence, and the New York Metropolitan Opera principal Lawrence Tibbett, who played the marine in question and—more importantly for Fields and McHugh—sang the title song.

Currently in the seventh of what would eventually turn out to be twenty-seven seasons at the Met, Tibbett was a powerful baritone, much celebrated for such roles as Rigoletto, Iago (in Verdi's *Otello*), and Valentin (in Gounod's *Faust*). A somewhat stocky, good-looking man, he possessed great expressivity both as an operatic stage actor and singer. However, this did not transfer entirely easily to the movie set despite his success the previous year in *The Rogue Song*, and he lacked the lightness of touch of such later popular classical screen singers as Nelson Eddy or Mario Lanza.

McHugh, however, was delighted to have the chance to compose for him. Recalling his own far-off Boston days, he wrote: "As long as I can remember, opera stars have had a greater glamor for me than any other people. I have always loved being around them and wanted to be associated with them.

When Lawrence Tibbett did *Cuban Love Song* at Metro . . . my knowledge of opera gave [the] producers confidence in me they wouldn't otherwise have had. For such singers, one had to have a knowledge of the range of voice and what could be done with them."[32]

For the title song, McHugh produced a catchy, memorable tune in three/four time, which works best over a rumba rhythm as the background music to the film's carnival scene. At the end of this sequence, Tibbett picks up the song and sings it several times more during the movie, including both an emotional duet with his fiery Mexican-born costar Lupe Velez and a "ghost" sequence where he duets with himself. Although the Latin vogue was already beginning in 1930, Tibbett's commercial recording of the song, made in October 1931 when the movie was finally released, has barely a hint of a rumba rhythm, and he sings it as a light operatic ballad, rather in the manner of John McCormack. To modern ears this seems a very stilted and unnatural performance, but this was clearly not the case at the time, as it briefly turned the opera star into something of a cult figure who was mobbed like a modern pop idol. According to the press report of a charity appearance in Baltimore, where he was promoting the film:

> Six women fainted, when Lawrence Tibbett, motion picture actor and opera star, sang his *Cuban Love Song* at a relief ball. Tibbett had barely finished his song before a crowd of 4,500 last night, when 200 women deserted their escorts and fought their way to him. Scrambling over chairs and tables, they sought to touch his hand and clothes. One woman lifted a trembling hand to his cheek: "Oh, Mis-ter Tib-bett!" she gasped. Then she swooned away. Five others, ranging in age from 20 to 40 soon joined her. Tibbett tried to stoop to the floor to help the woman, but the pressing throng thrust him aside. Policemen finally made their way through the crowd and carried the dishevelled but still smiling Tibbett away to safety.[33]

Plenty of effort went into the musical elements of *Cuban Love Song*. In addition to the theme tune, a nautical song, "Tramps at Sea" (also known as "Ship Ahoy!"), not only served as the basis for a show-stopping routine near the start of the movie but provided the thematic material for numerous musical cues as the story progressed. In his Broadway days, McHugh had seldom done his own arrangements. Indeed, at the Cotton Club he had paid Duke Ellington $50 apiece to orchestrate the new songs for each show, and for other revues he frequently used the African American composer William Grant Still to orchestrate his and Fields's songs. At MGM, orchestration was done by another division within the music section; once he and Fields had finished the lead sheet, it was whisked away to be arranged for the soundstage, with full-fledged cues written from his thematic sketches. In *Cuban Love Song*, the entire second verse of "Tramps at Sea" was cut from the final print, despite great care having been lavished on every step of its production by all the sections of the MGM Music Department.

This was minor, however, compared to *Flying High*, from which an entire song, "Love in the Air," was deleted not once, but twice. In a curt, if apologetic, letter to the songwriters, MGM's Martin Broones explained: "We had to cut down the entire opening due to excessive footage. As a result, Donald Novis singing 'Love in the Air' came out. And then in the middle of the story where we needed speed, we not only eliminated Kathryn Crawford's song on the lake, but also the love scene preceding it, due to the fact that the tempo of the picture was so terrific that the whole lake scene held it up. Anyway, the audience didn't seem to be particularly interested in her rendition of the above number."[34] Such perfunctory decisions, often after weeks of (albeit well-paid) work, were not exactly morale boosting, but they came to be a commonplace experience for all composers and lyricists who worked in Hollywood.

Flying High had been devised as a vehicle for the comedian Bert Lahr, so by coincidence Fields and McHugh found themselves supplying him with songs for what turned out to be his first movie, just as they had once given him "I Can't Give You Anything but Love, Baby" for his New York stage debut in *Delmar's Revels*. Although in the picture Lahr mainly combines a manic energy with an air of deep-seated stupidity—he had yet to reach the dizzy heights of his assured performance as the Cowardly Lion in *The Wizard of Oz*—his contribution is mainly remembered for a piece of comic business that had also been the highlight of the stage version of the show (scored by Da Sylva, Brown, and Henderson) when it played on Broadway the previous year. For the film, Fields and McHugh supplied the "Examination Number," a musical setting for Lahr's medical tests for fitness to fly. Strapped into a drum and spun rapidly to simulate the effects of flying, the dizzy Lahr is unprepared for the doctor then to demand a urine test and misses the entire point of the request, "I need a sample." He assumes the doctor wants an illicit drink. While the doctor is out of the room, he fills the sample container with amber fluid from the hip flask that (as it was still the Prohibition era) he carried as a matter of course. When the doctor returns to collect the brimming bottle, Lahr apologizes that he "could only spare a quart." In prudish, alcohol-free 1930s America, this line invariably brought the house down.

Lahr's other comic business, aloft on an "aero-copter" with the deadpan comedienne Charlotte Greenwood as his fiancée, satirized the kind of derring-do flying contests that McHugh had experienced firsthand as a Boston teenager. Maybe for this reason, he put considerable energy into revising and reworking the stage show's original "Happy Landings" number for a huge spectacular sequence choreographed by Busby Berkeley. Sixty female dancers took part in one of Berkeley's more impressive trompe l'oeil routines, as the *Los Angeles Times* reported: "What seems to be an aviation field with scores of planes taking off turns suddenly into a bewildering melange of chorines, each bearing a glass-covered airplane in her right hand."[35]

Fields and McHugh completed their work on these two movies in the allotted three months, and by March 1931 they were back on the East Coast, picking up their stage careers. Since *Hello Daddy*, Dorothy Fields had nurtured the desire to write another book musical with a full-scale plot, rather than contributing individual numbers to revues. The producers Alex Aarons and Vinton Freedley came up with just such a project, a musical version of Jack McGowan's "race" play *Singin' the Blues*. (McGowan, incidentally, was also the author of *Flying High* and almost certainly took a hand in introducing the songwriters to Aarons and Freedley, who had previously worked mainly with George and Ira Gershwin.) The plot was simple. Two low-life characters, Jim Williams and his pal "Knuckles," are accidentally involved in killing a Chicago cop, so they flee to New York and go to ground in Harlem, where Jim falls for a nightclub entertainer, Susan. The action concerns the two weeks that Jim and Susan spend together before his past (and the police force) catches up with him. With an evocative setting in a nightclub called "The Magnolia," there was plenty of opportunity for *Blackbirds*-style song and dance routines; and not only were these choreographed and rehearsed by Dan Healy, but the show's terpsichorean star was the exotic African American dancer Fredi Washington, who had recently headlined with Duke Ellington in the RKO short film *Black and Tan*.

The title song, "Singin' the Blues," was launched by the dancer's sister, the vocalist Isabell Washington. Other musical numbers devised for a team of Lindy Hoppers included two Cotton Club–style dances, "Gotta Skip the Gutter" and "Harlem Jungle," with Isabell featured again on a slower, romantic love song, "It's the Darndest Thing," thrown in for good measure.

The show opened for its out-of-town preview at the Apollo Theatre in Atlantic City on April 6, 1931, and perhaps as a refreshing antidote to his hands-off involvement in movies, McHugh took a close personal interest in the whole production. After attending the first run-throughs for the cast at the Broadhurst Theatre in Manhattan, he checked into the Shelbourne Hotel in Atlantic City and attended full rehearsals, just as he had been on hand for the tryout tour of *Blackbirds*. While the show was running in Atlantic City, grossing a healthy $8,800 for the week, he worked with the professional manager at Robbins, Jack Bregman, to fine-tune the arrangements for the following week's opening at the Majestic Theatre in Brooklyn, for which Eubie Blake, the venerable show composer and bandleader would lead the onstage band. On April 8, Bregman wired McHugh for instructions:

> VICTOR YOUNG READY TO ORCHESTRATE HARLEM JUNGLE STOP ADVISE ME WHAT KEY YOU WANT ARRANGEMENT IN STOP IN OTHER WORDS AFTER WASHINGTON GIRL THROUGH DANCING WHAT KEY ARE ROUTINES IN YOUNG WILL HAVE SAME READY ALSO CHORUS BUTTON UP YOU [*sic*] HEART ORIGINAL KEY FOR DANCERS BY SATURDAY MORNING WILL AWAIT YOUR ARRIVAL SO YOU CAN USE FOR BROOKLYN VARIETY AND SENSATIONAL WRITE UP ALSO NOTICED ATLANTIC CITY PAPERS CERTAINLY ENCOURAGING EVERYBODY TALKING ABOUT IT.[36]

Cables flew to and fro, and by the following week's opening in Brooklyn, the show was running slickly, grossing $8,013 in its first week. It was well received by the critics, with Rowland Field in the Brooklyn *Daily Times* complimenting this "interesting well-arranged Negro musical melodrama, that combines the best features of such topical subjects as dusky dice games and gunplay . . . with the carefree rhythms of Harlem nightclubs in their most syncopated state." Edwin Stein, in his *Stage and Screen* column, hailed "a combination of musical comedy and legitimate drama that retains the better features of each." All of the reviewers were unanimous in their praise of the singing and dancing nightclub sequences, in which McHugh's music and Healy's choreography brilliantly evoked the Cotton Club atmosphere on stage.[37] Once again, the songwriting team had proven its talent for writing convincing material for a high-energy troupe of African American performers.

Following this very successful pre-Manhattan run, the show was booked into the Liberty Theatre that fall, opening on September 16. But somehow, in reworking the play for this full-scale Broadway production, the baby got thrown out with the bathwater. New music was added by Harold Adamson and Burton Lane; Young's orchestrations were superseded with new ones by Robert Russell Bennett; and Dan Healy's dazzling Lindy Hop routines were replaced with new choreography by Sammy Lee. The result was not a success, and although the same principal cast members and Eubie Blake's band tried their best, the show folded on Broadway after just forty-five performances.

McHugh did at least ensure that his songs survived beyond the show's untimely end. "Singin' the Blues" and "It's the Darndest Thing" were recorded back to back during the April previews by Smith Ballew and Red

Nichols for Brunswick, and a second 78-rpm recording was made during the ill-fated Broadway run, for Columbia, by Fletcher Henderson's band. However, *Singin' the Blues* was to be the last book musical on which McHugh and Fields collaborated.

In the months between the previews and the arrival of *Singin' the Blues* on Broadway, Fields and McHugh contributed a song to a musical revue that was effectively a job-creation project for actors and musicians who had no work during the Depression. *Shoot the Works* ran from July until September 1931. It was the brainchild of Heywood Broun, who cajoled several songwriters, including Irving Berlin, E. Y. Harburg, and Ira Gershwin, into writing songs for the show, which featured sketches written by members of Dorothy Parker's Algonquin circle. "How's Your Uncle?" was the Fields and McHugh song, for which they received no share of the performance royalties, as all profits went to the deserving cast, but they retained the publishing and mechanical rights.

In 1931 the pair split their working lives between New York and Hollywood, but the two years that followed saw them dividing their time a little differently. They spent most of 1932 on the East Coast, penning a large number of individual songs that were published and plugged in the normal way but more importantly contributing to a couple of stage works, before heading West for a highly productive movie season in 1933. What is more, the 1932 stage pieces involved a rapprochement with Lew Leslie.

During the time that Fields and McHugh were first in Hollywood, Leslie had worked hard to salvage his career in the wake of the failure of the *International Revue*. In the fall of 1930, he mounted a new edition of *Blackbirds*, starting at the Lyric Theatre in Boston and starring Harriett Calloway, whom he had featured in the touring company of the original 1928 show and whose press clippings made much of the fact that she was a former Columbus, Ohio, newspaper delivery girl and no relation to Cab or his band-leading sister Blanche. With music by Eubie Blake and Andy Razaf, the show then ran for a respectable three months at the Royale Theatre on Broadway, with Ethel Waters taking over the starring role from Calloway, joining an all-star cast that included Buck and Bubbles, Cecil Mack's Choir, Flourney Miller (the original star of *Shuffle Along*), and Broadway Jones.

The show did much to revive Leslie's career and his fortunes, and it was followed in May 1931 by an even more ambitious revue called *Rhapsody in Black*, billed as "a symphony of Blue Notes and Black Rhythms," that ran for three months at the Sam H. Harris Theatre in Manhattan. Again, Ethel Waters was the star, alongside female trumpeter and singer Valaida Snow. One of the skits, called "Her Supporting Cast," was a direct crib of the plot from *Hello Daddy* and caused *Time* magazine to dismiss the entire evening as "an awful show,"[38] but there was praise all around for Miss Waters and the music by Pike Davis's Continental Orchestra. Among the musical offerings was a new song by Fields and McHugh called "I'm Feeling Blue," and this triggered the resumption of their working relationship with Lew Leslie. The show was sufficiently successful for it to be revived, and (after a tour to Chicago, Boston, and Pittsburgh) it ran for some weeks in the summer of 1932 at the Paramount Theatre in New York City.

For 1932, Leslie had plans for two shows, one to maintain his track record for successful African American revues and the other an attempt to prove that he could overcome his previous failure by creating a successful all-white revue as well. The all-black *Dixie to Broadway*, with Ethel Waters and the Mills Brothers among its "100 Sepian Stars," shamelessly reused Leslie's successful title from the 1920s, but it did not open until October. Most of the earlier part of the year was taken up with planning, casting, and sending on tour a revue called *Clowns in Clover*, which Leslie hoped to bring to Broadway.

Sadly, this effort was to fare little better than the *International Revue*, and first-night critic Robert Garland astutely summed up the position when he wrote: "Lew hit a home run with his *Rhapsody In Black*, [but] he has fanned out with its pale-faced successor."[39] The show's troubles began with the fact that its star, Walter Woolf, was not a particularly successful leading man, but the main problem was with the comedy sketches that suffused the production. They simply were not funny. Some of the routines, according to those who saw the first performances, had their "mirth quite destroyed, others are merely sordidly dirty."[40] During the previews in Detroit, where the show first opened, comedians Lew Hearn and Eddie Lambert struggled for laughs, with the former winning some applause for a sketch that had him thrown from a fifteenth-floor window, and the latter making a success of a comic piano recital by his stage persona of "a mugging, mispronouncing Yiddish comedian." The only consistently good thing the critics could find to say about the opening was that a very young man who played the harmonica "extracts effects that surprise the natives into stopping the show." The young man's name was Larry Adler, and he was still only eighteen at the time, two years before he first moved to London to begin his successful international recording career.

After struggling at the Cass Theatre in Detroit, the show moved in late June to the Apollo in Chicago. Fields and McHugh were receiving a percentage of the gross, but they cannot have been gratified by the paltry sums in the count-up sheets, which showed sizable parties being admitted at "special" rates. Furthermore, although Leslie was too old and wise a producer to be discomfited by poor reviews, when he set about his usual trimming and reshaping of the show, he dropped Adler, its major asset, and turned to the Merriel Abbott Dancers, the "40 most beautiful girls in the world," to play up the singing and dancing side of the show. Press releases stressed what today would be called the show's "feel-good factor" for the Depression years, with the Chicago advertisements emblazoned with Charles Collins's review in the *Tribune:* "Its spirit runs to smiling optimism and it undertakes to counteract the depressed psychology of the times . . . with gallant reassurance."

After a short run in Chicago, the planned opening on Broadway never materialized. Instead of the labored comedy of *Clowns in Clover*, New York crowds were treated to the sheer exuberant escapism of Leslie's African American show, *Dixie to Broadway*, also with songs by Fields and McHugh, which opened at the Paramount in the wake of *Rhapsody in Black* on October 28.

There was, however, to be one long-term legacy of *Clowns in Clover*, because among its otherwise forgettable musical numbers was one enduring masterpiece of a popular song, "Don't Blame Me." Even McHugh's formidable plugging skills failed to get it recorded at the time; but in 1933 he and Fields slipped it into their movie score for *Meet the Baron*, and with the extra push of the film's promotion, it was soon recorded by Ethel Waters and the Dorsey Brothers and went on to become one of the most recorded songs in Fields and McHugh's entire catalog.

One reason for this is that McHugh fitted some extremely ingenious chord changes into the normal thirty-two-measure sequence of the song. It opens with three descending chords that run down a simple chromatic scale from C to B flat to A, but by making the first two notes of the melody rise from G to B flat, he builds in a sense of contrary motion. The whole harmonic structure of the piece intrigued jazz musicians, in particular, and made them want to improvise on it, so that from Jimmy Dorsey's inventive clarinet solo on the first recording, they have been doing so ever since.

There was one other song in *Clowns in Clover*, which—although it became a minor hit at the time—is now memorable for quite another reason than any musical merit it may have had. "Hey, Young Fella (Will You Close Your Old Umbrella)" was the first song that Fields and McHugh ever performed together on stage in public, when they made it the centerpiece of their act at the grand opening of Radio City Music Hall in New York on December 27, 1932. Indeed, the lyrics were printed in the souvenir program (the only song to be so honored in a very lengthy evening of variety turns), undoubtedly so that McHugh's plugging instincts could be satisfied as the audience of over six thousand sang along with Miss Fields's smoky contralto.

Although Fields and McHugh had appeared in public as a couple in Los Angeles, being asked to do so on the New York stage by Roxy (Samuel Roxy Rothafel, the entrepreneur who had built the theater in partnership with the Rockefeller family and RCA) was almost too much for them. One account, describing Roxy at the dress rehearsal, bellowing out instructions through a megaphone to everyone from his dancers to his lighting designers, ran: "He called to his people on the stage: 'Now, Jimmy don't be that way. Put your arm around Dorothy, go on. And Dorothy, put your arm round his neck. Remember you're having a good time in this scene.' It was Dorothy Fields' stage debut. She blushed when she put her arm round Jimmy's neck. And both of them seemed rather shy. Roxy went up on the stage and took the young lady joyously round the waist, and skipped merrily away with her. 'Do it like that!' he said to Jimmy. But Jimmy simply couldn't."[41] Nevertheless, their double act was one of the high points of the show, and *Variety* complimented them by suggesting they had gone over far better than most of those on the bill who actually performed for a living.

After reviving their association with Lew Leslie in New York and making this high-profile stage debut, it was time for Fields and McHugh to head back to Hollywood. They had not been entirely overlooked by the movie industry in 1932, as individual songs had appeared in a couple of films—the "Goodbye Blues" in the *Big Broadcast of 1932*, and "It's the Darndest Thing" in *Dancers in the Dark*. Now, however, they were going back for a period of sustained work on several movies.

In the early part of the year, they were involved in creating the title songs for Joan Crawford's *Dancing Lady* (a picture that is mainly remembered now for being Fred Astaire's debut on screen as a dancer), and for *Dinner at Eight*.

Then they were featured on screen themselves, in a short film set in a music publishing office. This was shot during April and early May, before they returned briefly to New York. Following their stage appearance the previous year at Radio City, it seemed that they briefly nurtured the idea of performing as a duo, because within days of wrapping up the film shoot, they began a series of short broadcasts on WJZ in New York, with Dorothy singing excerpts from their work while McHugh "sticks to piano," as the press put it. For once, McHugh seemed slightly reticent in making newspaper copy out of his own exploits, because when asked about the movie they had just appeared in, he said: "Dorothy Fields and I have just made a short with Jack Osterman, Ben

Adey, the Pickens Sisters and a 10-piece band, and I guess it will be OK. . . .
Hope so. . . . At any rate we've been paid, so I guess it's OK."[42]

Dreams of performing for a living were short-lived, and the couple were
soon back in Hollywood behind their songwriting desks at MGM for *The
Prizefighter and the Lady* and *Meet the Baron*. The first of these movies featured
the boxer Max Baer. Just as McHugh had been delighted to work with his
operatic idol Lawrence Tibbett, the chance to compose for one of his heroes
of the ring was equally inspiring, and he wrote "Lucky Fellow" as Baer's featured number in the movie. He recalled: "Max and I became good friends.
He told me that before he was twenty-one, he used to bend hot iron rods
with his hands. He had a 24-inch waist and a 46-inch chest. If ever there was
a great specimen of manhood this was it."[43]

In 1933 "Madcap Maxie" Baer was twenty-four years old and in his prime
as a boxer. Although the deaths of fighters Frankie Campbell and Ernie Schaff
as a result of injuries sustained in fights with him had put a shadow over his
career, his fortunes had revived earlier that year when he defeated Hitler's
favorite boxer, Max Schmeling, during a bout in which Baer had deliberately
worn a Star of David on his trunks. The American public, particularly the
Jewish public, consequently adored Baer. The movie was a chance for him
not only to display his talents for singing and dancing but to promote his
forthcoming bout for the world title with the current champion, Primo Carnera, who appeared as himself in the picture in a fight refereed by former
world champion Jack Dempsey (also playing himself), while Baer played the
fictional role of "Steve Morgan." McHugh wrote: "Baer proved very talented
on the picture. We found he could do his own dancing and singing . . . and
then there were the fight scenes with Primo Carnera, which gave him a good
chance to feel out Carnera and vice versa. . . . When we were shooting the
picture, Max kept telling Primo, 'When I get you in the ring in New York,
I'm going to kill you!'"[44]

The title bout did not take place until June 14, 1934, and preceding it both
McHugh and Baer stayed in style at the Park Central Hotel. Before the fight,
McHugh wired Baer the lyric of "Lucky Fellow," with its line about "fortune
in my glove." As it turned out, Baer won convincingly, and Carnera ended
up in the French Hospital, where McHugh remembered him lying "like a
ludicrously large mammal," begging Baer for a return match. For the next
year or so, until he lost the world title to James Braddock, Baer combined
success in the ring with a growing sideline as a nightclub singer and dancer,
often in partnership with his brother Buddy. Fields and McHugh wrote the
song "Who Said Dreams Don't Come True?" for them. From 1935 onward,

Baer increasingly became a full-time actor and singer, appearing in one or two more movies, as well as making stage and club appearances. In McHugh's opinion, the club work "softened him up" for any further activity in the ring, which is why he never regained his former status as a boxer.[45]

Although working with Baer and hanging round the set with his heroes Carnera and Dempsey were experiences that McHugh remembered for the rest of his life, it was the other picture from the latter part of 1933, *Meet the Baron*, that tells us most about the input Fields and McHugh had on the movies for which they provided the score. The film itself was a vehicle for radio comedian Jack Pearl, the voice of the on-air character of Baron Munchausen, who told far-fetched stories topped off with the catchphrase "Vas you dere, Charley?" In Walter Lang's movie, Pearl was to re-create the role on screen, in the improbable setting of a women's college, and comedians Jimmy Durante and the Three Stooges were also in the cast. Female interest was provided by the exotic actress Zasu Pitts.

Large portions of the script survive in the McHugh family archives, and because whole sections of the story involved chorus singing or rhyming (rather in the style of the Munchkin sequence in *The Wizard of Oz*, when Dorothy arrives in Oz), many of these were drafted in their entirety by Fields. The opening sequence alone is eight pages of outline, with camera shots, scene directions, and descriptions of the action intertwined with some of Fields's most complex lyrics. As messages are shouted across the campus, each is misheard and subtly altered as it is passed on, so that "the Baron and his manager" becomes "the Baron and a staff of ten" and then mutates into "the Baron and a hundred men. . . ."

Some of her rhymes are outrageous ("Hey nonny noney / eau de cologney"), and she works in contemporary references to both Mae West and Cab Calloway, but all in all, Fields's work is a tour de force of rhyming invention set to music by McHugh, who enhances her allusions to Calloway's "Minnie The Moocher" and other passing parodies of popular songs in his score.

We also know that despite the easy flow of the sequence, it had to be filmed piecemeal because of the limited availability of the stars, notably Miss Pitts, who had previously had an illustrious career in silent films before making the switch to the talkies. On August 29, Harry Poppe in the production office asked: "Is there anything to prevent the shooting of the Zasu Pitts section of the opening recitative as a separate entity? As you know we have Miss Pitts for only a limited period, therefore we must clean up everything possible involving her before her departure date. She is scheduled to finish Friday, Sept. 1st. If we can do her section of the recitative by that time, we will have cleaned her up entirely."[46] And so it was back to the drawing board for Dorothy Fields, who had worked Miss Pitts's lines into some interactive scenes. These all had to be rewritten so that she was in separate shots throughout, without spoiling the flow of the lyrics or the music.

Meet the Baron is not remembered as a particularly good movie, but the opening scene, plus a bathhouse sequence in which the song "Clean as a Whistle" is titillatingly sung in the showers of "Cuddle College," and above all the big hit of "Don't Blame Me," provide a good example of how Fields and McHugh could transform a mediocre film into something better. And it also goes to show that while life in Hollywood might have seemed pampered and luxurious at a time when much of the country was still in the grip of the Depression, those who were employed in the movie industry had to work hard for their rewards. Rewriting, orchestrating, and setting complete scenes and then filming them in a couple of days were par for the course, but along with the hard work came the poolside lifestyle, the parties, and a thriving social circle of similarly creative people. The social scene was enhanced during 1933 when Dorothy Fields and her brother Herbert rented a palatial house on Rodeo Drive that became a focal point for all those members of the New York theatrical profession who had ended up in Tinseltown.

As light relief from their work on the studio lot, it is not altogether surprising that Fields and McHugh (still intimately bound up in one another's lives even when they were "off duty") got together to write an operetta that spoofed the style of Gilbert and Sullivan. It was performed that July at the Hollywood Bowl by the Civic Grand Opera Association of Hollywood.[47] Small sections of the score that survive suggest the show was a knockabout parody at several levels, but it is instructive that two of the most successful songwriters of the age spent their leisure time on a busman's holiday to improve their craft.

6

"Goodbye Blues"

THE SPLIT FROM DOROTHY FIELDS

BY 1935, AMERICA was beginning to put the hardships of the Depression behind it. To alleviate its remaining financial pain, the nation developed an insatiable thirst for entertainment. Once again Broadway was booming, as it had been in the 1920s, and Hollywood was churning out picture after picture, launching a new wave of stars in the process. Dorothy Fields and Jimmy McHugh were at the center of this revitalized show business industry on both sides of the country, with their growing catalog of hit songs among the most frequently played on stage or on film, and their new work going from strength to strength. So to the general public it was a shock when, halfway through the year, their partnership, which had seemed as close and stable as a longtime marriage, blew apart, never to be reunited.

There were few public signs in the months that led up to the split that such an outwardly successful partnership was under threat. Their last major Hollywood movie, released in late 1933, had been the high-profile *Dinner at Eight*, starring John Barrymore and Jean Harlow, for which they provided the title song. They then spent much of the following year back in New York, coming up with new numbers for a series of stage and cabaret shows. Yet even when they were absent from Tinseltown, they managed to maintain their presence on celluloid, because in true song-plugger style, McHugh and the couple's publisher Jack Robbins ensured that the best of the songs they wrote for these stage productions made their way into movies. Both *Fugitive Lovers* and *Have a Heart*, minor MGM features, included selected hits from their New York stage shows, with the result that their names remained prominent in the company's lists of film credits, although they did not return to Hollywood themselves until the fall of 1934.

By now they had settled into a well-established manner of writing together. In Hollywood they generally worked in a bungalow, complete with a piano, on the studio lot, whereas in New York they met at one another's apartments or at their publisher's premises. Pictures of them at work show that a sharp sense of style pervaded their offices. McHugh looked thoroughly businesslike with a crisp shirt, immaculate tie, and cufflinks, while Fields was always attired in the latest fashion. Their papers would be spread in orderly piles across the desk—indeed many of McHugh's friends and family have attested to his lifelong love of tidiness and order while at work.

If they were tackling a movie script, they would first identify the music cues and then start to rough out their ideas for songs. For a stage show, once they knew the singers or groups for whom they were writing, they would sketch out an outline of the book and identify the openings for new vocal numbers. Then Fields would start proposing titles. Between them, they would whittle these down to a short list, then agree on the one to be worked on first, and McHugh would buckle down to composing the tune.

For much of the time this was a question of simple perseverance, sitting at his desk or at the piano until he had a workable melody, but throughout his career, inspiration would strike at unusual moments, often as he was drifting off to sleep after a long evening of doing the rounds, visiting the clubs where his songs were being performed. Consequently, he kept a pad and pencil handy at all times, so that ideas that sprang into his head were never lost. In 1939, when he and Harold Adamson were writing together, a suitable melody struck McHugh in the small hours. Blurry with sleep, he could not find any manuscript paper, so he scribbled the tune on his bedsheet. In the morning he had forgotten all about it, and by the time he remembered, the sheet had been whisked off to the Beverly Hills Laundry. A few frantic phone calls later, the soiled linen was returned to him so that he could transcribe the tune. In later life, he would conveniently link the song "I Couldn't Sleep a Wink Last Night," written in 1943 for Frank Sinatra in the movie *Higher and Higher*, with this story, although he had first related it to the press some four years before the Sinatra movie was made.[1]

Although he often brought along notebooks with hastily jotted scraps of melody to their meetings, there were no moments quite as anxious as the laundry incident during his partnership with Fields. She recalled what generally happened once she had given him a title: "You listen to him make noises on the piano for a couple of days until he gives you a piece of paper scrawled over with markings which look as though they had been made by a fly fresh from the ink well."[2] Then it would be her turn to seek inspiration, which she usually did back at home, sitting with a yellow legal pad at a bridge table near the piano in her Upper West Side apartment in Manhattan, or in the house on Rodeo Drive in Hollywood that she shared with her brother Herb. She laughed: "You figure out that this is meant to be music, and learn to play it. Then you hum over the melody and the title and start writing the chorus. When you have that done, you start on the verse, being careful to avoid polysyllable words and to use a theme dear to the hearts of all, ie: LOVE. . . . When this is done, you take your beautiful, beautiful lyrics to Mr. McHugh, and then he arranges the melody to correspond more exactly with the words."[3] Before the song went off to the copyist, they would run through it together, McHugh embellishing the melody on the keys, and Fields singing the lyrics in her husky "cigarette contralto."

Despite the almost constant sense of pressure under which they worked, their partnership was full of fun, and their personal chemistry brought them together as effectively as did her words and his melodies. Sometimes lyrics and music came in a headlong rush, and papers survive—some of them hastily pressed into service, such as the backs of menus or hotel notepaper—where McHugh's rough scrawl of a new melody has a first draft of words penciled lightly under it. More often, and particularly during this period back in New York, the lyrics were passed to McHugh neatly typed out in block capitals, emphasizing what Fields hoped would be their final, definitive form, and avoiding any transcription problems when words and music eventually went off to the publisher.

While back on the East Coast during 1934, Dorothy Fields mainly lived at her family's apartment, but she also spent short periods of time at the homes she owned with Dr. Jack Wiener, her estranged husband, either their Manhattan apartment or a short distance away at their country house north of the city. They were never close (and divorced well before her second marriage in 1939) but were still officially married in 1934. Her comparatively lengthy stay in New York was a contrast to the long periods over the previous three years when she had been living in Los Angeles. Nevertheless, her constant appearances with McHugh at various functions in and around Manhattan, where they were often photographed together, and the fact that their names were linked in every press report about their shows, caused renewed public speculation about the precise nature of their relationship. The body language in photographs from that time is convincing evidence of their affair on the West Coast: McHugh appears brash and confident, eyes focused directly on the photographer and usually tilting his head slightly away from the camera to disguise his receding hairline, but Fields seldom looks at the camera. More often than not, her eyes are turned toward McHugh, giving the impression of adoration, and her heavily penciled, arched eyebrows add a sense of fun and whimsy. Certainly it always looks—at the very least—as if the two of them are enjoying themselves.

It was not unusual to find their names listed among the guests at functions as if they were a married couple. This happened so often that writing about this period years later, in a fragment of unpublished autobiography, McHugh felt compelled to write: "It has been suggested that I mention at this point that Dorothy Fields was married to a very fine doctor in New York, and that I was also married."[4] He glosses over the point that he and his wife had lived separate lives for many years, only communicating regularly with one another over the welfare of their son. Jimmy McHugh Jr. moved to Los Angeles in 1933, "in heaven no. 7" as one report put it, "now he's on the coast with his dad." He attended Beverly Hills High School, but his parents nevertheless continued to live apart.[5]

In and around both New York and Hollywood, McHugh was generally perceived as living a bachelor life, save for his very close relationship with Fields. His scrapbooks from this period do not contain the copious letters and cables from a circle of female admirers such as those that arose from his European visit in 1927, or the plentiful notes that he was later to receive from his young swimming protégés in the 1940s. Yet both songwriters worked hard to cover their tracks so that the press would be given no hint that McHugh's closeness to Fields was anything other than professional. He gave away his true feelings only in a private memoir, and even there, he crossed through the most telltale sentence, which reads: "Dorothy was married and had a family life of her own, but when we were on the road things were different."[6]

In an effort to assert her independence from him publicly, Fields appeared in various magazine features that stressed her home life, her marriage, and her hobbies, including a feature in the *Marksman* that reported: "Tiring of verse, she totes her six-shooter to her country home in Westchester County,

N.Y., where she is a revolver champion. Bangs away at a target, every bull's eye inspires a song hit!"[7] Making such public efforts to stress their separate personal lives had become almost second nature to the pair since 1928, even though they saw far more of one another than they did of their respective spouses. Gossip alone was unlikely to disrupt their working relationship at this point, any more than it had done throughout the preceding years. So why was it that cracks finally appeared in the Fields/McHugh partnership during 1935?

McHugh's stalwart efforts to generate a mass of solidly upbeat press reports make the reasons for the split hard to discover. However, in an interview with the *New York World-Telegram* in 1934, Fields was unusually candid about the strains that working with McHugh had placed on her domestic life. She recalled how she had been sitting in her New York apartment late one night, having just finished a set of lyrics, and decided that she had earned the opportunity to take time out to celebrate what she had calculated was her five-hundredth song. "Her husband, and her secretary, and even the cook agreed. Then along came Jimmy McHugh, her dynamic songwriting partner, 'We've got no time for celebrations,' he roared. 'As it is we'll have to work 'til tomorrow morning to finish that song we promised would be done by tonight.' 'And that,' sighs Miss Fields, 'gives you some idea of the songwriter's life.'"[8]

Ironically, by any normal standards, the two of them did not need to work quite so hard. That same press report mentions that Fields's "weekly earnings run into four figures," a small fortune in 1934. But in McHugh's mind, penury was always just around the corner. He felt compelled constantly to push the pair of them to work as hard as possible, ceaselessly plugging the songs they had already written, sending copious copies of sheet music to musicians he thought would perform their entire catalog of tunes, bombarding his leading ladies (and sometimes their mothers and sisters as well) with flowers, and constantly agreeing to write yet more music.

Whenever he let the frantic pace of his life slow enough to take a moment of reflection, McHugh was haunted by the prospect of returning to the relative poverty of his childhood in Boston. Looking back late in life, he talked of the 1930s as "years charged with memories of struggle, uncertainty . . . and a fair amount of anguish . . . the many times I had gotten what I wanted only to have it slip from my grasp."[9] This was, of course, mainly due to the fact that he was still paying off his share of the losses of the Bank of the United States. Although he had been only a minor stockholder, the paper value of his holding was close to half a million dollars (somewhere close to ten million in today's terms), and because of the way the bank's administrators had structured its debts, he, along with all the others who had traded its stock on the margin, was compelled to make regular payments to the bank's creditors from 1933 until 1940. Despite his considerable earnings, as a result of his habitual extravagance—sending flowers, attending the opera in a $100 box, or hiring a car in Hollywood for $350 per week[10]—he remained constantly anxious about meeting these installments.

As a result, he took every means at his disposal to avoid sliding back into what he regarded as poverty. Sitting at his desk each morning—once he had revived from the night before, showered, breakfasted, and dressed in his customary crisp attire—he went about his work just as a broker reviews his holdings. He never conformed to the popular image of the bohemian composer in search of mysterious inspiration, nor did he simply confront a blank sheet of manuscript paper to start the day's new tune. Instead, he began by reading carefully through the daily press and continuing the meticulous business habits that had made him a successful song plugger.

His scrapbooks are filled with the regular reports in *Variety* covering the frequencies of radio plays and the sales of recordings of his songs. Every mention of his work is assiduously ringed in red pencil, and there is a sense that as he scanned each newspaper report, his mental calculator was trying to work out exactly how many dollars it was worth to him. Every positive piece of news was an excuse to fire off more letters to artists and agents, place yet another advertisement for his wares in the press, or plant a further story in the gossip or business columns. He had no qualms about paying for his own advertisements. After all, he saw each one as an investment in his own success. Eventually, in exasperation, Jack Robbins wrote to ask him to refrain from constantly using the firm's name in his *Variety* display panels, because "a lot of songwriters think we are paying for the ads and should do the same for them!"[11]

This unrelenting pressure of work, McHugh's intensely acquisitive attitude, and his constant anxiety about where the next dollar was coming from were major factors in opening up the split in the songwriting team, and as 1935 went on they ceased to be as personally close as they had been.

McHugh's outer carapace of confidence was beset by dozens of niggling worries, uppermost among them his major concern about the method by which ASCAP paid its composers. This was the year that his anger with the system reached boiling point, and every press report concerning the issue got the full red-pencil treatment, with McHugh circling what he believed to be iniquitous, underlining the rewards due to composers, and heavily marking all items of news about the organization itself.

ASCAP, to which virtually all American composers of the day belonged, doled out shares of the revenue it received for performance of a piece not on a pro rata basis for the number of times a song was actually played on the radio or performed in public but according to the length of time its composers had been members of the society. The membership committee carefully orchestrated the slow progression of young writers through its ranks to protect the higher earnings of its most senior constituents. At the start of 1935, McHugh was still rated "A," which was the penultimate rung of the ladder. He felt that this was extremely unfair and had nothing to do with the merit of his songs, which were heard far more frequently than those of older, less-productive writers who had been elevated to "AA" status years earlier.

As well as feeling that he was being cheated of his just rewards, McHugh was in a particular hurry to rise to the most privileged level of membership, because ASCAP itself was under threat during the 1935–36 congressional session. Senator Ryan Duffy of Wisconsin had instigated an attempt to reform the music copyright law, with the intention of removing the existing statutory levy on every dance hall, club, or restaurant that presented live music.[12] This would have radically reduced the funds available for distribution by the society. Ultimately, the bill failed, but the proposed changes drew attention to the fragile consensus that allowed composers to be paid for the public performance of their work. As long as there was a possibility that the bill might become law, McHugh wanted as much of what he considered his due as possible, before it was too late.

Bizarrely, despite their completely opposing points of view, he shared several of Senator Duffy's forthright opinions about the antiquated structure of ASCAP. Whereas Duffy was concerned with the crude "racketeer" strong-arm tactics the organization used to extract its license fees from small regional clubs and dance halls, McHugh railed against the almost Masonic secrecy of its inner committees and decision making. His resentment against the organization constantly festered, in the wake of the rebuff he had received from Raymond Hubbell, its chairman, who fobbed him off a year or two earlier by saying: "You have been raised in classification as fast as possible according to your length of membership and the usual comparison which must be made."[13]

When *Variety* published the lists of radio plugs versus earnings for the first time in 1935, the reasons for McHugh's grievance were all too apparent. During the previous financial year, his songs were played a total of 27,317 times on the radio, and he was paid $5,390.48 by the society; whereas the relatively obscure "AA" rated songwriter Joseph McCarthy had only 5,873 radio plugs but netted $6,835. Even the estate of McHugh's fellow Irish-American, the late songwriter Victor Herbert, only got $6,835, despite even more airplay than McHugh, while the lesser-known Samuel M. Lewis, an even longer-term ASCAP member, received $7,043.83 in return for a paltry number of songs played on air.

McHugh's angry response was to work even harder, to bring himself and Fields to the point where their commercial success simply could not be ignored by the society, and they would have to be rewarded with top ranking. He was totally unprepared to put up with what he perceived as a mighty injustice, and he lobbied ASCAP constantly over the question, supported by a number of other major figures who felt similarly ill-treated. His efforts eventually paid off, and he was upgraded in September 1935,[14] but by then, his productive partnership with Fields was terminally broken, despite the fact that the pair had just created one of the year's biggest hits, "I'm in the Mood for Love."

Although the additional $1,500 or so to which he became entitled after his promotion within ASCAP was indeed a substantial sum in 1935, there is a strong argument for seeing McHugh's incandescent anger over the affair as somewhat over the top, considering that his increased income from ASCAP was largely irrelevant to his overall financial success. Taking into account sheet-music royalties, film royalties, and shares of the box office for their stage shows, Fields and McHugh already made a very comfortable income from their back catalog, let alone their current work. In 1934, they created considerable new rewards for themselves by writing book, lyrics, and music first for the *Palais Royal Revue* in Manhattan and then for the *Riviera Revue*, which was presented at a supper club across the river in New Jersey.

The way these shows came about serves as a perfect illustration of the frantic pace at which McHugh was prepared to push himself and his writing partner. They were the result of a fairly informal meeting with the promoter and former mobster Ben Marden—one of McHugh's old contacts from the Cotton Club—during January 1934. As McHugh told the story, one day when he dropped in at the Palais Royal supper club for a chat, Marden was ready and waiting for him:

When he saw me, he said, "That's my boy! Get a show ready in two weeks for me. Dream the entire thing up yourself!"

I said, "don't think I can do it in two weeks, possibly three . . ." I needed the money and was only too happy to do it.

He said, "I'll give you $50,000 to produce it, and you can write your own ticket."

I said, "Okay, can I have a little of that federal lettuce?"

He said, "Oh, sure, Jimmy, how much do you need? Is $1,000 all right?" I said, "Fine!"[15]

Inspired by the "federal lettuce," McHugh and Fields worked day and night to write half a dozen new songs and a book for the show, Ken McComber rushed out orchestrations, and within the two weeks Marden asked for, producer Walter Brooks, the man who had originally introduced McHugh to the Cotton Club, had pulled the entire presentation together. The resulting revue—"the smartest ever presented in a supper club" according to its advertisements—opened at the Palais Royal on Forty-eighth Street and Broadway on February 1, 1934, and starred the African American singer Ethel Waters, as well as a chorus line of "40 Gorgeous Beauties" (all of them white).

This latter fact was not without some controversy. The Palais Royal itself put out a news sheet that drew attention to the fact that most of these girls were society beauties but behaving in a way not normally expected of debutantes: "Society Belles found posing as nudist models!" trumpeted the headline, followed by: "Park Avenue had a fright last night when fond mamas and papa's [*sic*] were unable to find their daughters home at dinner time. . . . The sixteen young, fresh, lovely, talented girls when interviewed said they were extremely happy they had started to occupy their minds now, and could avoid dull society affairs in the evenings." The girls themselves appeared in various stages of undress in several photographs accompanying the article.[16]

In the musical part of the show, as the climax of her short set of vocals, Waters sang "You've Seen Harlem at Its Best," one of the numbers freshly written by Fields and McHugh. At that stage in her life, the dainty, exotically dressed, and light-skinned Waters had precise theatrical diction, combined with a charming, lilting, high voice that could—on occasion—open up to great volume. Normally she held this in reserve, relying on her sweetness, stagecraft, and guile to win over audiences both black and white, and adopting in her most celebrated performances almost a conversational style of singing. McHugh was already aware of Waters's formidable ability to put across his numbers, as she had made highly successful recordings of "I Can't Give You Anything but Love, Baby" and "Porgy," from *Blackbirds of 1928*, and later starred in Lew Leslie's *Rhapsody in Black* and *Dixie to Broadway* shows in 1932, for both of which he and Fields had contributed songs. Since then, with a number of movie appearances to her credit and her recent hits with "Heatwave," and "Suppertime," from Irving Berlin's 1933 Broadway success *As Thousands Cheer*, Waters had become a hot property, capable of pulling in a substantial crowd.

With Waters supported by the amiable English comedian Oliver Wakefield, whose hesitant uncertainties invariably and hilariously turned into double entendres, and featuring the band of Emil Coleman, the show did good business. As a result, it was held over for a second month, reopening on March 6, although Ethel Waters's commitments meant she had to leave the production. Nevertheless, she recorded her principal number for Brunswick the following month, and "You've Seen Harlem at Its Best" went on to become one of her most enduring discs, still in the catalog in the twenty-first century, not least because its all-star backing band included Bunny Berigan, the Dorsey Brothers, and jazz violinist Joe Venuti. At the time, Waters also starred on a network radio show that took her singing coast-to-coast, and the song was one that she frequently featured on air.

Knowing that there would be a change of cast, and that Waters would take her hit song with her rather than leave it for another singer, McHugh and Fields wrote a further set of songs for the "second edition" of the Palais Royal revue. This revised version of the show had a radically increased musical content, as a result of replacing Coleman and his band with the charismatic singer Phil Harris and his Orchestra from the Cocoanut Grove in Hollywood. The "wavy-haired" Harris and his "vivacious" female vocalist Leah Ray were featured in a new Fields and McHugh song, "Thank You for a Lovely Evening."[17] With his alligator-wide grin and rough-timbred vocals, Harris was just entering his period of greatest fame, although today he is remembered more for providing the voice of Baloo the Bear in Disney's *Jungle Book* than for the decades he spent as a top nightclub singer and bandleader. Written as a dialog between the lead singers, the new song was ideal material for the gruff Harris and the coquettish Ray to spark off each other.

The song quickly caught on and was still finding its way into recorded medleys of Fields and McHugh songs over twenty years later.[18] At the time, it was so popular that its sheet music was exploited by the Hotel Montclair on Lexington Avenue, which placed advertisements in the New York papers showing a male and female character singing the lyrics and music to one another as they reminisced about the superb dining and dancing at this "new and beautiful" hotel.[19]

With this show up and running, Ben Marden came back to McHugh and asked if he and Fields could provide the music for a similar new revue at his Riviera Club, across the George Washington Bridge in Fort Lee, New Jersey. McHugh agreed, and with a budget of $1,400 per week and the help of NBC's Harry Kemp, he hired the Dorsey Brothers Orchestra as the backbone of the show.

That band had only recently been formed by the two multi-instrumentalist brothers from Shenandoah, Pennsylvania, who had been among the most prolific of New York's studio players since the late 1920s. Brought up by a bandmaster father, the brothers were technically brilliant musicians and early converts from brass band music to jazz. The pair had played in the celebrated orchestras of Jean Goldkette and Paul Whiteman, holding their own against such jazz stars as Bix Beiderbecke, and as the economy picked up, it was only logical that as they entered their thirties they would try to front their own band. The tall, bespectacled figure of Tommy, whose specialty was languid ballads, and the shorter, darker-haired Jimmy, who preferred generating excitement with the amazing speed of his playing, made a very potent contrast, and great things were forecast for them. They had lured some of their most accomplished colleagues from the studios into their lineup, and the moment McHugh heard them on the launch of their weekly NBC radio show, he knew this was the band he needed.

It ought to have been the launching pad that the band needed as well. However, the fiery temperaments of both brothers led to a very public breakup a few months later, as immortalized in their film biography, *The Fabulous Dorseys*, but during the group's short life, the Riviera Club was one of its major club engagements in the New York area. It was also virtually the first opportunity for local audiences to hear the band's singer, the future bandleader Bob Crosby, Bing's younger brother. His Fields/McHugh feature, "Lost in a Fog," was strongly promoted in the local press as "the new song sensation from the Riviera of America."[20] The show itself continued at the Riviera for several months; and in this case, although there was a complete cast change as time went on, the Fields/McHugh format and repertoire remained intact, even after Harry Richman had come in as the star and Harry Berrens's more stable, if less exciting, band replaced the warring Dorsey Brothers.[21]

Despite these successes, it was not always obvious to the writers which of their songs would click with the public. McHugh was acutely aware of this, saying, "Every time I've done a score . . . I've been asked what tune was going to be a hit. I wouldn't dare take a bet on it. Nobody can say, because one person's guess is as good as another's. Sometimes the setting makes the song. Sometimes it's the star, and sometimes it's just because the song—words and music—has everything."[22]

Consequently, McHugh usually gave in to his irresistible urge to plug every note he had ever written, on the grounds that any song might prove to be a hit, but the less-volatile Fields was also sometimes deaf to a song's potential. Neither of them shared their publisher's judgment of the Palais Royal show. Both she and McHugh badgered Jack Robbins to bring out full sets of orchestral parts for "I Love Gardenias" and "I'm Full of the Devil," which they felt were their strongest offerings in the revue, although nowadays these are among the most obscure of the entire Fields/McHugh canon. Robbins's instincts were entirely at odds with theirs. He thundered: "If you did not get so excited about getting out orchestrations of 'Gardenias,' and 'Devil,' you would realize that the only number that looks good in the revue is 'Thanks for a Lovely Evening,' copies and orchestrations of which we are now preparing to issue. It is the only logical, possible, hit in the whole show."[23] Sadly, the song was not to become the major hit that Robbins hoped for, and he was later forced to discount a large number of copies of the sheet music he had printed.[24] Nevertheless, the song received plenty of live performances and airplay and was recorded by, among others, the novelty pianist and bandleader Frankie Carle.

"Lost in a Fog," despite a short-lived lawsuit claiming that it plagiarized the work of one Juanne Arliss,[25] was far more successful, and it was immeasurably helped in the short term by the Dorsey Brothers' publicity machine. In the show at the Riviera, Bob Crosby's pleasant singing was buoyed by his accompanying band, which was packed with future stars of the swing era. Both of the Dorseys themselves—trombonist Tommy, "the Sentimental Gentleman of Swing," and saxophonist Jimmy—were ultimately to lead highly successful bands. Their joint lineup also included the future bandleaders Glenn Miller and Ray McKinley, plus pianist Axel Stordahl (who later became Frank Sinatra's arranger). This distinguished cast, with the exception of Stordahl, appeared on the Dorsey Brothers' September 21, 1934, recording of the song; but for good measure—not least because the perfectionist Tommy never really liked Bob Crosby's singing—the brothers recorded it again a week later, in a pickup band with vocalist Chick Bullock and star trumpeter Bunny Berigan. Both versions sold well and kept the names of Fields and McHugh in the public eye.

After this return to the theatrical stage from late 1934 until May 1935, the songwriting team was hard at work back in Hollywood on the movies *Hooray for Love* for RKO and *Every Night at Eight* for the producer Walter Wanger.

Today, the first of these is largely celebrated for the screen appearances of Fats Waller and Bill "Bojangles" Robinson, who have small cameo roles that steal the picture. Fats—who journeyed all the way from New York for one day's work on the set—sang "Livin' in a Great Big Way," and Robinson contributed his brilliant dancing. The musical content of the film both prevented it from being a complete flop and gave it its title, as the movie had originally been called *Four Stars to Love*. When Fields and McHugh came up with the song "Hooray for Love," as *Variety* reported: "Execs liked the title so well that the handle of the picture has been changed to embrace it."[26]

Slammed by *Variety*'s "Hollywood Reporter" as "weak on story," the movie was a typical backstage romance, starring Gene Raymond and Ann Sothern, in which a young man's efforts to get his show staged on Broadway are frustrated by crooks, defaulting lenders, and a host of other increasingly unlikely impediments. "The show does go on . . . and on and on . . ." ran one review, further suggesting that "it could stand a lot of cutting and there are no punchlines to induce any laughter." However, all the film's critics agreed that "the main contribution to the picture is that of Fields and McHugh, and they have written what seem like three grand numbers: 'I'm Falling in Love All Over Again,' 'Livin' in a Great Big Way,' and 'You're an Angel.'"[27]

Every Night at Eight was a higher order of movie altogether, and it yielded two of Fields and McHugh's finest compositions, "I Feel a Song Coming On," and "I'm in the Mood for Love." Starring George Raft as a bandleader and Frances Langford, Alice Faye, and Patsy Kelly as singers, the story was a lighthearted romp in which the vocal trio is runner-up to Raft in a radio talent show but goes on to become a far greater success than his band. Reported *Variety:* "Top notch entertainment from start to end. Six musical numbers are woven through the story, each brought in legitimately."[28]

The biggest hit song in the film was not, in this case, influenced by anything as romantic as the penniless couple who apparently inspired "I Can't Give You Anything but Love, Baby." A couple of years earlier, McHugh had awoken in his room in New York with the idea for a melody buzzing around his head. He recalled: "I got up at about ten o'clock, walked to the window and looked out. Then I went back to my piano and sat down and wrote the melody of 'I'm in the Mood for Love.' It took me about twenty minutes. I phoned Dorothy Fields and told her, 'I've got a great tune.' Dot hurried over. The song was finished within half an hour, but then we sat on it for two years because my music publisher didn't think the middle strain was any good."[29]

As we know from chapter 1, McHugh's mother liked the tune, and it was she who persuaded him to ignore Jack Robbins's criticism and not to throw it away. This proved to be sound advice when Walter Wanger summoned Fields and McHugh to show them Frances Langford's screen test. *Every Night at Eight* was to be Langford's first movie, and Wanger wanted a ballad that would secure her reputation as a romantic screen vocalist. "For her test, Frances sang 'Night and Day,' which was rather stiff competition," wrote McHugh, who, remembering the song they had written back in New York, suggested to Wanger that they did indeed have a ballad that might fit the bill. "Frances made another test, singing 'I'm in the Mood for Love,' and that was it." In the movie, the song is heard first on a phonograph record, played by George Raft's band, but it swiftly becomes Langford's signature melody. What is more, in her subsequent commercial recording of the piece with Harry Sosnik's Orchestra, she makes the most of the middle eight measures, contrasting "Now we are one" with a hushed "I'm not afraid" in such a way as to consolidate the very section of the song that Robbins was unsure about into the core of her performance.

When the film was released, "I'm in the Mood for Love" rocketed into first place as the most popular song in America.[30] By September it was being played more frequently on air than its nearest rival, Irving Berlin's "Cheek to Cheek," and it beat the same song into second place in terms of sheet-music sales. It was to go on to become the second most broadcast song of 1935, beaten only by Sigmund Romberg's "When I Grow Too Old to Dream" from the movie *The Night Is Young*.

First to record the song commercially was Bob Crosby, who by the summer of 1935 had left the warring Dorsey Brothers to form his own high-powered swing orchestra. Soon more and more discs appeared, by Putney Dandridge, Chick Bullock, Adelaide Hall, and a host of lesser-known artists. But it was the definitive recording of October 3, 1935, by Louis Armstrong and His Orchestra that brought the song its greatest public attention. Armstrong's magisterial phrasing of the melody on trumpet and the relaxed poise of his singing made it not only one of the finest big-band records of the 1930s but one which went way beyond his adoring circle of jazz admirers to conquer the general entertainment market.

Consequently, "I'm in the Mood for Love" became far and away the biggest hit for Fields and McHugh since "I Can't Give You Anything but Love, Baby." Given that the movie that spawned it also included "I Feel a Song Coming On," which also became one of the year's top one hundred songs (and included in its lyrics a daring paraphrase of the British national anthem), Fields and McHugh had once again demonstrated their knack for producing hit songs with universal appeal.

There was no advance warning that *Every Night at Eight* was to be the last full-scale project on which Fields and McHugh ever collaborated. To the outside world, all was going well. Their names were linked once again in the press when they returned to New York in May, after finishing work on the movie, to make a charity cabaret appearance at the Waldorf-Astoria, on behalf of the Bronx Committee of the National Council of Jewish Women, in a show called *A Night in Japan*.[31] They performed a selection of their songs after the more authentic Japanese offering of George Hirose singing "Kimiyago," then the Japanese national anthem.

However, at the time of that trip back to New York, the partnership was already under professional threat from the unlikely figure of Jerome Kern, although he was entirely innocent of conceiving the idea to poach Fields away. She had by then flexed her songwriting muscles with one or two composers other than McHugh, setting lyrics to melodies by the great violinist Fritz Kreisler and producing words to a song by Max Steiner. When the RKO bosses—noting her ability to work independently of her longtime partner—proposed that Fields might help Kern with a song, Kern was initially not even aware that she had been asked.

In 1935 Kern was universally admired as one of the world's finest composers for musical theater and films. He was fifty years old, a senior figure in the industry who ranked alongside Gershwin, Berlin, and Romberg. His halo of receding curly hair, round spectacles, and aquiline nose made him an immediately recognizable figure, but Kern led a fairly private, straightforward life, as his subsequent film biography *As Clouds Roll By* revealed—no scandal, no tantrums, just a string of wonderful melodies. The closest he and his English wife Eva came to appearing in the gossip columns was when their daughter Betty became one of Artie Shaw's sequence of wives in 1941.

Socially, he had a somewhat distant air except to his inner circle of close friends, with whom he played poker long into the night. His shows played to packed houses on both sides of the Atlantic, and his repertoire ranged stylistically from Edwardian operetta in London to the full-scale Broadway musical *Show Boat*. In 1935, he was still writing book musicals for the stage but was increasingly feeling the pull of Hollywood, as were his card-playing friends Berlin and Gershwin.

A case in point was Kern's Broadway show *Roberta*, which had run for a respectable 259 performances at the New Amsterdam Theatre in 1933–34 and was being transformed into a movie by RKO in the spring of 1935. The book and lyrics (including the great hit "Smoke Gets in Your Eyes") were by Otto Harbach, but he had left part of the job unfinished for the movie. At this point, Fields had never met Jerome Kern, whose original score to *Roberta* contained a short melody to which there was no lyric. This tune was not the usual thirty-two-measure length of a popular song but a mere sixteen bars. The producer, Pandro Berman, wanted this to become a song that would serve a double purpose, both as a love song and as a vehicle for the film's star Irene Dunne to sing at a fashion show, so he asked Fields to provide some lyrics without clearing this with Kern in advance. By her own account, Dorothy Fields herself was a little shocked: "Would you believe that Berman had the temerity to film the new number and then send the sixteen bar song to Mr. Kern? It took a lot of guts to put one over on a man as eminent and discriminating as Jerome Kern. I heard he was very severe and critical, [but] he was a dream. One day at lunch I asked him why 'Lovely to Look At' only had sixteen bars, and Kern replied, 'Because that was all I had to say.'"[32]

Both her work on the song and the lunch with Kern took place before Fields and McHugh returned to New York for their cabaret appearance. Because they were technically under joint contract to RKO, McHugh's name also appears on the song copy of "Lovely to Look At," despite the fact that it was entirely written by Fields and Kern, and the same is true of "Jockey on the Carousel," from Kern's next movie for the singer Lily Pons, *I Dream Too Much*.

With two songs in two successive movies by the new team, McHugh immediately sensed that his long-standing partnership was under threat. To keep his name publicly linked with Fields's, particularly as *Every Night at Eight* had yet to be released, McHugh was astute enough to send to the papers some press shots of himself, Fields, and Pons, with the tenor Tito Schipa, taken a couple of years before in New York. The caption artfully ties him to Fields's work on *I Dream Too Much* and also states, somewhat inaccurately, "Mr. McHugh recently completed . . . several numbers including 'Lovely to Look At' for the musical film *Roberta*."[33]

The bond between Fields and Kern was immediate. It gave her the chance to work with an established writer twenty years her senior who had proven he could compose what she dreamed of working on—full-length book musicals, instead of the revue songs and musical interludes that made up most of her work with McHugh. It gave Kern the chance to work with a lyricist who was more in touch with the times than he was, who would encourage him to aim at a wider stylistic range, and who brought with her a touch of the jazzy instincts she had learned with McHugh (shown on such songs as Kern's "Bojangles of Harlem").

Any lyricist, however successful, would no doubt have shared Fields's satisfaction at producing words for one of the finest of all show composers. However, Fields also managed to achieve something that even the most experienced of his other collaborators never did. Somehow, her personality broke through the layers of reserve in Kern, an effect she achieved almost at once. He had always kept his distance from Oscar Hammerstein II, with whom he had written *Show Boat* and many of his earlier successes. Johnny Mercer recalled addressing him as "Mr. Kern" throughout their professional relationship. But once Dorothy Fields turned her gaze on him, he was "Jerry" from the outset, and she later referred to him affectionately as "Junior."[34]

By the end of the year, she was hard at work with Kern on his next full-length screen musical, *Swing Time*, which featured Fred Astaire and Ginger Rogers. From her recollections of their work together, Fields clearly found writing for Kern an altogether more relaxing business than collaborating with the hyperactive McHugh. She would take home a lead sheet and then write and rewrite her lyrics over and over until she felt they were worthy to be submitted to Kern. There was a wistful note in her voice when she recalled the process in 1972: "He was most particular. . . . In 1936 we wrote *Swing Time*, and a situation called for a song which Jerry loved to describe as a sarcastic love ballad. For one of only two times in our collaboration, I wrote the lyric first."[35] The song turned out to be "A Fine Romance," one of a string of hits contained in the movie. Both "Pick Yourself Up" and "Waltz in Swing Time" were equally fine songs, but the film's other great number, "The Way You Look Tonight," won an Academy Award for the best song of the year. This was something Fields never achieved with McHugh and did much to cement her partnership with Kern.

Perhaps Fields and McHugh would have resumed their collaboration in due course, but for two reasons—one financial, the other personal—this became unlikely. The financial problems are further discussed below, but the personal reasons were simple. After years of being involved with McHugh at a variety of levels, Fields fell in love—but not with him. Rumors began to reach McHugh that she was being seen with someone else, and his friends in the press called to ask about the truth of the story. "They wanted the lowdown. I begged them to hold off. 'Don't print it,' I said, 'I'm sure it's not true.' But it was true, and it was the end of our work together."[36]

Once the news was out, McHugh, who always preferred to be the one giving out the story, fed his favorite journalists a little more detail: "Maybe it's never been printed before . . . but it is being now. Reason the song team of Jimmie [*sic*] McHugh and Dorothy Fields sundered was her boyfriend Felix Young. 'I can't write with a regiment,' McHugh confides to cronies."[37] The film producer Young was to have a long-running relationship with Fields over the months that followed.

The breakup of the Fields/McHugh team was formally announced in *Variety* on August 16, 1935: "The definite breaking point came over an offer for the team to do the music for Shirley Temple's next picture *The Littlest Rebel*. Miss Fields and McHugh could not get together on a satisfactory arrangement, so the Fox deal had to be passed up. First indication of their professional separation was when Miss Fields went without McHugh to Radio to write the lyrics for the Lily Pons picture. Jerome Kern is writing the music."

In later life, McHugh always put a positive spin on the separation, saying, "It was around this time that Dorothy and myself split up our partnership after having a wonderful association of about eight years."[38] In other accounts, he tended to push the line that "Dorothy Fields decided that she liked Broadway better than Hollywood and returned to New York." This is a slight economy with the truth, as she was clearly already planning to remain in Hollywood to spend time with Young and to work with her new writing partner. And who could blame her? Writing with Jerome Kern for Fred Astaire and Ginger Rogers and winning an Academy Award were clearly good career moves compared to crafting songs for the child star Shirley Temple, even though Temple already had thirty movies under her belt and was big box office. As it turned out, McHugh was actually to do very well writing for Temple in the following year, but by then Fields had irrevocably moved on.

For someone as outwardly tough but inwardly fragile as McHugh, the split was devastating. During the next twelve months, he made some of the most uncharacteristically poor professional judgments of his life. His rock, the foundation of his professional stability, had gone—albeit to a composer he greatly admired—and his attentions veered from stage to film and back again with none of the urgent sense of purpose that had guided his work since the Depression. In the spring of 1936, this vacillation got him into a huge problem with his former colleagues, as part of the continuing fallout of the split.

McHugh only knew one way out of trouble, and that was hard work. It is typical of his workaholic character that almost as soon as he lost the woman with whom he had written all of his greatest hits, he immediately picked himself up and got on with the job of writing songs with a range of new partners, of whom the first was the lyricist Ted Koehler. And it is typical of his luck that whereas he came out of his 1935 visit to New York minus a collaborator, he acquired something else that became central to the McHugh legend. In his own words:

> With those pictures done and our shows doing well in New York, the money was beginning to come in again from motion picture scores, royalties on the songs, and things had a brighter look all round. So I got myself a penthouse when I returned to New York. I thought, Gershwin has one. McHugh, you have to have one too. I started looking around, and found one on 76th Street directly across the street from George Gershwin. It was a small place and I got busy furnishing it up. I was talking with George Gershwin about it one day, and he asked me if I needed a piano. I said, "Yes I do," and he gave me

the modernistic upright which I still have today. As a matter of fact, many of my hits were written at this piano.[39]

Today, this art deco gray piano is in the Jimmy McHugh Music offices in Los Angeles. When he returned to the West Coast in the fall of 1935 to work with Koehler on their first major movie together, *King of Burlesque*, the piano went, too. It remained in the den at his California home for the rest of his life.

King of Burlesque, one of the first musicals to be produced by the newly merged Twentieth Century-Fox Studios, is not a bad film. The plot features Warner Baxter as a burlesque impresario who has made his name in variety but tries his hand (disastrously) at legitimate theater. Urged on by the film's star, Alice Faye, he rescues his career, and his fortune, by returning to the kind of show he knows best, an all-singing, all-dancing revue. Once again, Fats Waller—this time cast as an elevator operator—has a big production number in the final revue; and in due course he not only recorded his hit song from the film, "I've Got My Fingers Crossed," for Bluebird but went on the road with his little band, the Rhythm, playing the tune at black cinemas across the country where the movie was showing. (It is also rumored that Waller's penchant for using any excuse to throw a party played havoc with the schedule, as the cast and crew suffered such severe hangovers after the shindig he organized on his arrival that shooting was suspended for a day.)[40]

In addition to this hit from the film, McHugh and Koehler had an equally great success with "I'm Shooting High," a widely recorded song that also became a jazz standard. Koehler's pedigree and experience as a songwriter had, in many respects, paralleled McHugh's, not least because he had a long association with the composer Harold Arlen, and the two of them had provided songs for the Cotton Club in the immediate aftermath of McHugh and Fields's departure for Hollywood. Koehler's lyrics had a similar feel for contemporary nuance and jazzy atmosphere as those of Fields, and he had supplied several extremely popular songs for Cab Calloway, Lena Horne, and Ethel Waters. Whereas Fields had the ear to catch street slang and transform it into credible lyrics, Koehler achieved his jazzy effects by writing short, choppy phrases that mirrored the effect of jazz horns on numbers like "Get Happy." He had also learned a thing or two about blues lyrics, taking inspiration from the cataclysmic meteorological descriptions in standards like "Backwater Blues" or "Rainy Weather Blues" for the words of his best-known song, "Stormy Weather." Arlen had made a determined attempt in 1934 to move away from writing the kind of catchy, jazzy tune that he had made his own, for fear of being typecast,[41] but Koehler, who had followed his former collaborator to Hollywood, remained best suited to writing jazz and blues lyrics.

When their collaboration achieved instant success, it certainly seemed as if with Koehler's help, McHugh had bounced back from his little setback and was once more in the business of producing hit songs. The new team was unsuccessful in persuading studio boss Darryl Zanuck that *Shooting High* would be a better title for the movie than *King of Burlesque*, but the film still gets occasional showings today, albeit more for Waller's humorous cameos than for the work of its original headline stars.

In the spring of 1936, McHugh still harbored the possibility of once more working with Dorothy Fields, but during March he managed a spectacular piece of contractual bungling that was not only the last straw in his relationship with Fields but nearly cost him his good relations with Jack Robbins as well.

He enjoyed the life that Hollywood offered him and had managed gradually to improve his financial rewards with each film and each move from studio to studio. Yet with his habitual insecurity about finances, he was unsure how long this could continue. Although MGM had approached him and Fields about providing a sequence of musical numbers for a new movie featuring Joan Crawford and Clifton Webb, because of Fields's new association with Kern, nothing had come of this offer.[42]

Consequently, when Lew Leslie got in touch with him to suggest that they revive their old partnership and collaborate on yet another *Blackbirds* revue in Europe, backed by C. B. Cochran, the most famous of all English theatrical entrepreneurs, McHugh talked terms—but even as a flurry of telegrams crossed the continent, bringing his latest demands to Leslie's room at the Waldorf Astoria in New York, he was simultaneously negotiating with Twentieth Century-Fox for a new contract. When the film company finally confirmed that he was needed to write another movie, albeit for less immediate reward than the money proposed by Leslie, McHugh could not resist the charms of his California lifestyle. Although he had already telegraphed his agreement to Leslie, instead of setting off for Europe, he sent a cable attempting to retract the deal and stayed put in Beverly Hills.

Since the dizzying heights of his success with *Blackbirds of 1928*, Lew Leslie had constantly been attempting to repeat that magic formula. Following their work on *Clowns in Clover* and *Dixie to Broadway*, Fields and McHugh had also written songs for *Blackbirds of 1933*,[43] although the major hit in the latter show was Victor Young's "A Hundred Years from Today." So Leslie had decided to try his luck in Europe, hoping that he could repeat his international touring success of the 1920s, and he first sounded out McHugh from London in early March of 1936.

By the time Leslie was back in New York later in the month, negotiations were moving apace, with Jack Robbins also involved. The final deal to which McHugh agreed on behalf of himself and Ted Koehler was an advance of $4,000, with $100 for living expenses during the rehearsal period, and 3 percent of the gross, including first-class travel in both directions to and from London. When McHugh tried to pull out, Leslie sent him a desperate message from New York: "PLEASE JIMMY YOU MUST CANCEL COMMITMENTS OR YOU PUT ME IN AWFUL JAM HAVE WENT THROUGH BIG EXPENSE COMING HERE AND PHONING LONDON TO OKAY TERMS ALSO HAVE SIGNED TREMENDOUS BIG CAST STOP. . . . PLEASE DO NOT FAIL ME."[44]

McHugh was unrepentant. He and Koehler were going to write for the new Shirley Temple movie *Dimples* and that was that. Jack Robbins weighed in on the following day:

CANT FOR THE LIFE OF ME UNDERSTAND HOW YOU COULD NEGOTIATE OR CLOSE DEAL WITH ANY PICTURE COMPANY WHILE MAKING DEAL WITH LESLIE WHO IS BACKED BY COCHRAN STOP. . . . THE LEAST YOU COULD HAVE DONE IS TO WIRE ME TO WARN LESLIE IN VIEW OF FACT THAT I STARTED NEGOTIATIONS THAT YOU WERE CLOSING OTHER DEAL. . . . THE LORD KNOWS THAT I HAVE NEVER BEEN PLACED IN SUCH A POSITION BEFORE. . . . LESLIE CAN DEFINITELY HOLD YOU TO YOUR CONTRACT ON STRENGTH OF YOUR WIRE OF MARCH THIRTY FIRST EVEN THOUGH YOU CANCELLED ON APRIL THIRD STOP PLEASE WIRE ME WHAT ITS ALL ABOUT[45]

In McHugh's drawer of neatly filed contracts, his agreement with Twentieth Century-Fox for *Dimples* is dated April 3, 1936. He and Koehler would get $750 per week for writing the film, and his Hollywood lifestyle could continue undisturbed. Lew Leslie nearly went broke again as a consequence of the affair, which left the trust of his London backers in tatters. As it was, until he could mount a replacement show that earned him a worthwhile amount, he was kept afloat by an advance against the royalties that Robbins deducted from the earnings of the original *Blackbirds* songs, in which Leslie retained stage rights, until the debts incurred by McHugh's actions were paid off.

This unhappy episode might not have concerned Dorothy Fields too greatly, but for the fact that for some years afterward a percentage of her own royalties on the numbers she and McHugh had written together were used by Robbins to compensate Leslie. Innocent of any intrigue herself, she was far from delighted to find that instead of increasing her earnings, McHugh's hyperactivity had actually reduced them.

As a consequence of McHugh's pullout, Robbins moved quickly to provide substitutes from his stable of writers, and the young Johnny Mercer, together with Koehler's previous songwriting partner Rube Bloom, got a trip to Europe to write songs for the show that Leslie eventually rescued from the collapse of his original plans.

When the dust finally settled, McHugh's skill and luck gradually returned, along with his judgment. The Shirley Temple movie saw him once more reviving his Hollywood fortunes, but without fully intending to do so, McHugh had made a substantial break with the world of theater, decisively throwing in his lot with movies for the next few years. He also lost the goodwill of both his agent and his former collaborator. He eventually regained the trust and friendship of Robbins, but the successful hit-making team of Fields and McHugh was broken forever.

7

"Dimples"

WITH HER HALO OF bouncing curls, slightly exaggerated dance movements, and cute manner of delivering both dialogue and lyrics, Shirley Temple was dubbed "America's adorable little sweetheart" by the press. In the entire history of motion pictures, there had been nothing to compare with this "amazingly incredible youngster."[1] In the first few years of the 1930s, feel-good movies had been the order of the day in a Hollywood doing its best to counteract the doom and gloom of the Depression, and an effervescent, immensely talented child star who could help to heal the country's ills by focusing on the innocence and goodwill of childhood itself was a national asset to be treasured.

Shirley Jane Temple was the daughter of a Santa Monica bank manager, and she had been recognized as a child prodigy from the moment when, little more than a toddler, she started to sing and dance at Mrs. Meglin's Dance Studio in Hollywood. Temple celebrated her eighth birthday on April 23, 1936, just three weeks after McHugh and Koehler signed the contract to provide the score for *Dimples* (then carrying the working title of *The Bowery Princess*), and McHugh sent her a rag doll named "Taps" both to mark the event and to underline his enthusiasm for her dancing skills. She was to be the first of a number of child stars for whom McHugh was to write songs as a result of his decision to stay in Hollywood.

Temple's first screen appearances had been in a series of short films, *Baby Burlesks*, made when she was only five years old. She was spotted in these by Charles Lamont of the Educational Film Corporation and in due course started making movies for Fox in 1934. By the time McHugh worked with her, she was already famous for her songs "On the Good Ship Lollipop" (from *Bright Eyes*) and "Animal Crackers in My Soup" (from *Curly Top*), the latter song written by Ted Koehler with Ray Henderson and Irving Caesar. Indeed, it was McHugh's new association with one of Temple's most successful lyricists that meant he had again been asked to compose for her, and this time he accepted the invitation.

Ironically, despite her extreme youth, Temple was one of the more experienced screen stars McHugh had worked with. In 1935 she had been presented with a special Oscar for her services to screen entertainment, and within the industry she was renowned for grasping the most complex dance maneuvers and lyrics so quickly that she often did all that was required of her in one take.

Even so, her career was not without controversy. In 1935 she had made two pictures in which she sang and danced with the former *Blackbirds* star Bill "Bojangles" Robinson. In the first of these, *The Little Colonel*, she accompanied him, hand in hand, on his famous tap-dancing up-and-down-the-stairs routine. This scene caused the Fox studios such anxiety that the sequence was cut for theaters in the southern states, where such easygoing racial integration was considered far from acceptable to white audiences.

Although Robinson does not appear on screen in *Dimples*, he was on hand backstage to work with Temple on her choreography for the final scenes, notably a couple of tap dances that bore all the Robinson hallmarks and were hailed in the press as "new intricacies," delivered with "precision and verve."[2] These are neatly worked into the plot, which has Shirley starring in a production of *Uncle Tom's Cabin* alongside Stepin Fetchit, the African American comedian.

As a further part of her preparation for the movie, McHugh and Ted Koehler diligently ran through her songs at the soundstage piano. The publicity shots, posed carefully for the press, were not far from what actually occurred, with Temple sitting atop a studio upright while McHugh played for her, with Koehler sitting at the side taking notes. Any tweaks and twists that were needed to the lyrics or the melody line could be dealt with immediately to ensure that she made the best of her material. The scruples that had apparently prevented McHugh and Fields from writing the music for Temple's earlier picture, *The*

Littlest Rebel, owing to their disagreement over publishing rights, had disappeared with the prospect that this new movie contract would allow McHugh to remain in Hollywood. He and Koehler had worked for Darryl Zanuck at Fox before, when on loan to the studio for *King of Burlesque,* and so now McHugh threw himself into the work with enthusiasm.

McHugh was immediately impressed by his very young star. He said at the time: "Shirley is absolutely unspoiled. For one thing, she has absolutely no idea of her own prominence. When the President of Cuba comes to dinner with her, she is polite and sweet. When the King of Belgium sends an artist to paint her portrait, she is the same. The idea that such honors don't come to other kiddies has never entered her head."[3]

The whole plot of *Dimples* is somewhat contrived, and it is not among Temple's best films. Cast in the title role, as the granddaughter of a Fagin-like character, played by Frank Morgan, she opens the picture by dancing for crowds in the Bowery, holding their attention as her grandfather and his cronies pick the spectators' pockets. Rescued from this life of crime by a society woman, Mrs. Caroline Drew (played by Helen Westley), "Dimples" is then cast by Mrs. Drew's nephew to play Little Eva in a musical stage show of *Uncle Tom's Cabin.* This allowed McHugh and Koehler to write songs in a variety of styles, from minstrel-show parody to sentimental ballads, and also to include some rousing dance numbers.

In one of Temple's more simpering ballads, "Hey! What Did the Blue Jay Say?," McHugh returned to the device he had used in "Love in the Rough" and had Temple sing to a chorus of harmonicas. There were no golf caddies on hand this time. Instead, dressed in her urchin clothes, with a cap over her blond curls, Temple sings and dances between two slightly older African American boys who play the accompaniment. In another return to ideas from the past, McHugh and Koehler went back to the territory of "There's a New Star in Heaven Tonight" for the tear-jerking "Oh, Mister Man up in the Moon," in which "Dimples" recounts how the angels took her mother away to keep them company in heaven.

More successful by far, musically speaking, is a song from later in the film, the rousing and energetic "Dixie-Anna," which is almost a one-song reprise of everything McHugh had learned from Lew Leslie. Opening with a dramatic tap-dance sequence, performed to a brisk, jazzy orchestral backdrop, the piece moves into a segment for a black choir, not unlike the Cecil Mack Singers who had worked with Leslie. This choral segment then ushers in the main chorus section of the song.

This might well have been one of McHugh's most memorable songs, had it received wider exposure. In place of the thirty-two-measure sequence that is usual for this type of song, McHugh employs just twenty measures, with two eight-bar sections divided by a contrasting four. The effect is absolutely in keeping with the Stephen Foster tradition that he is parodying, but the song is one of his most instantly memorable, perhaps because it defies one's normal expectations of its structure. In the movie, the song shifts effortlessly from the choir to a couple of choruses performed by Temple, in the second of which she jokes with Stepin Fetchit, and then the scene ends with a wild and exciting dance. The music for the final sequence of the film ran to twelve pages of piano score and ranks as one of McHugh's fullest through-composed scenes.

However, Fox's tight grip on Temple's contract, and the steely control with which her mother ran her career, meant that the song-plugging avenues that McHugh had explored all his life were on this occasion closed to him. Normally he would have encouraged the company to allow the song to be recorded by Temple and also by a variety of other performers, thereby setting up a competitive market for airplay and disc sales. In this case, there were no opportunities for Temple herself to record any of the songs commercially, because the studio was so keen to reserve her energies for movie making that it vetoed a recording contract. The British film researcher Geoff Milne has unearthed correspondence between Jack Kapp at Decca in New York and E. R. Lewis at his head office in London that demonstrates how Fox refused to allow Temple to sign a record deal. Apparently even having her sing on the radio was banned.[4] With the star herself unable to make any recordings, there was little point in setting up lots of cover versions, and so the only surviving record we have of this music is from the film soundtrack.

In later life, Temple's own memories of the film mainly centered on the upstaging tactics of Frank Morgan, her costar (who remains most famous for playing the title role in *The Wizard of Oz*).[5] In her autobiography, she portrays her childhood self as isolated from the fiercely commercial Hollywood world around her, just as McHugh described her at the time, but the reality of her status within the industry was very different. In 1935 she had become the top-grossing box-office star in the United States, almost single-handedly rescuing Fox from bankruptcy on the eve of its merger with Twentieth Century and securing a position she was to hold for the next three years. As the press reported in the early spring of 1936: "Unofficially and secretly, Shirley Temple had her salary raised a month or so ago. Also Maria Temple collected a little extra cash on her weekly check. . . . Daryl [*sic*] Zanuck wants above everything else to keep the baby goldmine and her mother happy. Shirley's next is *Dimples*, an original story by Arthur Sheckman and Nat Perrin, with music by Jimmy McHugh and Ted Kohler [*sic*]."[6]

When *Dimples* opened in October 1936, it set an all-time attendance record for its first weekend.[7] On the whole the critics were kind to it, largely on account of Temple's charming performance. One typical review declared: "Miss Temple has a grand time, singing, dancing, making wisecracks, keeping her grandfather out of trouble and patching up a lovers' quarrel. So grand a time indeed, that it becomes infectious, and you enjoy it almost as much as she does."[8] The songwriters were singled out, too, for providing "splendid opportunity in the music and lyrics. . . . [Temple] sings them with growing professional assurance, yet without losing the childish charm which is her most ingratiating box office asset."[9]

Although this movie could definitely be counted a success, McHugh was not to compose for Shirley Temple again. For his next picture—which had already been shot by the time *Dimples* was released—he not only returned to RKO, where he had done the majority of his scores with Dorothy Fields, but changed lyricists, working briefly with Gus Kahn, a writer who seems to have had more compositional partners than almost any other. McHugh did not, however, abandon working with child actors, because his first venture back at his old studio was *Let's Sing Again*, the debut movie for the Canadian boy soprano Bobby Breen.

Like Temple, Breen was eight years old in the summer of 1936, and he had made his name as a guest singer on Eddie Cantor's weekly radio program. However, RKO took a very different marketing approach to selling their young star from the protective attitude that Fox adopted with Temple. Producer Sol Lesser actually delayed the release of the film to make the most of Breen's radio appearances with Cantor and establish the boy's name with the public. He also ensured that McHugh and Kahn's title song was released on disc well ahead of the movie. The song was "haunting of melody, appealing of lyric and of certain hit caliber," according to *Variety*, and it was given a much greater plug than any of the songs from *Dimples*.

The plot of *Let's Sing Again* revolves around the character played by Breen running away to join the circus, where the boy is taught to sing by has-been clown (and former opera singer) Henry Armetta. RKO featured Breen in another seven pictures, during which time he became a minor child star and Hollywood's leading young male singer, but his "rudimentary" acting in this debut picture did not help the film, and McHugh had already moved on before Breen's next foray onto celluloid.[10]

At first he continued the association with Kahn, writing "With All My

Heart" for the Paramount movie *Her Master's Voice*, before teaming up with Harold Adamson, initially at MGM for *The Voice of Bugle Ann*, starring Lionel Barrymore, and then at Fox for *Banjo on My Knee*, with Barbara Stanwyck and Tony Martin in the leading roles. This latter picture produced the song "Where the Lazy River Goes By," which was a best-seller for jazz pianist Teddy Wilson, among others, and confirmed that the McHugh/Adamson partnership had hit-making potential.

Although they did not work continuously as writing partners, Harold Adamson was to be McHugh's major collaborator for the next decade and a half, not least because in 1937, rather than hopping from studio to studio, both men opted for a long-term contract at Universal, thereby creating a secure basis on which they could work together in several movies each year.[11] This kind of staff contract was a little more restrictive than the movie-by-movie agreements McHugh had previously signed, but the basic terms still allowed him to collect his own royalties on sheet-music sales and to take around 30 percent of the total income received by the company on recordings.[12]

Adamson was originally from Greenville, New Jersey, although contemporary press reports suggested origins as far removed from one another as North Carolina and Brooklyn. A somewhat stocky individual with dark swept-back hair, slightly prominent eyes, and strong features, he had contracted polio as a child, which restricted the use of his right arm and hand for the rest of his life. After high school, he took a pre-law course at the University of Kansas and then went on to study law at Harvard. However, the lure of stage and screen proved too strong to resist, and instead of pursuing a legal career, he came to Hollywood in 1933 at the age of twenty-seven to write lyrics.

He had written for all manner of amateur dramatics during his college years and also tried his hand at serious verse, so by the time he teamed up with McHugh, he already had some substantial hits to his name, of which the best known was "Time on My Hands," written with Mack Gordon and Vincent Youmans. This partnership had clearly been very influential for him, as he revealed when he summed up his attitude to songwriting in an interview shortly after he and McHugh began working together: "The important thing in writing a song is to convey an emotion. A single, simple, vibrant emotion. Vincent Youmans once advised me to visualize a couple dancing to a tune and hearing it sung. Music is a big help to romance."[13]

In the first months of their contract, McHugh and Adamson turned out a considerable number of songs for a variety of pictures. The majority of these compositions do not rank among either man's best work, but this did not deter McHugh from whipping up his usual collection of frequent (and usually adulatory) mentions in the press. That October his erstwhile lyricist Gus Kahn wrote, not entirely jokingly, from his office at MGM, "any time you get tired of struggling at Universal, maybe you would like to be my press agent."[14] As ever, the straight-talking Jack Robbins saw through McHugh's purple prose: "For Christ's sake, it's about time both you guys got wise, and stopped giving us manufactured songs. Everybody here in New York feels that nothing is outstanding in *Top of the Town* and nothing new in *When Love Was Young*. So by God and by Jiminy, try to get something outstanding, something with life and character."[15]

Despite these strictures, and the workaday nature of most of McHugh and Adamson's early output, there were a couple of substantial hits buried in what are now otherwise long-forgotten movies. First, Gertrude Niesen managed seven weeks on the radio hit parade with "Where Are You?," a tear-jerking ballad from the movie *Top of the Town* (which also received a best-selling treatment from Mildred Bailey with Roy Eldridge's swing band from Chicago). Then Alice Faye followed her into the hit parade for eleven weeks with the title song from *You're a Sweetheart*. This eventually become the number one song of 1938 in terms of radio plays, something that was immeasurably helped by Jack Kapp at Decca taking a liking to it and assigning it to Ethel Waters, whose recording did almost as well as Faye's original.[16] The top-selling version, however, was by another almost forgotten figure, the big band singer Dolly Dawn. In addition, there were discs by Tommy Dorsey (the first to record it), Woody Herman, Artie Shaw, and Lee Wiley, which did a lot to establish the piece as a swing-era standard, and jazz drummer Kenny Clarke cut a version of it in Stockholm just a few weeks after the movie was released.

Despite these minor successes, McHugh must have been aware that he and Adamson were not creating the kind of immortal standard that he had so often managed with Dorothy Fields. When he cabled his congratulations for her 1937 Oscar success with Jerome Kern on "The Way You Look Tonight," her reply was very sweet but must have rubbed salt in the wound of their separation: "I can only say—and I mean it—that the award is yours next year. Your new stuff is wonderful, especially 'Where Are You?' . . . Always, Dot."[17]

Yet even the more obscure "manufactured" songs that McHugh and Adamson produced were well crafted, and some of them achieved a life beyond the films for which they were written. A good example is "You're My Dish," written in 1937 and originally featured in the movie *Merry-Go-Round of 1938*, which, despite the presence of Bert Lahr, flopped at the box office. It displays one of Adamson's greatest gifts as a lyricist, which was to take a simple metaphor and then load the idea with puns and related references, pushing the original idea to the extreme. In this case, the plethora of food and drink imagery, taking in flavors as varied as Yorkshire pudding, angel cake, and French pastry, was ideal for Fats Waller, who (partly on account of his generous girth) specialized in such food-and-drink numbers as "Eep, Ipe, I Wanna Piece of Pie," "The Rump Steak Serenade," "Hold Tight, I Want Some Seafood Mama," and "All That Meat and No Potatoes." With a simple melody from McHugh that backs up Adamson's patter-song lyric, Waller turns in a performance in which he sounds completely enraptured by all the foodstuffs about which he sings. Not surprisingly, his version of the song reached the *Billboard* top twenty.

"About this time, Deanna Durbin came on the horizon," recalled McHugh.[18] More mature than Temple or Breen, Durbin was the Canadian-born teenage soprano who had won over audiences both with her acting skills and her agreeable singing in the movies *Three Smart Girls* and *One Hundred Men and a Girl*. McHugh had met her three years before at MGM, when—at age fourteen—she had been signed to that studio alongside another teenage hopeful, Judy Garland. The two girls had appeared together in a musical short called *Every Sunday*, but Louis B. Mayer decided to let one of them go, as he felt his firm did not need two adolescent singing stars. His decision was to retain Judy Garland and to try and keep her a child (at least in movie terms) for as long as possible. He may have, on occasion, referred to her as "the fat hunchback,"[19] but his choice was vindicated with her 1939 starring role in *The Wizard of Oz* and in the many films she made opposite Mickey Rooney.

Mayer's preference turned out to be a stroke of good fortune for Universal, which picked up Durbin's contract. Just as Shirley Temple had helped rescue the fortunes of Fox, Universal was rewarded when the commercial success of *One Hundred Men and a Girl* (in which Durbin persuades Leopold Stokowski to conduct an orchestra of out-of-work musicians) helped stave off a threat of imminent bankruptcy for the studio. Her successive movies put the company on an altogether sounder financial footing. As the firm's in-house songwriting team with numerous current hits to their names, McHugh and Adamson were assigned to Durbin's first movie of 1938, namely, her third full-length feature, *Mad about Music*.

Still just sixteen, Durbin was a far better actor than Breen and a much better singer than Temple. She was also easy and agreeable to work with, took direction well, and applied a sparkling intelligence to all her roles. Like Breen, she had appeared on Eddie Cantor's radio show, but unlike him, her appearances were not limited to one or two song plugs. Instead, she starred in her own regular weekly spot on Cantor's Texaco-sponsored program during the season that started in September 1937. Her ability to span the stylistic range from Tin Pan Alley standards to light classics, sung in her clear, unaffected soprano voice, and to sound entirely at ease with the material was a remarkable asset, both on the air and on film, something about which the *New York Times* commented when *Mad about Music* appeared. The paper's film critic, Frank S. Nugent, wrote: "[She] seems to have cajoled Mother Nature into compensating her for being at the awkward age for misses. Aside from that extra-special compensation of a fresh and flexible soprano, she has succeeded in turning a 14-year-old's coltish gangliness to charmingly comic uses, and she remains as far as we can see, a natural, unaffected, sunshiney little person."[20] The *Hollywood Reporter* agreed, saying, "this lovely child has lost none of her naturalness and appeal and has gained in poise."[21]

The movie's plot is far-fetched and flimsy, based on the idea that Durbin is the teenage daughter of a successful Hollywood actress (played by Gail Patrick) who banishes her to a finishing school in Switzerland, lest her mother's fans discover her existence and put an end to the myth that Patrick is a single, glamorous star. Durbin's screen father, a navy pilot, had died, necessitating the invention of a fantasy father to keep her school contemporaries off the scent of her real parents. When she fantasizes to her friends about a visit from her father, she inveigles a visiting English composer, played by Herbert Marshall, to pretend to be him.

The concept that Marshall is a composer allows Durbin to sing along with him at the piano, and as was usually the case in each of her films, the musical high point is provided by the classical repertoire, with a sterling performance of Gounod's "Ave Maria" in which she is accompanied by the Vienna Boys' Choir. At the other end of the spectrum, Adamson and McHugh's chirpy ditty "I Love to Whistle" was hardly high art, but after Durbin was seen cheerily singing it as she rode through the Swiss landscape on a bicycle, the number caught on with the public (along with the movie's other major new piece, "Serenade to the Stars")—although it never quite survived the merciless lampooning of Fats Waller, whose best-selling recording with his Rhythm is one of the most savage deconstructions of a popular song in his entire repertoire. Yet as *Variety* said at the time, "I Love to Whistle" "is so sprightly and catchy that one can hear it repeatedly during the hour and a half of the movie without tiring of it. It is refreshingly rhythmic and yet simple."

The ingenious way that Universal's music director, Charles E. Previn, and his orchestrator, Frank Skinner, wove the theme into the soundtrack won them an Oscar nomination for best musical scoring. However, the song almost achieved a very different type of notoriety for Adamson and McHugh, when

Dave Hoffman, the deputy city attorney for Los Angeles, together with his fellow lawyer Myron Glauber, launched an infringement of copyright suit on the grounds that the movie's hit song was little more than a brisk makeover of a number called "I Can Only Whistle," which they had cowritten and frequently performed for their legal friends at various parties in and around the city. They claimed that a rumor was going around that they must have sold their song to Universal, so close was it in content and style to Adamson and McHugh's composition. However, the action was unsuccessful, and Universal's relentless plugging of the song meant it continued to be heard on radio and records for much of 1938.[22]

For Durbin's next movie, which also had new songs by McHugh and Adamson, Universal decided to play to her strengths and beef up the classical content of her performances. As a result, *That Certain Age* featured her singing Gounod's waltz from *Romeo and Juliet* and Delibes' "Maids of Cadiz." This time, however, it was not the studio's backroom music staff but McHugh and Adamson themselves who were nominated for an Oscar, for Durbin's featured song, "My Own." She sings it beautifully, with a maturity far beyond her sixteen years, but for once her classical training with its slightly mannered delivery worked against the natural relaxation that she achieved in her finest recordings. In any case, that year's Academy Award for best song went to Ralph Rainger and Leo Robin for "Thanks for the Memory," with Harry Warren and Johnny Mercer's "Jeepers Creepers" becoming the best-known runner-up.

The plot of *That Certain Age* is just about as feeble and far-fetched as that of *Mad about Music*. This time Durbin is the daughter of a newspaper magnate who invites his leading war reporter (played by Melvyn Douglas) to his country retreat, in order to help the writer recuperate from injuries sustained while sending home dispatches from the Spanish Civil War. Durbin, who is using her father's guesthouse to rehearse a play with her boyfriend (played by another child star of the era, the *Our Gang* actor Jackie Cooper), gradually falls for Douglas, until things get so serious that her parents and the reporter's girlfriend contrive to put an end to her puppy love.

Durbin won the October movie critics' poll for her performance, and McHugh and Adamson achieved the feat of winning both first and second slots in the same poll for "song of the month," with "My Own" and the film's title song, "That Certain Age," the first time that any songwriting team had done so.[23] Despite the flimsiness of the plot, the critics were virtually unanimous in their praise of the film. *Variety*, hailing it as "four in a row" for Durbin and Universal in terms of commercial success, pointed out how the whole picture was crafted to allow Durbin to grow up a little, both physically and emotionally, from her previous roles. "Providing a well-tailored and carefully-planned story, studio brilliantly bridges the adolescent period at one crack, and launches her into the broader fields of youthful romance and adventure, where story material is more plentiful for future adventures."[24]

The same paper was dismissive about the new songs, suggesting there was "not much chance" of any of the McHugh and Adamson pieces becoming hits, but nevertheless the Universal song-plugging machine whirred into life, and this time McHugh decided to indulge in a little additional plugging of his own. Earlier in the year, Tommy Dorsey's orchestra had been resident in Los Angeles for a few weeks, and McHugh had helped Dorsey and his wife Bobby to find a house to rent for the summer, during the band's stay. Ever since the *Riviera Club Revue* in 1934, McHugh had remained on good terms with Dorsey, and there were regular invitations for McHugh to join the Dorsey family on their all-too-rare vacations at their Bernardsville farm in New Jersey, plus a standing request for McHugh to supply new songs for Dorsey's frequent broadcasts. Tommy wrote: "If you have any other material that you think we might be able to use, send it along, as I guess we shall need everything we can get." Now, in August 1938, cables flew between McHugh and the Congress Hotel in Chicago, where Dorsey was launching a new season of his Wednesday night NBC radio show, prior to the band's opening the following month at the Paramount Theatre in New York. As a result, the band previewed all four of the original songs from the movie on national radio, shortly before the film's late-September release.[25]

Apart from the fact that "My Own" was a song well worth plugging, one reason McHugh put extra effort into the Durbin movie was that it was a major, full-length, big-budget picture, a comparative rarity in a working life at Universal in which he and Adamson were otherwise turning out B-movie musical potboilers. These are now largely forgotten films, such as *Hitting a New High* (which starred Lily Pons), *Breezing Home*, *The Devil's Party*, *Youth Takes a Fling*, and *Reckless Living*. For another of these now very obscure movies, *The Road to Reno*, McHugh was reunited with the former silent movie actress Hope Hampton, for whom he had written "Heroes of the Air" during his 1927 transatlantic crossing.

Unlike any other time in his entire working life up to that point, McHugh spent 1937–38 doing as close to a nine-to-five office job as was possible for a composer. The financial and social rewards were comfortable, and even when Jack Robbins sold his publishing interest to MGM and Twentieth Century-Fox, leaving McHugh in the hands of Jack Bregman at Leo Feist,[26] his financial stability remained on an even keel; and as well as mingling at the highest levels of Hollywood society, he continued to pay off his Bank of the United States debts. He also set about building himself a new home on Sierra Drive in Beverly Hills, which he commissioned from local architect Harry B. Aarens. Meanwhile, in his working life, he and Adamson grew to understand each other thoroughly and were able to turn out well-structured songs on almost any subject. But there are clear signs in his memoirs and letters that the normally hyperactive and energetic McHugh was getting bored.

For the seven years of his partnership with Dorothy Fields, she was the only female to whom he had been linked in the press. But in August 1937, McHugh's name appeared for the first time alongside that of the beautiful heiress to a sugar-importing fortune, Geraldine Spreckels. In January of that year, on the death of her father Claus Spreckels, she had inherited $51 million, and although by the end of the year she confessed candidly to a reporter that most of it had "slipped through my fingers like quicksilver,"[27] when McHugh met her she was still possessed of considerable funds. She was also separated from her husband, her cousin Adolph Spreckels, whom she was soon to divorce on grounds of cruelty.

The fact that she was still technically married, and therefore McHugh could squire her around town with a measure of propriety, had parallels with his moral logic regarding Dorothy Fields. The parallels went further, too, because just as he had once planned amateur opera performances with Fields, culminating in their pseudo–Gilbert-and-Sullivan Japanese spoof, the Associated Press now reported that "under the sponsorship of James F. McHugh, songwriter, and Geraldine Spreckels, sugar family heiress, Beverly Hills Civic Grand Opera Association will present operas at Beverly Hills High School auditorium on a one-night-a-month basis."[28]

It is not difficult to detect the hand of McHugh in the raft of press announcements that subsequently appeared about Spreckels, confirming first that she had "recently completed a screen test for one of the major studios. In spite of her youth, Miss Spreckels is a lyric soprano of no mean ability," and then that she had "signed a Warner Brothers contract as a featured player."[29] She auditioned and occasionally acted under the name of Anna Johns, and she was frequently photographed for the gossip columns under her own name, both with stars such as Bing Crosby and—in what was to become a typical McHugh publicity device in years to come—stepping from her backyard swimming pool, clad in a bathing suit. McHugh's interest in and social contact with Miss Spreckels continued into 1938 but finally ended when his Universal contract expired, and in 1939 he briefly returned to New York and the world of Broadway shows.

Spreckels herself ended up on Broadway somewhat later, playing for a year and exercising her "lyric soprano" voice in the long-running *DuBarry Was a Lady*. Her film career was undistinguished, and few today remember the former heiress for the biggest speaking part she earned, namely, her role in the 1942 movie *Secrets of a Co-Ed*.

Maybe one reason that McHugh's interest in Miss Spreckels waned, in public at any rate, was the fact that his son Jimmy Jr. married Edna Cantor, the daughter of comedian and singer Eddie Cantor, on September 17, 1938. As the Hollywood press columns reported on the engagement and then the wedding, drawing attention to the fact that McHugh was a father and that his son was twenty-two years old, it was not such a good idea for McHugh to be portrayed as a gadabout bachelor, fostering the movie career of an eligible heiress. "Mrs. McHugh is the comedian's second daughter to marry," ran an Associated Press report, "and her husband is the son of old friends of the Cantor family."[30]

This was a slight economy with the truth, as in reality Bess McHugh had had little to do with the Cantors, but Eddie was well known to McHugh himself, and their professional paths had crossed many times, not least when Cantor was involved in making a movie short about the *Midnite Frolics* at the time Fields and McHugh were writing songs for Ziegfeld's after-hours shows. Cantor had replaced the *Frolics* star Maurice Chevalier on the Chase and Sanborn radio show in 1931, which had launched his broadcasting career as a comedian. By the time of Edna Cantor's wedding, her father's NBC radio show was heard coast-to-coast, and he was also well-established in Hollywood, having appeared in numerous movies, including *Whoopee!*, *Roman Scandals*, and *Ali Baba Goes to Town*.

The Cantor radio show had been instrumental in launching the careers of both Bobby Breen and Deanna Durbin, but once McHugh arrived in New York, some six months after his son's wedding, the time had come to leave child stars behind him. He was to take a hand in launching the stage career of one of the most charismatic international performers of the coming decade, Carmen Miranda.

In the summer of 1939, war clouds were gathering over Europe, but in the world of American show business, this was hardly noticed, although, ironically, the Broadway show that McHugh was invited to write for was to be an old-fashioned variety revue called *The Streets of Paris*. It was to feature acts from around the world to demonstrate international cooperation. The show was scheduled to open during the summer on Broadway, and then a splinter production was to transfer in the fall to a specially adapted pavilion at the New York World's Fair. The idea came from Harry Kaufman of the Shubert Theatres organization, with financial backing from Ole Olsen and Chic Johnson, who were currently starring in the Broadway run of Nat Perrin's madcap stage show *Hellzapoppin'*. Kaufman suggested that Al Dubin, who by this time had spent several years at Warner Brothers studios, would be the ideal lyricist.

Maybe Kaufman was innocent of Dubin's excessive lifestyle, or maybe he thought that reuniting a hit-making partnership of the 1920s was more important than worrying about the unreliability of a man whom Jack Warner had more than once had to have paged at every railroad station in the country. Whatever his motives, he can hardly have anticipated the difficulties there were likely to be with this outsize wordsmith. As overweight and untidy as ever, Dubin seemed to have added further complications to his already byzantine life with each year that had passed since he and McHugh last worked together.

Hollywood suited Dubin, who was well known around town for his vast red convertible, driven by an African American chauffeur and allegedly equipped with a gun in every seat-back compartment to keep his many creditors at bay. He was still living wildly beyond his means, and according to McHugh: "[He] needed between three and five thousand dollars a week to keep from going into debt. Between advances from music publishers and loans, this wonderful genius somehow got along. He had a list of five hundred prospective names for borrowing, which he called his 'A' list. 'You're on my preferred list,' Dubin would tell you. By his standards, this was a great honor."[31]

Kaufman paid McHugh a $5,000 advance, and somewhat against his better judgment, McHugh split it with Dubin, who immediately set off for New York but somehow contrived to arrive there, by way of several bars, two days later than McHugh. The show was to introduce several new stars to Broadway, notably the comedic duo of Abbott and Costello, the French singers Jean Sablon and Yvonne Bouvier, the American comedian Bobby Clark, and the "Brazilian Bombshell" Carmen Miranda, with a classically trained dance troupe directed by the leading Broadway choreographer Robert Alton.

For a couple of weeks, based at the Warwick Hotel, McHugh and Dubin worked on the core songs for the show, although Dubin had become something of a prima donna when it came to McHugh's spidery lead sheets. Perhaps spoiled by Harry Warren, his partner at Warner Brothers, with whom he had written such evergreens as "I Only Have Eyes for You" and "September in the Rain," Dubin insisted on having the notes written out clearly and plainly or he would, as McHugh put it, "squawk and scream."

Then he disappeared, to be found a few days later indulging in a low-life ménage-à-trois with a nurse and her daughter. To those who inquired as to the precise nature of the relationship, he passed the nurse off as his assistant and even went so far as to issue a press release to say that the daughter was his protégée, a wealthy Boston debutante. Hauled back to work by McHugh, he completed one or two more songs for the new show's Boston tryouts, but then he disappeared again. This time Kaufman tracked him down to a clinic for recovering alcoholics on Central Park West, where Dubin had paid $300 for a fortnight's treatment. McHugh and Kaufman packed him up and discharged him to the Madison Hotel, where they kept him under lock and key until all but one of the songs were done.

This time it was McHugh who was unable to finish the final song. Despite being shown color photographs of Carmen Miranda, and having her act described to him by Kaufman, no ideas for a suitable tune for her main song would come to mind. McHugh even suggested to Kaufman he find another composer to write for her. Kaufman refused and called for a run-through of all the music, to be held a few days later at McHugh's suite at the Warwick. Gathered round the piano, McHugh and Dubin played through all the material, including Bobby Clark's song "Robert the Roué from Reading, PA." But although she was due to arrive for rehearsals in a matter of days, there was still only a blank sheet of paper for Carmen Miranda. At the end of the run-through, Kaufman invited McHugh and Dubin to join him for supper in order to discuss the problem. As McHugh went into the bathroom to freshen up, he sang to himself a fragment of a tune to the syllables "Ay, ay, ay, ay."

Through the door of the bathroom he heard Kaufman shouting, "That's it Jimmy! Hang onto that tune, don't lose it! Come out right away!" When nature had taken its course, McHugh emerged, went over to the piano, and sketched out what he immediately titled "South American Sway." Dubin jotted down some lyrics and in the process turned the name of the piece into "South American Way." The entire song was written in less than half an hour.[32]

In May 1939, at the time the show started its previews in Boston, Carmen Miranda was already a phenomenon in Brazil. Just thirty years old, she had already had an extensive recording career with the South American branch of RCA Victor and had also appeared in six Brazilian movies; the most recent was *Banana Da Terra*, in which she became the first internationally famous singer since Josephine Baker to don a costume consisting principally of bananas. Her outrageous fruit-adorned hats were a regular feature of her publicity photos, and she became an object of fascination to theatrical manager Lee Shubert and the former figure skater Sonja Henie, who between them persuaded her to break her contract at the Urca Cassino in Rio de Janeiro and try her luck for the first time in the United States.

Shubert was convinced that Miranda would be a huge star with the American public, particularly the Hispanic population, and as befitted a prima donna who would headline in his major theaters, he had also taken a hand in ensuring that she would have a lucrative merchandising deal with Saks Fifth Avenue to sell branded accessories. Macy's also got in on the act with special Carmen Miranda headgear, although their exotic turbans were supplied to customers without additional fruit. She set sail from Rio on May 4 with her group, the Bando da Lua.

In the days preceding her arrival, Kaufman discovered that Carmen Miranda spoke no English, so McHugh had the new song translated into Spanish, only to realize that he should have opted for Portuguese. In the nick of time, it was translated again, and the Brazilian star arrived in New York, ready to take the lengthy train journey to Boston, where the previews were due to start rehearsals at the Shubert Theatre. In the 1960s, McHugh remembered: "The first time I met Carmen was as we got on the train. She looked gorgeous. Much the same style as now—high shoes, eccentric colors, electric personality."[33]

In Boston, McHugh was back in his element, well away from the nine-to-five routine of studio composition. Rehearsing a stage performance, tweaking the songs as they gradually came to life, changing a key here or a note there, working closely with the orchestrator and bandleader, as well as adjusting the running order of the sketches and musical numbers, were skills he had learned both at the Cotton Club and with Lew Leslie, and now he felt confident of his instincts about how to make this somewhat unwieldy revue a success. Even when Dubin persuaded Lou Costello, who had not had a drink for years, to go and get blind drunk on the night of the dress rehearsal, it failed to dampen McHugh's spirits. He had to join forces with Kaufman in resisting the Shubert family's anxieties about whether Abbott and Costello's vaudeville-style slapstick was too dated for the late 1930s, and he had to be equally persuasive that Carmen Miranda's soft-toned version of "South American Way" was a better first-half closer than an all-out, rowdy production number.

On the first night, May 29, McHugh was confident enough of success to invite Maurice Tobin, the city's mayor, to be his guest. Also in the party were Eddie and Ida Cantor. "I came to town," explained Cantor, "to see a show composed by my son-in-law's father." Press reports made much of the fact that "the Cantors are naturally biased in favor of a McHugh opera, [as] all three are prospective grandparents of the same baby."[34] Once his party had been dispatched to its limousines following the show, McHugh, leaving the darkened theater well after midnight, spotted a familiar bulky figure skulking in the shadows by the box office.

> It was Dubin. His opening remark was "I've heard all about it. It's the lousiest show that ever hit Boston."
> "Did you see it?" I asked him.
> "I wouldn't see the dirty show."
> "Al, sweetheart, I've got news for you," I said. "You'll collect royalties for this show for two to three years."[35]

McHugh was almost right. *Streets of Paris* ran for 274 performances, continuing well into February 1940, after its official Broadway opening at the Broadhurst on June 19.

The Boston critics had been unanimously kind about the show, although some of the lesser acts got more column inches then they deserved, such as the conjuror Dr. "Think-a-drink" Hoffman, whose magical cocktail shaker would instantly pour out anything from a chilled martini to a hot coffee and cream for members of the audience who shouted out their beverages of choice. Sablon's Gallic charm was widely praised, as were the knockabout antics of Abbott and Costello, who, as the *Boston Herald*'s Elinor Hughes noted, were firmly under the spell of the show's principal backers, Olsen and Johnson, as the "*Hellzapoppin'* influence is rampant this year."[36] Sidney B. Whipple's review (once the show moved to New York) went so far as to say that Abbott and Costello were "the second great comic invasion of Broadway." But although that duo's comedic genius was to take flight in the years that followed, the more prescient New York writers all focused their columns on what they saw as the real potential star of the show. The *Variety* notice was typical: "There's buried treasure in *Streets of Paris*, the new revue which opened at the Broadhurst on Forty-fourth Street last night. That treasure is Carmen Miranda, a Brazilian beauty whose song style, grace, personality and other indefinable qualities, earned her New York bravotes in her all-too-brief premiere session. She is a sensation, and the word is employed in the New York and not the Hollywood sense in this report. In other words, the show is really terrific and colossal, and we mean that oomphatically."[37]

It took six months from the opening night for Miranda herself to record "South American Way," but the disc, cut on December 26, 1939, for Brunswick, is a little masterpiece. Featuring the Bando da Lua e Garoto, which provides the underlying rumba rhythm and some splendid acoustic guitar playing, the record demonstrates all her subtle seductive powers, as she woos her audience with mystery and guile. It also shows how, by combining the simple syllables "hi-yi, hi-yi" with the repeated tag line "South American Way," the song could work with any audience in any language as a memorable, hummable standard. McHugh's subtle incorporation of samba material underpins a Portuguese verse, complete with some authentic-sounding call-and-response, but then—obviously having learned the English words by rote—Miranda sings a classic set of Dubin lyrics that combine all his verbal ingenuity with his highly personal, and somewhat autobiographical, vein of romanticism.

> Why don't you do
> The way they do in Peru
> Have a good time while you may
> Make love at night,
> And dream all day.

But it is Dubin's subsequent, more convoluted rhyme scheme that really sticks in the mind:

> The Latin scheme of love
> Is like a dream of love.
> A Latin stream of love
> Is in their veins.
> They'll buy a jewel for you
> Or fight a duel for you
> Or drive a mule for you
> Across the plains.

With the same effortless ingenuity that he had demonstrated for Gallagher and Sheen a decade and a half earlier, or with which he had endlessly extended "Hinky Dinky Parlay Voo?," Dubin hit exactly the right note of contemporary sophistication and Latin exoticism to complement McHugh's entirely convincing pastiche of a Brazilian melody.

Ironically, given her importance to the revue, Miranda ended up being just about the last person to record her featured song. The publishing rights in this show were vested in Harms Inc., and that firm went to work plugging the score with the same fervor that McHugh himself had once displayed at Jack Mills. "South American Way" was recorded prior to the Broadway premiere by Al Donahue, Sammy Kaye, Guy Lombardo, Ozzie Nelson, and Ray Noble. In addition, the show's other major songs, "Rendezvous Time in Paree" and "We Can Live on Love," were cut by a host of bands, ranging from Glenn Miller to both Jimmy and Tommy Dorsey and their respective orchestras. Not surprisingly, given such a buildup, the *New York Enquirer* hailed Dubin and McHugh's songs as "the best work of this sort they have ever turned out."[38]

McHugh placed a few press stories of his own relating to the show, including one that said that "the man termed the goodwill composer," owing to the international flavor of *Streets of Paris*, had been invited to Buenos Aires by its chamber of commerce as a gesture of thanks for a song "classed as one of the most popular in the Latin American countries."[39] The piece went on to suggest that consequently McHugh planned to spend Christmas 1939 in Argentina. In fact he did no such thing but returned to his newly built home and comfortable Universal contract in California.

Had he ever entertained serious plans to visit Latin America, it is likely these would have been postponed anyway, because Edna McHugh was expecting Jimmy's first granddaughter. On January 19, 1940, Judy McHugh was born at Cedars of Lebanon Hospital and a few hours later was photographed for the press in the arms of Nurse Harriet Aleshire, who smiled away the baby's screams at the camera by saying, "It shows she's healthy!"[40]

Although McHugh had never been a close father to Jimmy Jr., living away from home from the time his son was five years old, he was still extremely proud of him, and the two men grew closer as Jimmy Jr. moved into adulthood and a career as an agent for MCA, at one point running the firm's London office. The arrival of his first granddaughter was gleefully celebrated by McHugh, who wrote: "Judy has filled a great gap in my life, because she resembles the only lasting love of my life, my mother."[41]

Soon after he got back to Hollywood, as a result of the success of *Streets of Paris*, which was safely settled in for its Broadway run, he and Dubin were asked to work together on a Universal movie that picked up both the Parisian and the Latin American themes of their stage collaboration. *Rio*, directed by John Brahm and starring Basil Rathbone as a criminal financier in a role very much at odds with his famous casting as Sherlock Holmes, was an early example of film noir. There were nightclub scenes set in Paris and Rio de Janeiro featuring Rathbone's screen wife, played by the singer Sigrid Gurie, which offered plenty of opportunity for McHugh and Dubin to extend their new vein of inspiration. However, as was so often the case, the Universal music staff had reckoned without Dubin's unreliable temperament. McHugh recalled: "After a few days' work on the picture Dubin disappeared again. For three weeks nobody could find him. The nurse and her daughter were still with him. Finally Dubin was removed from the picture, and I worked with Ralph Freed instead."[42]

The arrangement with Freed was only temporary, producing the song

"Love Opened My Eyes." For his next film, made in the first months of 1940, McHugh teamed up with a new lyricist, Frank Loesser. The picture, *Buck Benny Rides Again*, was a vehicle for the comedian Jack Benny, in which he satirizes the entire cowboy-movie genre; but among the songs that Loesser and McHugh turned out for Benny and bandleader Phil Harris (who somewhat improbably played himself) was "Say It Over and Over Again," which was widely recorded, most successfully by Ray Eberle with Glenn Miller's band. McHugh was to write again with Loesser in the years that followed, during a brief break in his partnership with Harold Adamson.

As far as movie-goers were concerned, his partnership with Al Dubin was still alive, and the results were evident on the big screen when Carmen Miranda came to Hollywood late in 1940 to reprise her stage performance in *Streets of Paris*. She sang "South American Way" in a picture called *Down Argentine Way*, which also starred Betty Grable and the Nicholas Brothers.

During work on *Buck Benny*, an incident took place that underlines McHugh's abilities as a musical chameleon, able to write convincing jazz songs for African American artists as effectively as he could create a Brazilian standard for Carmen Miranda. He was at a party one night at the Beverly Hills home of the opera singer Tito Schipa, who had recently performed in *Manon* in Los Angeles. Among the other guests was the Metropolitan Opera House diva, Brazilian soprano Bidu Sayao. McHugh played and sang "South American Way" for her, because back in Rio de Janeiro, Sayao had been a friend of Carmen Miranda, and she was much amused by this subtle tribute. McHugh recalled what followed: "Some of the maestros present were called upon to play for Schipa. For some reason or other, he couldn't find the *Manon* score, so the former office boy of the Boston Opera Company played the 'Dream Song' for him, and between faking and remembering, I got along. It wasn't half bad."[43]

Once work on *Buck Benny* was completed, McHugh found himself back in New York for another Broadway revue and a final reunion with the wayward Al Dubin, although Howard Deitz was called in to work on some of the songs that Dubin never quite got around to finishing. The show was *Keep Off the Grass*, which went into the Broadhurst a couple of months after *Streets of Paris* closed, opening its run on May 23. It reunited McHugh with Larry Adler, who was now far better known than he had been during the early previews of *Clowns in Clover*. More important for McHugh, it allowed him to work with one of the figures from the classical world he so admired, the choreographer George Balanchine.

The stars of the show were the dancer Ray Bolger and singer Jane Frohman, but head and shoulders above the rest was Jimmy Durante, whose mere entrance on stage at the first Boston tryout stopped the show. But despite Durante's comic excellence and Balanchine's exquisite dance routines, there were ominous signs in the Boston reviews. Elliott Norton, writing in the *Post*, recommended cutting half an hour from the running time and giving Bolger better material, as well as tightening up the whole direction and stagecraft. He also singled out the score as "probably not the best that Jimmy McHugh has ever written," which—to those in the know—might have had more than a little to do with McHugh's having to keep Al Dubin focused on the job in hand, although their song "Crazy as a Loon" was singled out as "very pretty."[44]

The New York reviewers seized firmly on the weaknesses their gentler colleagues in Boston had identified in passing and were merciless even to Durante, who was featured in numerous types of sketch material, but "none of it quite reaches the violence of those mad, mad moments when he and everything else gets suddenly out of control, the moments when he seems to be practically in a trance and carrying himself frenziedly out with feet, elbows and colors flying."[45] On Broadway, *Keep Off the Grass* turned out to be a sizable flop, and it closed after just forty-four performances.

McHugh returned to Hollywood once the show opened and was quickly back in the world of the studios, joining forces with Johnny Mercer, first at RKO and then at Paramount. Dubin remained—for the time being—in New York, accompanied by his nurse and her daughter. His dissolute lifestyle and excessive weight (over three hundred pounds) finally began to catch up with him, however, and he began to suffer bouts of ill health. One of these stymied what seems to have been his final attempt to collaborate with McHugh.

In August 1943, Dubin cabled Nat Finston in the music department at MGM, saying:

> COLLAPSED IN TAXI GOING TO STUDIO. TRIED TO HIDE THE FACT I WAS VERY ILL. AS I DID NOT WANT TO LOSE PICTURE. OF COURSE WE CAN'T GO ON AS WE HAVE BEEN DOING HAVE SEVEN CHORUSES FINISHED. WILL GET PUBLIC STENOGRAPHER TOMORROW TO TYPE WHAT I HAVE AND GIVE THEM TO JIMMY. PLEASE DON'T GET ANYONE ELSE UNTIL YOU LISTEN TO THESE. SORRY THIS HAD TO HAPPEN IN THE MOST CRUCIAL POINT IN MY CAREER. I WAS ON THE FAIR WAY TO RECOVERY BUT OVER ANXIETY SET ME BACK. AFTER YOU GET LYRICS YOU CAN DECIDE EXACTLY WHAT TO DO.[46]

No songs by McHugh and Dubin appeared in any 1943 film from MGM, so one must assume that his appeals to Finston were in vain and that he and McHugh lost the picture. Although he was ill, Dubin did turn out lyrics for other composers and his songs were heard in the films *Santa Fe Trail* and

Stage Door Canteen, but in February 1945, back in New York, he succumbed to pneumonia and barbiturate poisoning and died. He was just fifty-two.

McHugh was unable to travel back to New York at the time, but he recalled: "His funeral took place at Campbell's Mortuary, with a handful of his old pals. Lester Jacobs and Sammy Chapman told me that Clarence Gaskill, who used to fight with Dubin all the time, took out his rosary and laid it in the casket. Later we arranged a catholic [*sic*] burial for him in California." It was a sad, if entirely predictable, end to one of the more brilliant wordsmiths with whom McHugh ever collaborated, and they had been through a lot together. After Dubin's death, McHugh wrote: "I always admired him, and we were dear friends. Dubin had a great theory that it was a great idea to take the first three notes from any old hit song, and go on from there."[47]

8

"My Kind of Country"

BECAUSE JOHNNY MERCER and Jimmy McHugh shared a Gaelic background—the Mercer family's forbears originally hailing from Scotland and McHugh's from Ireland—one might have expected that they would get along well when they teamed up at RKO. Yet they had extremely different temperaments, and it seems that Mercer, an affable, relaxed Southerner, was at the least irritated, if not downright vexed, by the hyperactive Bostonian McHugh. We know from Mercer's subsequent partnership with Harold Arlen that he took an extremely easygoing attitude to crafting his lyrics.

"After we got a script and the spots for the songs were blocked out," Arlen recalled, "we'd get together for an hour or so every day. While Johnny made himself comfortable on the couch, I'd play the tunes for him." This was seldom a lengthy process, because, as Philip Furia, Mercer's biographer, points out, the lyricist's memory was so retentive that he often only had to hear a song once before he went away to write the complete lyrics.[1]

This laid-back approach, which was to produce "That Old Black Magic" and "Blues in the Night," was totally at odds with McHugh's method of writing movie songs, which had settled more than ever into the nine-to-five office routine of "10 percent inspiration, 90 percent perspiration" during the years of his Universal contract with Harold Adamson. This was the schedule to which he reverted after the ups and downs of his stage work with Dubin, but to it he added a frenetic energy that had been rekindled by his brief return to Broadway, with its world of rehearsals, last-minute changes, and urgent demands for new songs or the reshaping of entire scenes.

McHugh was no longer tied to a single studio after he returned from the premiere of *Keep Off the Grass*, but when he began work at RKO Radio, where he was hired with Mercer to score *You'll Find Out*, his attitude was that every minute spent at the lot could be used to search for new melodies. Mercer was not impressed: "I'd come into the office at the studio and maybe I'd say, 'Mornin' Jim, how's it goin'?' He'd start tinkling away on the treble echoing 'Mornin' Jim, how's it goin'' to a dozen strains until I thought I'd go daffy. There was no way to break the spell either, or if you said, 'I guess I'll go to the men's room,' he'd switch to *that* theme and we'd be going to the men's room for half an hour in waltz time, rumba and foxtrot."[2]

The bizarre plot and hectic pace of the movie itself may have fueled McHugh's level of activity, because *You'll Find Out* was a piece of comedy mayhem. It featured the bandleader and entertainer Kay Kyser, whose madcap "Kollege of Musical Knowledge" was a national hit on radio, and whose first movie, *That's Right, You're Wrong*, had been a surprise runaway success at the box office. Although one reviewer of *You'll Find Out* wrote that "the daring venture of combining the rollicking and somewhat zany Kyser and his band in the same story with so sinister a trio as Boris Karloff, Bela Lugosi and Peter Lorre at their most menacing is highly successful," the movie demands a massive suspension of disbelief. The plot requires that the bespectacled and mild-looking Kyser and his entire orchestra of tuxedo-clad players stand idly by in a "gloomy country mansion" while a young heiress is potentially defrauded out of her inheritance by three somewhat ghoulish characters.[3]

The film contains one slightly unsuccessful legacy of McHugh's immersion in the world of child stars in "The Bad Humor Man," a song written for the comedian Ish Kabibble about a grumpy ice-cream seller and the children who flock to his cart, but remarkably, the rest of the score holds up well and betrays little of the working tension between McHugh and Mercer. Indeed, both songsmiths collected an Academy Award nomination for the song "I'd Know You Anywhere," which Kyser's vocalist Ginny Simms performs with the band. It was just plain bad luck that the winning musical film of the year was

Disney's *Pinocchio*, which took the best song award hands-down for "When You Wish upon a Star."

The collaboration between McHugh and Mercer continued into 1941 with a transfer to Paramount and the movie *You're the One*, which was a vehicle for another society bandleader, in this case Orrin Tucker. Whereas Kay Kyser had made his name on radio, Tucker had come up the hard way, touring with his band around the theaters and white dance halls of the South and Midwest. A former law student, Tucker played the saxophone and sang. His band began its run of success in New Orleans and then came to Kansas City, where he hit on the idea of having stage risers and illuminated music stands that flashed in different colors according to which section of the band was being featured on an arrangement. One number they played everywhere they went was a German drinking song, in which the musicians held aloft steins with the name of the town in which they were playing picked out in fluorescent letters.

While the musicians McHugh loved to work with in clubs and theaters, from Duke Ellington and Paul Whiteman to the Dorsey Brothers and Ethel Waters, had made their reputations on musical ability and talent, in this 1941 Hollywood venture he was asked to provide musical fodder for a band that had made its reputation with flashing lights and gimmickry. Not surprisingly, Tucker and his diminutive singer Bonnie Baker, who had a hit in 1939 with her unusual revival of a World War I song, "Oh, Johnny!," failed to conjure much distinguished music from McHugh, or indeed from Mercer. *You're the One* was the last picture on which they worked together, McHugh returning thereafter to RKO Radio and to his earlier partnership with Frank Loesser, while Mercer moved on to work first with Walter Donaldson and then with Harold Arlen.

In the meantime, with his Bank of the United States debt finally written off in 1940, and money coming in from various movies that reused some of his older songs, together with strong sheet-music and record sales, McHugh was able to throw some of his considerable energies into activities other than the relentless pursuit of wealth. He became active at a local level in the Beverly Hills Chamber of Commerce and at a national level in ASCAP, which had now elevated him to its highest possible ranking. He eventually joined the board of the chamber of commerce in 1946 and became its vice president in 1948.

After losing so much money in the stock market crash of 1929, McHugh now sought other forms of investment. As the 1940s went on, he amassed a sizable art collection, including examples of such European masters as Modigliani, Renoir, Utrillo, and Toulouse-Lautrec, and American paintings by the likes of John Decker and Julian Ritter. All these paintings hung in his home on North Sierra Drive, but he was generous in allowing the best of them to be loaned from time to time for exhibits in public museums and galleries.

Nevertheless, he still took his greatest interest in promoting his own output, and early in the 1940s he formed a company called "Songs by Jimmy McHugh," the precursor to what eventually became Jimmy McHugh Music, to take care of his burgeoning catalog of material, which by the middle of the decade had reached well over five hundred songs. The office was managed by his secretary, and it was about this time that he first employed the formidable Lucille Meyers, who remained with him for the rest of his life. McHugh's firm subscribed to "three services which tell him to the moment and to the dollar how well his old songs are doing." According to a contemporary press report, there were also several additional secretaries employed from time to time. His publicity activities were coordinated with a public relations agent, Maurice Soladair, who issued the relentless stream of press releases McHugh confected about himself and his wares and also ran numerous stories in the trade papers "letting the music world know that 'Sunny Side of the Street' was played by seventeen bands last week." The legal side of the office was overseen by McHugh's brother Lawrence, now a qualified attorney, who—on the formation of the new music publishing company—moved his practice permanently to Beverly Hills from Massachusetts, where he had had a successful ten-year career as a state senator. He now took care of his brother's royalty accounting and scrutinized all publishing, movie, radio, and recording contracts.[4]

This in-house support left McHugh free to be something of a man about Hollywood, attending every first night, club, and theater opening, just as he had once done in New York during his plugging years. As he had also been wont to do in those days, he kept a shrewd ear to the ground as to how his own work was going over with the public. One report ran: "To keep the rhythm, Jimmy still drops around to four or five Hollywood hotspots every night, waving cheery greetings to movie stars and bartenders. When bandleaders see him coming, they strike up his latest tunes. Jimmy, his own best press agent, may sit down at the piano and play a few himself."[5]

As ever, he was always dressed to the nines and sporting the latest smart fashion. Whereas other songwriters met their colleagues and did business at such fashionable watering holes as the Brown Derby on Hollywood and Vine, McHugh tended to entertain at Cabana No. 5 at the Beverly Hills Hotel, next to its opulent swimming pool. In later decades, he was to entertain at his own poolside, but in the 1940s he felt it was easier to fall back on the resources of the region's grandest hotel. The upshot of his renewed social activity was that he was elected one of the top ten best-dressed men in Los Angeles, the only songwriter so honored amid film stars, singers, bandleaders, and politicians.

The war in Europe was beginning to make an impression on Hollywood, and in February 1941, McHugh became involved with the Permanent Charities Committee of the Motion Picture Industry in organizing a concert for the Greek War Relief Fund. He was photographed with the child star Alicia Adams, who donned Greek national costume in "admiration of the courage of the Greeks," and the accompanying press pieces announced further stars who would appear, including Jack Benny, Bing Crosby, Eddie Cantor, Judy Garland, Bob Hope, Frances Langford, and Mary Martin. This was the earliest of what would become a series of patriotic and fundraising events in which McHugh took part throughout the war, particularly after the shocking attack on Pearl Harbor on December 7, 1941, when the United States was drawn into the conflict. His correspondence files contain copious tributes to both his energy and generosity, whether donating prizes of giant cartons of cigarettes to the Al Jarvis Variety show that toured hospitals with the likes of Peggy Lee and the Blue Blazers, giving sizable checks to fundraising broadcasts and celebrity dinners, or coaxing stars to turn out in aid of such good causes as the War Aid Group, temporarily based at the Beverly Hills Hotel. In due course, he turned his attention to raising money through sales of War Bonds, both as a composer of attention-grabbing songs and an energetic organizer of special events.

Soon after the United States went to war, and before McHugh turned his attention more fully to fundraising and morale-boosting, there was another movie score to be written with Frank Loesser. *Seven Days' Leave*, made by RKO, starred Victor Mature and Lucille Ball. The seven days in question referred to the period of time the newly enlisted Mature had on furlough in order to woo a socialite played by Ball. The wartime mood was immediately conjured up by the title song, "Please Won't You Leave My Girl Alone," which is sung in the opening credits by soldiers in barracks and at the end of the movie by Mature and his fellow servicemen as they set off by ship for battle and wave goodbye to the civilian crowd on the docks.

The musical mix of new songs and light classics was not unlike the Deanna Durbin films McHugh had scored with Harold Adamson, as there were soundtrack versions of Beethoven's "Moonlight Sonata," Wagner's "Wedding March" (from *Lohengrin*), and Johann Strauss's grand waltz, "Tales of the Vienna Woods." Such a broad musical palette also allowed McHugh and Loesser an element of pastiche with their new songs "A Touch of Texas" and "Puerto Rico," which were played by Freddie Martin's orchestra, one of the two resident big bands on the picture. And it was Martin's band, too, that backed up Ginny Simms in the reflective ballad "Can't Get Out of This Mood," which ranks among both McHugh's and Loesser's finest songs and deserves to be far better known than it is, buried in this somewhat obscure movie. Overall, the musical content of the film is surprisingly good, with Les Brown and His Band of Renown playing much of the remainder of the score, including a further three original songs from the Loesser–McHugh partnership.

The urban, Jewish, street-smart, gravel-voiced Loesser could not have been more of a contrast to Mercer. He loved words and witty wordplay, and although his daily speech was often peppered with Yiddish, German, and the occasional obscenity, he had a sure ear for the niceties of the English language. The result was that many of his lyrics take pleasure in the sound of words for their own sake. One of his most amusing pieces written with McHugh, "Sing a Tropical Song," takes a Gilbertian delight in an island population who "put the ac-CENT on the wrong syl-LA-ble."

While Mercer took a laid-back approach to writing, Loesser's activity level matched McHugh's. Fidgety, a compulsive doodler, fueled by coffee and cigarettes, Loesser often rose to jot down lyrics at four or five in the morning and worked in short, sharp bursts throughout the day, sustaining himself with catnaps punctuated by more caffeine and nicotine. According to his former collaborator Burton Lane, Loesser liked to have the composer play the tune they were working on "over and over . . . till ya hated it."[6] He also found inspiration while at the wheel of his automobile, although his daughter Susan remembers that "he used to get so involved in his thoughts that he would drive through red lights, sit through green ones, turn the wrong way on one-way streets, drive past his house when coming home, and generally behave like an absent-minded highway menace."[7]

There is every sign that after *Seven Days' Leave* this partnership would have developed into a team as productive and successful as McHugh's association with Fields, had not the war itself intervened. As 1942 drew to a close, Loesser, then aged thirty-two, decided to enlist in the army. This brought to an end his day-to-day partnership with McHugh, but he nevertheless managed to spend most of the time he was in uniform working on music in one form or another, first in a California-based radio production unit that put together special broadcasts for troops overseas, and second in a special services department in New York City where he was posted in 1943. This operation created what came to be known as "blueprint specials"—variety shows in kit form, for troops to present for themselves, with ready-made scripts, song sheets, and even do-it-yourself sets and costume designs.

Fortunately, before he joined up, Loesser worked with McHugh during the final months of 1942 on another picture to be released the following year, *Happy-Go-Lucky*, that included what turned out to be the finest of all the numbers they wrote together, "Let's Get Lost." Indeed, there were few weak links amid the several good songs in this film, but Betty Hutton's feature "Murder, He Says!," a skit on contemporary hipster slang which caught on with the public as a series of catchphrases, and "Let's Get Lost," sung in the movie by Mary Martin and Dick Powell, were the longest-lived. The former, which was recorded by Dinah Shore as well as by Hutton, was built around a plethora of "romantic vocabulary," including such terms of affection as "dig," "zoot," and "hep, hep," and it quickly slipped into the argot of conscripted troops, who used the phrase "it's murder, he says" to describe the toughest commands of superior officers.[8] The latter song was less modish and became a jazz standard, particularly identified in subsequent years with the trumpeter Chet Baker. He recorded it in his romantic, breathy voice, imbuing the idea of "let's defrost, in a romantic mist" with an ironic double meaning, given that he was a serious heroin addict. The song eventually became the title of a movie about Baker's tragic, drug-addicted final years, which ended with a fatal fall from a hotel window in Amsterdam in 1988.

In the run-up to Christmas 1942, McHugh wrote, with obvious affection, to the newly enlisted Private Loesser, who was at that stage posted to West Coast army headquarters in Santa Ana, California.

Dear Frankie

A few lines to let you know how our songs are doing. "Touch of Texas," and "Can't Get Out of This Mood" are among the big hits of the country, with "I Get the Neck of the Chicken" following. I saw Kay Kyser last night, and he said that his Columbia recording had sold 301,000 on "Can't Get Out of This Mood." This is wonderful considering the shellac rationing. I was with Freddie Martin at the Cocoanut Grove Xmas last night. He told me his recording of "Can't Get Out of This Mood" was No. 1 seller for the Victor list for the country, "White Christmas" second and "Touch of Texas" third. Looks like we have a two million record sale on this score from *Seven Days' Leave*.

Paramount will start on our songs from *Happy-Go-Lucky* on February 1st. "Let's Get Lost," and "Happy-Go-Lucky" will be the first plugged with Betty Hutton's "Murder," and "I Don't Know How He Does It but He Does It" following. We have 100% recording on these. Looks like we are OK for the first half of 1943. My love to you,

Jimmie [*sic*] McHugh[9]

Paramount did an excellent job plugging the songs from *Happy-Go-Lucky*, and as a result, the Mary Martin / Dick Powell recording of "Let's Get Lost" spent twelve weeks on the *Your Hit Parade* radio show.

With Loesser in the army, McHugh teamed up again with Harold Adamson. This second period of collaboration was to produce their most successful songs; and although their first 1943 movie at RKO Radio was another vehicle for Kay Kyser (once more with Ish Kabibble in support) called *Around the World*, containing few memorable numbers apart from "Candlelight and Wine," which the trumpeter Harry James promoted heavily, their second full-length film of the year was *Higher and Higher*, which is now mainly remembered because it featured Frank Sinatra's first starring role.

Before that, however, they produced one of the most memorable of all wartime songs, "Comin' In on a Wing and a Prayer." When he first came up with the idea, McHugh had intended to write this as a one-song reunion with Frank Loesser, who was still in regular touch with McHugh from his California posting. Soon after joining the army, Loesser himself had written and composed a remarkably successful morale-booster of his own, called "Praise the Lord and Pass the Ammunition," a song inspired by a navy chaplain who had been called up on the deck of an aircraft carrier to minister to two gunners fatally injured in action. After doing what he could for them and giving them the last rites, he took over on the gun himself, uttering the famous phrase that became the song title.

However, when McHugh produced what he thought was an equally brilliant title, Loesser turned down the chance to write the lyrics, saying, "I don't like it."[10] The idea for the song was inspired by a young scholar and football player, Sonny Bragg, whom McHugh had met at a Los Angeles civic reception in 1939, when the Duke University football team, for whom Bragg played, had taken on the University of Southern California at the Rose Bowl. As Bragg's career as a promising footballer developed, he corresponded from time to time with McHugh, who had by the early 1940s begun to develop an interest in football that would become almost as passionate as his fondness for boxing and his later love of competitive swimming. In early 1943, Bragg wrote out of the blue to McHugh, apologizing for not being in touch but telling him that after being drafted he had been flying bombing missions over Europe from a U.S. Army base in North Africa. "On my last trip, half a wing was shot away, but we managed to return on one wing and a prayer."[11]

When Loesser refused to collaborate on the song, McHugh bet him that it would outsell "Praise the Lord and Pass the Ammunition." He called Adamson, who was delighted to assist and polished off the lyric for "Coming In on a Wing and a Prayer" in a matter of minutes. Later, McHugh would tell interviewers that the melody struck him "like a bolt from the blue," and it was one of the quickest songs from start to finish they ever wrote.[12] Opening with a firm and urgent on-the-beat verse, rather like Morse code, backing up the lyric "one of our planes was missing, with all its gallant crew," the chorus then takes flight, so that "with one motor gone, we can still carry on." Adamson's lyrics press all the right emotional, patriotic, and religious buttons for the period, ending triumphantly on:

> With our full crew aboard
> And our trust in the Lord
> We're comin' in
> On a wing and a prayer.

It sold over eight hundred thousand copies in sheet-music form in the United States, and the recording by the Song Spinners spent three weeks as a number one hit at the top of the charts. It was also recorded by various other artists—notably by Bing Crosby in the United States and Ann Shelton in Britain—and this meant that in addition to the several weeks of 1943 that the original version spent on the hit parade, outlasting "Let's Get Lost" by nine weeks, its overall record sales were extremely high. With these two songs, McHugh achieved the unusual feat for a songwriter of occupying both the number one and two positions on the chart simultaneously. According to McHugh, "Wing and a Prayer" also outsold the sheet music of "Praise the Lord and Pass the Ammunition" globally by some two hundred thousand copies, and he thereby won his wager.[13]

In the same early period of 1943, he also composed another patriotic song, when Universal called him to contribute a number for Deanna Durbin to sing in the movie *Hers to Hold*. The result, written with Universal's Herb Magidson, was the Oscar-nominated "Say a Prayer for the Boys over There." Durbin was cast as a wartime factory worker who loves an air force pilot, and this was the tear-jerker written for her to sing to her absent boyfriend (played by Joseph Cotten). McHugh made the extravagant gesture of donating his royalties from both these songs to war relief funds, but the most successful outcome from his career point of view was that "Comin' In on a Wing and a Prayer" reunited him with Adamson, enabling them to hit their stride with songs very much better than the "manufactured" variety that Jack Robbins had complained of so vehemently a few years before.

This was just as well, because RKO gave McHugh and Adamson just six weeks to write the songs for *Higher and Higher*, instead of the three months that was the industry average. McHugh later wrote: "The picture had to be out while Frank [Sinatra] was still the nation's newest sensation. Sinatra in himself is a great inspiration, because of his great delineation of words and trick phrasing. We had to give forth with something that would make the bobby soxers swoon, but we didn't have time for much moongazing or the like."[14]

At this point in his career, Sinatra, billed as "the singing voice that is thrilling millions, the man of the minute in every young feminine heart,"[15] had just finished his three years as the singer with Tommy Dorsey's orchestra, after starting out with the similar swing band of Harry James. He was an electrifying performer, and musicians who worked with him, such as Dorsey's lead trumpeter Zeke Zarchy, recalled the way in which he dominated the band's stage shows and also completely revised the way in which popular singers sang and phrased, so that he sounded entirely natural but simultaneously managed to inject a sense of jazzy timing into his work:

> When he was still with Harry James, a bunch of us from the Dorsey band went to see the show one night, and this skinny kid was up there on the stage, stopping traffic. All the old ladies, and everybody else, wouldn't let him off the stage. It was a big hit. Word got back to Tommy very quickly about this kid, and Tommy was always looking for fresh talent in the vocal department. The vocalist in a big band was more or less somebody who was there to help a tune get more popular, because somebody had to sing the lyrics. There were really very few top band singers. Tommy instantly saw how Frank would enhance his band, and the rest is history. We had this arrangement on "East of the Sun," and Frank sang that tune with a jazz feel, like he was playing a horn. We'd never heard anybody take a ballad and sing it like that, but that was Frank.[16]

Sinatra's mature, mellow voice was somewhat at odds with his thin, almost gangly appearance, and in this first movie he had yet to acquire the relaxed assurance in front of the camera that was to be the hallmark of his later appearances on screen. Nevertheless, his enormous popularity—so great that the film previews were apparently drowned out, Beatlemania-style, by the screams of hordes of bobby-soxers—ensured that this first venture on celluloid would be a landmark in his career.

Originally, *Higher and Higher* had been a 1940 Broadway show, written by Rodgers and Hart, but for its film incarnation virtually all of their original score was thrown away, not least because in mid-1943 there was a major rift between Richard Rodgers and Lorenz Hart. This led to Rodgers's new collaboration with Oscar Hammerstein II but also, after a brief reunion of the two original partners, culminated in Hart's death from alcohol-related pneumonia in November 1943. Consequently, the film producers started afresh with new songs by McHugh and Adamson, billing the movie as "a glittering and glorious gem of romance, songs, dancing and laughs, adapted from the sensational Broadway stage success by Rodgers and Hart."[17] Only "Disgustingly Rich" survives from the stage musical—even the excellent "It Never Entered My Mind" was cast aside.

The star of the stage show, Jack Haley, playing a scheming butler who hatches a moneymaking scheme among his fellow domestic servants to help their suddenly impoverished ex-millionaire boss, was not happy about being upstaged by the hurriedly sketched-in part for Sinatra as—literally—the boy next door. As it turned out, it was Sinatra, "the hottest big-time attraction in show business right now,"[18] who helped the movie achieve box-office success; and film buffs also treasure it for the bit parts played by Victor Borge (as another impoverished gentleman), Barbara Hale (as an heiress), and Mel Tormé (in his first movie role as Marty, one of the servants).

Although McHugh spent time with Sinatra on and off the set and got along with him extremely well—not least on account of McHugh's long friendship with Tommy Dorsey and with Sinatra's musical director and arranger, Axel Stordahl, who had been in the Dorsey band for the *Riviera Revue*—he was destined never to write another movie score for him. He did, in his customary way, stay in touch by letter and cable, and over the decades that followed Sinatra recorded a significant number of McHugh songs (including his 1961 EP, *Sinatra Sings Jimmy McHugh*). For a time they were also close socially, particularly during the late 1940s and the final years of Sinatra's marriage to his first wife, Nancy, who would sometimes confide to McHugh that she yearned for the simpler life they'd enjoyed during the Harry James era, before Frank became a star.[19]

McHugh's immediate challenge in 1943, however, was to come up with material for Frank to sing that was as distinguished as the Rodgers and Hart score that had been jettisoned. He recalled:

Adamson and I trekked into our office at RKO and found the script glaring coldly at us from the top of the piano. It informed us that there'd be a minor lover's quarrel in the story, also the need of a big production number. Nothing happened with us that first day, but at 3 a.m. the next morning, Adamson phoned me and said he'd been listening to a swell musical shortwave program that suddenly had been cut off for a news announcement.

"There's our title for the production number, Jim," he said, "'The Music Stopped.'"

Then I began concentrating on the lovers' spat and came down with insomnia. As the thousandth sheep jumped over the fence, both tune and title landed: "I Couldn't Sleep a Wink Last Night."[20]

In McHugh's subsequent accounts of his own life, this became the song mentioned in chapter 6, which McHugh jotted down on his bedsheet and which had to be rescued from the Beverly Hills Laundry the next day, in order for McHugh to transcribe it. In fact, McHugh had already used this story in a press piece about himself as early as 1939, long before he met Sinatra. But from this point onwards he neatly worked it into his accounts of writing *Higher and Higher*: "Harold and I finished the song up in 15 minutes, and it proved to be the hit of the picture. In general, that's how it goes. You think and think, and somehow the idea of a melody comes along. But remember, that's just the song. It isn't a hit yet. It's got to be rehearsed and recorded by the singer for whom it was written. In the case of Frankie, he recorded the next day after his arrival in Hollywood. He did three recordings in one day which is very good for anyone in the picture industry."[21]

In the end all three songs made the hit parade, the two mentioned by McHugh and also "A Lovely Way to Spend an Evening." The commercial recordings by Columbia of this song and "I Couldn't Sleep a Wink Last Night" now seem like rather curious oddities in the Sinatra canon, because they are sung to the vocal accompaniment of the Bobby Tucker Singers with no additional instruments. This was not some bizarre aesthetic judgment on behalf of Sinatra's record company but an act of necessity, because 1943 was the year in which James C. Petrillo, the head of the American Federation of Musicians (AFM), had called a national ban on recording by his members. From August 1, 1942, no new discs could be made by commercial record companies using AFM players (with the exception of V-Discs made for American troops overseas), until, one by one, the firms agreed with the union to pay a tiny percentage of sales income to its members. The first companies to settle, Decca in September 1943 and Blue Note during the same month, were able to return to conventional instrumental discs by the fall of 1943, but Columbia held out for some time longer and so (as singers were unaffected by the ban) had to resort to unusual means to make what turned out to be a very substantial hit record for Sinatra.

"I Couldn't Sleep a Wink Last Night," in its more conventionally played soundtrack version (AFM studio musicians were allowed to continue recording for movies), resulted in McHugh's second Oscar nomination of the year for best song. Yet again, however, he was beaten, despite also being nominated for "Say a Prayer for the Boys over There," this time by "Swinging on a Star," written by Van Heusen and Burke, and sung by Bing Crosby in the movie *Going My Way*.

However, by the time of the Oscar ceremony in the spring of 1944, there were other things on McHugh's mind than the Academy Awards. Since his return to Hollywood after staging *Keep Off the Grass*, McHugh had developed a new romantic involvement, of a far deeper and more lasting nature than his dalliance with Miss Spreckels. He had fallen for Maria Feliza Pablos, the great-niece of the Mexican dictator Porfirio Diaz, and even in the 1960s he was still referring to her as "the big thing in my life." As with most of the women to whom McHugh's name would henceforth be linked romantically, she was less than half his age.

Things got so serious that during 1941 the press began reporting that he was seeking a divorce and would marry the "24-year-old Mexican beauty," Miss Pablos. The *Boston Post* reported: "The exact facts were buried in a welter of rumors and denials. In Hollywood close friends . . . insisted the bald song-writer had been making arrangements for some time to become a bachelor. They even named the church and the priest who would make Senorita Pablos the new Mrs. James F. McHugh." From their homes, both Bess (the existing Mrs. McHugh) and the songwriter's brother, Lawrence, issued flat denials, saying such reports were "unfounded"; and Bess went so far as to point out that there had been numerous rumors circulating some months before in the press, including an alleged liaison with a girl in Hartford, Connecticut, but that while McHugh was supposedly visiting this enamorata on the East Coast, Bess had spoken to her husband in Hollywood. McHugh himself point-blank refused to speak to reporters, telling them, "I'm still married."[22]

However, as he later recalled, there was more truth to the rumors about Senorita Pablos than he cared to admit at the time:

> I met Pablos at a party in Beverly Hills. Across the room I saw a black haired beauty with aristocratic ankles and an aristocratic nose. The next thing I knew, she took my plate and served me. This impressed me. I'm usually treated like a bum by the women I consider the most desirable. I don't know what she wore. We talked about music. She had been educated in Rome and had a wide knowledge of music. She spoke five languages. We became wonderful friends. Her father was Spanish, a wealthy rancher in Mexico, and her mother was a descendant of Diaz.

She had a white piano. I used to play it. I composed the starts of many tunes on it. I don't remember that I ever finished one. . . . We fought a good deal. She was hot tempered and high strung, and so am I. Our fights were mostly on account of certain moronic individuals that I believed I had a better knowledge of than she did. She would defend them and we would launch into one or two hour arguments. . . . I discovered that I wrote better when she was away on a trip. All the time I was writing the Frank Sinatra score for *Higher and Higher*, she was away in Mexico. When she was here, I was mad at her most of the time. And it was mutual. The busier I was, the harder it became for us to remain on friendly terms.[23]

One thing that did help to keep Pablos and McHugh on friendly terms, even when he was at his busiest, was that she formed a close friendship with McHugh's mother, who now lived permanently with him in Los Angeles. One of the great local customs that began during the mid-1940s was that after Sunday morning Mass at the Church of the Good Shepherd, McHugh would take his mother to brunch at his regular table at the Beverly Hills Hotel, joined from week to week by other members of his circle and the Cantor family. Mrs. McHugh and Pablos shared the same birthday, January 1, and they clucked and cooed over McHugh together.

Pablos was McHugh's regular companion throughout the first half of the 1940s, and they attended shows, movie premieres, operas, ballets, and concerts. He disliked her social ambition, her love of "people in furs with insincere 'I love yous' and 'darlings' . . . people I didn't believe in," but it seems that the attraction of opposites kept them together, even on such memorable occasions as when she mixed up all the sheet music for the annual Los Angeles orphans' party at which McHugh was both to play the piano and act as Santa Claus. The collision between his innate—almost neurotic—tidiness and her casual approach to such orderliness nearly brought them to blows. His observation that he wrote better when she was away had more than a grain of truth in it, and not just the score for *Higher and Higher* but some of his other best songs from the early and mid-1940s were written while she was out of town.

Nevertheless they remained an item. He wrote: "For the first time I had someone capable of sharing my innermost thoughts and dreams. She was well educated and had a good mind. We discussed literature and the classics and wept together over the music of Puccini, especially *La Boheme*, which we both adored."[24]

This continued until the fall of 1946, when McHugh reacted with some disbelief to the news that for some months she had been simultaneously dating Cornelius "Neely" Vanderbilt. As McHugh was wont to send flowers at almost any excuse to ladies from all walks of life, he read nothing too serious into another man doing the same thing. He recalled:

> One night I sat on her bed, at the head of which were four dozen roses from Vanderbilt. The following Sunday she phoned me.
> "*Life* magazine is in the other room taking pictures," she told me.
> "What for?"
> "I just got married!"
> "Congratulations to you both," I said.[25]

McHugh played it cool but was definitely stunned by the news that she had married this "silver-spoon socialite turned roaming tinsel journalist and *New York Post* columnist."[26] Yet he remained on good terms with Pablos, and when her marriage ended just five months later in February 1947, he helped her to obtain the first of what eventually added up to four divorces. Soon the Hollywood gossip columnists were able to report: "Phyllis [*sic*] Pablos who 'went steady' with Jimmy McHugh until she married some other guy is back with McHugh again."[27]

Such gossip took its toll on Bess McHugh, and in the mid-1940s she quietly filed for divorce on the grounds of desertion. Technically, as a Roman Catholic, McHugh remained married for life. According to his granddaughter Judy, he "bought the church off" by donating a window to the church in Toluca Lake where he and Bing Crosby were frequent members of the congregation, and he also gave generously to the Church of the Good Shepherd in Beverly Hills, where he took the collection most Sundays and was nicknamed "the Bishop of Beverly." Despite whatever deal he made with the church, McHugh remained ambivalent for the rest of his life over his marital status and never entirely accepted the fact that he was legally divorced, although in the years to follow, rumors of a return to the altar surfaced more than once.[28]

McHugh passed his fiftieth birthday at the height of his affair with Pablos in 1943, although by this time he had already shaved a year off his life and was claiming to have been born in 1894. He seems to have been every bit as energetic as he had been at the age of thirty, when he started writing his first successful songs. A review of his year in *Weekly Variety*[29] shows a simply astonishing amount of work, although he slightly exaggerated his total output of "sixty tunes" by claiming one or two numbers that had actually been written in 1942. The same article also claims that during the year his songs achieved total sheet-music sales of two million units and record sales in excess of five million.

One reason for this was—despite, or perhaps because of, the Petrillo ban—there was a huge revival of interest in the songs he had written with Fields, resulting in renewed sales of their older recordings. So, for example, "Diga Diga Doo" was featured in the African American movie *Stormy Weather*, and "On the Sunny Side of the Street" was used in both the Ted Lewis feature *Is Everybody Happy?* and the Mary Lee / Gladys George film *Nobody's Darling*. The newer songs that Kay Kyser and Freddie Martin had recorded just before the ban started in 1942 also continued to sell strongly. Furthermore, as the ban gradually ended, two songs McHugh had written with Ralph Freed were released: "My Mother Told Me" for Gloria De Haven and "In a Moment of Madness" for Harry James and his vocalist Helen Forrest, both to be featured in the forthcoming MGM movie *Two Girls and a Sailor*. Meanwhile, the music for Twentieth Century-Fox's similarly titled *Four Jills in a Jeep* was largely finished, with a complete new score consisting of songs by McHugh and Adamson and featuring Dick Haymes, Jimmy Dorsey, Alice Faye, and Carmen Miranda.

All the while McHugh was writing at this pace and continuing his liaison with Pablos, he was still following the habits he had established in the 1920s and spending a good portion of his working time plugging his wares. In 1943, after a gap of some dozen years, he resumed a lively correspondence with Louis Armstrong, who had brought his big band to the Trianon Ballroom in Los Angeles. Replying to a note sent to the dressing room, Satchmo told "Brother McHugh" that "it has always been a pleasure to run into you or hear from you," before cramming his letter with ribald and largely unprintable backstage anecdotes of the kind they had apparently shared at the Cotton Club many years before, together with encomiums for his current laxative. But the key to McHugh's reason for restarting the correspondence is in Armstrong's sign-off paragraph: "The tunes (of yours) you named in your letter from your catalog shall always live with me. . . . I'll never forget them. . . . And you either, my friend. . . . 'Heah?' . . . Goodnight and God blessya. . . . Am Pluto Waterly Yours, Louis Armstrong."[30]

Armstrong's manager, Joe Glaser, was also a recipient of McHugh's plugging letters and wrote reassuringly: "It will be a pleasure for me to make sure that Louis Armstrong has every one of the tunes you mention in his books—and I will also see that Lionel Hampton and Les Brown have them. No doubt you are aware of the fact that I also have Russ Morgan under my personal management. . . . He opens at the New York Strand Theatre for five weeks in March, and even though he has written enumerable [*sic*] tunes himself, I am sure he will be able to do some for you."[31] And so it went on. There were wires to Bill Stern ensuring that he considered McHugh songs for breaks in his sports program on NBC, there were roses for Irene Dunne to remind her of his songs, and there was a rosary (apparently blessed by the Pope himself) for Jo Stafford, sent along with a similarly ingratiating reminder about McHugh's recent catalog.

However, effective as these regular and efficient nudges to the show business community were in ensuring that his record and sheet-music sales continued, it was another of his activities altogether that brought him the greatest recognition during the war years. As early as March 1942, McHugh had turned his hand to writing songs to help with the government drive to raise funds for the war. That month he made a personal appearance at Victory House in Pershing Square, Los Angeles, where the U.S. Treasury Department was based, to play a selection of his songs for the public. To the "huge throng" that appeared he also launched a new piece called "I'm Buying Bonds for My Baby."[32] Now as 1944 began, the Treasury Department approached McHugh and Adamson once again to see whether, in the wake of their success with "Comin' In on a Wing and a Prayer," they would consider writing a song to help with the mission to sell war bonds.

The result was "Buy, Buy, Buy a Bond," a number recorded by Bing Crosby and Frank Sinatra and included in a special short film, *All-Star Bond Rally*, that Darryl F. Zanuck produced at Twentieth Century-Fox for the War Activities Committee. Advertised by another of the movie's stars, Bob Hope, this "greatest bond-selling movie the industry has ever turned out" carried the following personal message from Hope: "Your theater manager has gone from show business into the grim business of war. Here he helps the War Fund, the Red Cross, March of Dimes. Here he sells War Bonds any time . . . Saturdays, Sundays or Holidays. Your theater manager has a red, white and blue streak up his back."[33] Also featured in this "19 minutes of big-time entertainment" were Betty Grable, Harry James and his band, Harpo Marx, and Carmen Miranda.

The following year, after VE Day, in an effort to raise further funds toward the continuing conflict with Japan, Bing Crosby and Bob Hope recorded McHugh and Adamson's "We've Got Another Bond to Buy." Indirectly this led to McHugh's most extravagantly staged fundraising effort at the Beverly Hills Hotel, which involved another of his sporting passions, competitive swimming.

In future years, when McHugh was promoting regular swimming galas in Los Angeles, these often looked like little more than excuses for him to be photographed with rows of scantily clad, extremely shapely women at numerous poolside publicity events. However, the origins of his involvement in swimming promotions actually dates to 1945 and a more serious purpose.

It began with a cocktail party he promoted at the Beverly Hills Hotel pool, to which he invited (at his own personal cost) half a century of champions, including Esther Williams, Johnny Weissmuller, and Buster Crabbe. He said: "Throughout the years, I had met a good number of the champion swimmers and somehow felt they were a forgotten group of people who weren't receiving the respect due them."[34]

In terms of McHugh's longer-term involvement with swimming, it was this party that inspired him to make a play for (and win) the 1945 Women's National Swimming Competition, which he staged at the Los Angeles Olympic Pool. But it also gave him the germ of an idea when the Treasury Department asked if, having written three bond-raising songs, he would organize a proper fundraising rally. He suggested a meeting between the Treasury fundraisers, local members of the chamber of commerce, and Mr. Courtright, the managing director of the Beverly Hills Hotel, at which he proposed a giant aquacade with supporting entertainment.

Courtright suggested that the hotel would be pleased to be involved if the event could guarantee a minimum sale of $5 million in bonds. At this point the innate hustler in McHugh took over.

> I just looked at him and said, "Mr. Courtright, I'm sorry, unless we can do $25 million, I don't think we should touch it."
>
> Naturally, all these big businessmen from downtown were rather startled and started gasping. Then one of them asked me, "How do you intend to make this amount?"
>
> I said, "Well, I'll tell you. I happen to know a little about raising bond issues. I know that all of the big department stores here have collections, and all the money goes in individually. If we make this one general pot, and put in all the collections from the large stores, I guarantee you I'll give you the greatest show you have ever had in the history of Bond Drives!"
>
> They said, "All right. We can't guarantee $25 million, but that's what we are going to shoot for."
>
> At this time, Justice Frank Murphy was staying at the Ambassador, and I made him move out and stay at the Beverly Hills Hotel. I flew in every great champion swimmer from all over the country, had Tommy Dorsey's band, got all the stars to appear . . . singers to perform. I sold cabanas for half a million each, charged $1,000 admission, threw red, white and blue spotlights in the air for the first time. It was more than a huge success. We ended up doing $28 million worth of Bonds.[35]

The Aquacade took place on July 2, 1945, and was indeed an extraordinary success, in which McHugh's lifelong ability to generate self-publicity was a major factor. Senior generals were photographed being served ordinary G.I. meals at $1,000 a plate. Justice Murphy wrinkled his craggy eyebrows at the hordes of swimsuit-clad beauties, and Olympic diving champion "Dutch" Smith was snapped in his marine captain's uniform, surrounded by the most glamorous of female diving competitors. McHugh himself featured prominently in pictures of the event, with champion swimmer Esther Williams rubbing his bald pate affectionately as they jointly addressed the audience. At the afternoon competitive meet that preceded the events at the hotel, McHugh performed his recently written song, "There's a New Flag on Iwo Jima," and veterans of that particular battle, some of them in wheelchairs, appeared in support.[36]

In March of the following year, the magnitude of McHugh's contribution to the war effort was recognized with the U.S. Treasury's Silver Medal. "This award is being given to a handful of persons in radio who have made substantial contributions to the War Finance Division, in the course of the various bond drives," wrote the Treasury's David Levy, whose congratulations were followed just a few days later with a similarly complimentary letter from Vernon Clark, the director of U.S. Savings Bonds, along with the medal itself. As Levy made clear, this recognition was mainly to reward McHugh for the fundraising effect his songs with Adamson had had via the medium of radio, but after lobbying behind the scenes by several of McHugh's friends and allies, including Justice Frank Murphy and Senator Olin D. Johnstone, McHugh was also presented with the President's Certificate of Merit. He flew to Washington for the ceremony in February 1947, and General Edward F. Witsell, the adjutant general, commended him at the Pentagon for "outstanding fidelity and meritorious conduct in aid of the war effort." Overall, ran the citation, McHugh's fundraising, composing, and organizing, not just of the Beverly Hills rally but of "Hollywood Canteen" events, had contributed over $38 million to the war effort. The Canadian government also staged a dinner in McHugh's honor in Hollywood in thanks for the effect his songs had had on its war loans drives.[37]

In some respects, this recognition at the end of the war was not the best thing that could have happened to McHugh. He had indeed done a lot to raise the national consciousness and promote saving. He had produced a handful of patriotic songs, one of them Oscar nominated and another the source of a phrase that would live on in the English language long past the topical wartime imagery of "a wing and a prayer." He had proven himself an influential and energetic member of the Hollywood business and professional community. But he had not yet done what almost all his fellow Hollywood composers and several of his former collaborators had done or were about to do: write a full-length musical. Dorothy Fields felt the urge to do this and was to fulfill her dreams by participating in the writing of the book for Irving Berlin's *Annie Get Your Gun* in 1947. She eventually was to write the lyrics for several more shows, culminating in her most famous latter-day work, *Sweet Charity.* Frank Loesser would in due course create several of the most enduring of all musicals, starting with *Where's Charley?* in 1948 and including the 1950 show *Guys and Dolls.*

By contrast—with the exception of his unsuccessful past efforts and the 1948 Broadway show *As the Girls Go,* which was to be a flimsy vehicle for the comedian Bobby Clark combined with what was more or less a Mike Todd girly revue, followed eight years later by the disastrous flop *Strip for Action*—McHugh was never to go beyond producing individual songs for movies and stage variety shows. By becoming a mover and shaker in the film community, getting involved in promoting swimming meets, charity fundraisers, and similar events, he settled for the life of an occasional songwriter, living comfortably on his past royalties and the handsome remuneration he would periodically earn from the studios for writing a few new songs. Henceforth, he focused his considerable energy and creative skill not so much on furthering his own craft but on gradually transforming himself into a Hollywood personality.

Hand in glove with this change of direction came a slow but inexorable decline in the quality and appeal of his work. He and Adamson turned out dozens of songs, for pictures like *Four Jills in a Jeep, Something for the Boys, The Princess and the Pirate, Nob Hill, Bring on the Girls, Doll Face,* and *Do You Love Me?,* but the creative spark that had ignited so successfully with "Comin' In on a Wing and a Prayer" and the score of *Higher and Higher* was seldom there. Furthermore, as the war came to an end, and television began to challenge cinema as the main form of popular entertainment, Hollywood looked for other, less costly products than full-length musical films. This meant that its composers, arrangers, and lyricists were asked to score shorter, B-movie projects, most of which failed to get the same initial marketing push as the big-budget pictures that had been made to keep audiences on the home front happy. A second Petrillo ban on recordings by AFM members also depressed the market for composers such as McHugh for almost all of 1948. Only a few of the individual songs that McHugh and Adamson produced between 1944 and 1948 have stood the test of time.

Of these, "How Blue the Night?" from *Four Jills and a Jeep,* a movie about a USO tour that played to troops in Britain and North Africa, was the earliest success. It was sung by Dick Haymes and elbowed its way past other songs in the film, including those performed by guest stars Alice Faye and Carmen

Miranda, to spend a number of weeks on the hit parade. McHugh then pro-duced "Chico Chico (from Puerto Rico)" as Miranda's featured song in the film *Doll Face*, but although he demonstrated yet again that he could produce a rumba that was more than mere pastiche, the piece lacked the naive charm of her previous McHugh hit, "South American Way." The star who emerged from this movie was Perry Como, whose film career McHugh and Adamson had launched the previous year (1944) with their rewrite for Twentieth Century-Fox of Cole Porter's score for *Something for the Boys*. In that picture, Como had sung one of their better ballads, "I Wish I Didn't Have to Say Goodnight," and in *Doll Face* he was featured on "Here Comes Heaven Again." He also sang with Martha Stewart on "Hubba-Hubba-Hubba (Dig You Later)" which made use of hipster slang in much the same way as Frank Loesser's lyrics to "Murder, He Says." Perhaps their best cinema song from the period was also one of their last, "It's a Most Unusual Day," from the 1948 movie *A Date with Judy*, which was written for Jane Powell.

This film was composed during one of McHugh's final contracts at MGM, after almost two decades of writing movie songs. Debbie Reynolds, whose own MGM contract started just a bit later, remembers McHugh returning for an individual project after she had joined the company in 1950. She said:

> When I was under contract to MGM he was independently hired to do the songs for a movie. It was the same thing with Sammy Cahn. They'd be hired to write on a particular movie. They weren't under contract at that time, just hired film by film. We had a lot to do with the music department where they worked. Most of us would go over there for rehearsal. Johnny Green was in charge of the music department at MGM, and on the staff were Roger Eden, the lyricist, composer Connie Salinger, and Andre Previn. They were all there all the time and had their own bungalows on the lot. It was a huge lot, and in the music area, everyone had their own territory. You'd also see all these famous actors, Esther Williams, Gene Kelly, Kathryn Grayson, Mario Lanza. They were all at MGM, plus, plus, plus. Even Greer Garson took singing lessons, so we'd see her in and out of the bungalows.
>
> We worked between there and the building where all the writers, directors, and producers were. We might have to go there for script meetings, but MGM was in two different sections, and the music was on the main lot, along with wardrobe and publicity, which was all handled on the lot. That's because we stars were there. We each had our own dressing rooms. So on a typical day, you might go from a singing lesson in one bungalow to wardrobe, to the main set, and back again, sometimes several times in a day.
>
> It wasn't competitive. When you arrived everyone wanted to know about the new kid on the block. It was as if you were a new baby and everyone

came along to take a look. We were, in the best sense, one big family. It was an extraordinary time.[38]

Yet it was a time that, for McHugh at least, was almost over. As the economic climate altered in the studios, to some extent forcing the pace of the transformation in McHugh's professional life that was already underway, an even bigger change occurred in his personal life. Julia McHugh, who had in her latter years lived with her son in his home at 631 North Sierra Drive, died on June 20, 1947, at age eighty-three. In the aftermath of her death, he sold the house and auctioned many of his possessions, including some choice items from his valuable art collection. The Gershwin piano survived, as did some of his particularly favorite mementoes, but now he started all over again on the domestic front. Deanna Durbin bought his former house, and—after a period in the Sunset Towers apartments—he moved to a new bachelor home not far away from his old one at 709 North Sierra Drive, where a large swimming pool in the backyard became every bit as important to his social life and entertaining as was the grand piano that lived on the ground floor of the building (the Gershwin upright was once more consigned to his private quarters).

He was now the senior member of the McHugh family, and he made efforts to maintain a strong relationship with his son and granddaughter. Jimmy McHugh Jr. was already divorced from Edna Cantor and had married the actress Shirley O'Hara, but they had then moved to London, where Jimmy Jr. ran the MCA office. A new grandchild, Jimmy McHugh III, was born at King's College Hospital in London on August 23, 1948, and from then onward, his father became known as Jimmy McHugh II. The family returned briefly to the United States in the spring of 1949, and a regular flow of letters and postcards from their travels kept McHugh in touch with his grandson's progress.

McHugh also began to develop a closer family bond with his nieces Judy and Dorothy, the daughters of his sister Helen, the only one of his siblings (apart from himself) to have had children. The younger niece, Judy Kashalena, recalled: "He was very devoted to my mother. My father left when I was six months old, so my Uncle Jimmy became like a father to me. He sent her a monthly check for twenty-seven years. He supported her all the way through and gave her enough to take care of her children."[39]

Her sister Dorothy agreed.

Jimmy took very good care of his own mother and brought her to California after my grandfather passed away. Then when she died, he became like a surrogate father to me. [When I was] a little girl he wanted me to take piano lessons, but I said, "We don't have a piano." We lived in a third floor walkup, but he made sure we had one, although they had to bring it in through the window. He was wonderful to our family. We didn't have much money, but he was always there and very interested. We thought he was the most wonderful man in the world, and he made a real difference to our lives, something which our own father wasn't able to provide.[40]

McHugh was not a very frequent visitor to Boston, particularly after his son moved to Los Angeles during his teens, but he returned to his hometown to visit with all of his extended family during the fall of 1948. He had also come to town for the tryouts of the stage show *As the Girls Go*, directed by Mike Todd and with music and lyrics by McHugh and Adamson. For its first night the usual welter of telegrams from family members was now joined by official congratulations from the Los Angeles Chamber of Commerce, from Sigmund Romberg on behalf of fellow composers, and from a mysterious girlfriend who called herself "Spider."

The show was written for Bobby Clark, a comedian whose name was connected to McHugh's earlier, as one of the stars of *Streets of Paris*. Clark's career went back to the early days of the talkies. He and his comic partner Paul McCullough started out with the Ringling Brothers Circus as tumblers and clowns before bringing their stage act to movies, notably in a series of shorts for RKO that featured the mustachioed, raccoon-coated McCullough playing straight man to Clark's manic invention. With spectacles painted on his face and a series of outlandish hats and costumes, Clark's spontaneous wit and comic innovation were such that the studios kept two cameras running the entire time he was on set, lest they missed any of his most inspired moments. He pioneered elaborate stunts, and complex sets were devised that allowed him to create highly original routines around McCullough's stolid, mystified bulk. But in 1936, after falling ill with depression, McCullough slashed his own throat in a barber's shop, killing himself and the duo's film partnership in one fell swoop.

Clark reinvented himself as a stage actor, returning to his roots as a live entertainer, and by 1948 he was capable of carrying an entire show with a brilliant mixture of prepared routines and ad-lib departures from the script. However, all did not quite go according to plan when *As the Girls Go* began its run of previews. McHugh remembered: "This show opened at the Boston Opera House, the scene of my first job. It was such a flop. I lost all my great thrill that I had with the thought of returning to this great theater, and I must say that I did not enjoy the limited time I spent there, other than on one Sunday when I sat at the piano in the pit and played in a very empty theater some melodies from Puccini."[41]

The local press reported on McHugh's return to his musical alma mater and his solo recital from the pit. Ever the hustler, he had invited one or two reporters to the "very empty" auditorium. Only a few pages after these clippings in his scrapbook, photographs show a wrecking ball finally demolishing the Opera House on Huntington Avenue, prior to the opening of its present-day successor on Washington Street.

The *Boston Herald*'s senior critic Elinor Hughes, by now no stranger to McHugh previews in the city, was direct about the shortcomings of the opening night of *As the Girls Go:* "There are quite a few laughs, but it is in this department that Mr. Todd and his cohorts are going to have some work to do. . . . The book of the show . . . is going to need some help."[42]

However, the gloom surrounding Bobby Clark's opening in Boston was, on this occasion, swiftly allayed by director Todd's adept pruning of the show and his decision to give the comic his head. "Upon our opening in New York," wrote McHugh, "the reviews were most fantastic."[43] Photographs show Clark doing a clever routine where he sits astride a girl's legs, giving the impression he is wearing fishnet stockings, until she sits upright and he falls sideways, giving the impression she is wearing male attire from the waist downward. There were other costumes, other hats, and other running gags, peppering a book by William Roos that rather presciently looked forward to an era when women held political power. The plot revolved around Lucille Wellington (played by Irene Rich), the nation's first female president. Clark played her husband, whose dim-wittedness ensured that however hard her political opponents tried to tempt him into impropriety with a succession of ever more scantily clad maidens, he remained scandal free, and she held on to office. One of the favorable notices ran: "It's a straight Broadway show, an old-fashioned Mike Todd evening—the girls as beautiful as he could get, the gags as broad as he could get away with. Taken by itself, it's altogether ordinary. But it does have pep and the sense to let the plot go hang; and, with massive assistance from one of the funniest fellows in show business, it proves a thoroughly cheerful evening."[44]

The music was not the most significant element of the press reviews, although Adamson and McHugh did manage to introduce two minor hits into their score, "You Say the Nicest Things, Baby" and "Nobody's Heart but Mine." In addition, their novelty number "I Got Lucky in the Rain" was staged in a setting that anticipated Gene Kelly's famous waterlogged routine in the movie *Singin' in the Rain* four years later. With the exception of a mid-50s hit from the otherwise disastrous *Strip for Action*, these were the last songs McHugh wrote specifically for Broadway that made an impression on the public at large. Their success was helped by the fact that despite the flop in Boston, New York theatergoers took the revised version of the show to heart, and it swiftly recovered its investment of over $340,000. This in itself was an achievement, given that the same season saw strong competition from Cole Porter's *Kiss Me Kate*, Frank Loesser's *Where's Charley?*, and Rodgers and Hammerstein's *South Pacific*.[45]

Although it has not enjoyed the subsequent fame of any of those shows, *As the Girls Go* ran for a healthy 414 performances until January 1950, except that there was a hiatus of a few weeks in the summer of 1949, when Clark was briefly taken ill and the play was unable to continue without his central performance. The songs themselves were the first McHugh–Adamson pieces to be issued by their own newly formed publishing company, McHugh, Adamson, and Blondell, which they started with Mike Todd's wife, Joan Blondell, as an affiliate of the Sam Fox Publishing firm, using its existing network of agents and pluggers.

In 1948, as this show was in preparation, McHugh celebrated his twenty-fifth anniversary as a "tunesmith," presumably taking "Out Where the Blue Begins" from 1923 as his starting point, although this seems to have been quite an arbitrary decision. However, it allowed McHugh to send out plenty of press releases and to solicit testimonials that no doubt helped his record and sheet-music sales considerably. In Los Angeles, Frankie Carle organized a Jimmy McHugh night at the Cocoanut Grove; the Fortnighters, sponsored by Jane Powell, put on a party at the Mocambo; and McHugh himself threw what was to be the first of many a poolside party for the Hollywood elite, a "cocktail swimming soirée," at his new home, hosted by columnist Harry Crocker.

As his lavish series of pool parties began with this event marking McHugh's quarter century as a hit songwriter, it was, somewhat ironically, almost the final curtain on that particular act in his life—but confirmation of his new role as a Hollywood personality.

"A Lovely Way to Spend an Evening"

THE GREAT YEARS
IN BEVERLY HILLS

JUST WHEN JIMMY McHUGH first met the columnist and broadcaster Louella Parsons is hard to pin down, but for a musician of his self-promoting talents, and a columnist with her appetite for a story, it is likely to have been soon after he first arrived in Hollywood. Over seventeen million people read Parsons's daily Hollywood column, which appeared in the *Los Angeles Examiner* and was reproduced in more than four hundred other papers throughout Randolph Hearst's worldwide publishing empire. She also had a substantial fan base among the listening public for her weekly radio show *Hollywood Hotel*, on which she interviewed stars and recommended movies. It was on the successor to this show, which was broadcast at 6:15 every Wednesday evening on the ABC network, that McHugh was first heard publicly with her in December 1945, plugging the songs from his current crop of movies.[1]

Until the emergence of Hedda Hopper, who was employed by Hearst's competitor, Luce Publications, and wrote for the *Los Angeles Times*, Parsons had wielded unparalleled and extraordinary power in Hollywood since the 1920s. Studios granted her exclusive stories, the biggest stars appeared for free on her radio show, and she was reputed to have negotiated a twenty-four-hour moratorium on the release of any news item from any studio in order to allow her to publish it first. Although throughout the 1940s Hopper became an ever more serious rival, Parsons nevertheless remained the senior journalist. She was known to check her stories with more care and was regarded by many stars and their agents to be the more responsible and trustworthy reporter, despite many anecdotes about her wayward spelling of actors' names and occasional infelicities of grammar, and more serious concerns about her propensity to take offense against certain individuals on account of slights real or imagined.

Having direct access to several heads of movie companies meant that she could ride roughshod over publicity directors and press agents, and according to her biographer, Samantha Barbas, Parsons was usually the first to publish anything that came out of Warner Brothers, Columbia, and Twentieth Century-Fox. As the 1940s went on, Paramount and MGM tended to favor Hopper, although Walter Selzer at MGM attempted to apply a strict policy of alternation in feeding news items to the two doyennes of Hollywood reporting.

Hopper was a somewhat exotic character who had once been an actress and favored glamorous gowns and eccentric headgear for her public appearances. By contrast the homely figure of Parsons, with her characteristic broad smile, was more down-to-earth, and her love affair with movies had not begun in front of the cameras but in the early days of silent films as a scriptwriter. In 1948, much as McHugh had done with his celebration of twenty-five years of songwriting, Parsons marked her quarter century as a columnist for the Hearst organization with a big testimonial party thrown in her honor at the Cocoanut Grove.

The timing of this event was about as spurious as McHugh's own, in that Parsons herself pointed out in her speech that it was actually her twenty-seventh year with Hearst. The press releases gave her age as fifty-five, although she was really sixty-six, but given that Hollywood never cared too much about the accuracy of a date when there was a party at stake, nobody seemed to mind, and after speeches from such luminaries as Sam Goldwyn, Louis B. Mayer, Darryl Zanuck, Jack Benny, Bob Hope, and Louella's husband, Dr. Harry Martin, the Broadway singer Betty Garrett premiered a new song written especially for the occasion by McHugh and Adamson. "Louella, Louella, Louella" is hardly their greatest work, but not least by wildly exaggerating the number of outlets for her column, it achieved a bull's eye in terms of perfectly directed flattery:

Louella, Louella, Louella,
Everyone loves you;
Louella, Louella, Louella,
And Dr. Martin, too. . . .
Press agents live for your column,
Everyone's hustling you,
Oh, how we love you, Louella,
And your nine hundred newspapers, too!

Randolph Hearst's son David presented her with a memorial plaque, and then newsboys ran through the room with a "special edition" of the *Examiner*, followed by a cabaret that featured Dinah Shore, Eddie Cantor, and a raft of other stars whose names were regularly featured in Parsons's column.[2]

The unqualified success that McHugh and Adamson's new song had with Parsons herself meant that in the months and years that followed, the name of Jimmy McHugh featured far more frequently and prominently in her column than it had done before.

In April 1949, however, the news that Parsons imparted to her readers about McHugh came as something of a surprise to most of Hollywood. Ever since the 1945 Aquacade, McHugh had become more and more involved in the world of competitive swimming, and by the end of the decade he was regularly promoting several events a year in Los Angeles. Now, however, his involvement in the world of swimming suddenly got a little more personal, and it came to a head when the Associated Press sent out a news flash that "Songwriter, 54, plans to wed swim star, 17."[3]

It was Louella Parsons who got the exclusive interview with McHugh about his would-be bride, Anita Lhoest. "Composer Jimmy McHugh . . . is vocalising one of his own songs, 'You Say the Nicest Things, Baby,' these spring evenings. Object of Jimmy's serenading is statuesque, blonde and beautiful Anita Lhoest, United States swimming champion of the Olympics 300 meters womens event. The composer has confided to his close friends that he and Anita will be married this summer."[4] Photographed at poolside in her white swimsuit, and with her blond tresses pinned up as she sat demurely in a high-necked dress next to McHugh at the keyboard, Lhoest was the daughter of a Hollywood socialite couple, Mr. and Mrs. Fermand Lhoest. In addition to her 300-meter success, she also held "the senior 100 yard individual medley swim record" and was described as "an accomplished cellist." McHugh himself, in contrast to his tightlipped behavior regarding Feliza Pablos, confided "enthusiastically" to Louella Parsons that Lhoest was "just my type."

By the spring of 1949, McHugh had finally broken up for the last time with Feliza Vanderbilt (as she now called herself), who was being squired around Hollywood by Sonny Chalif. However, the erstwhile sweethearts still attended many of the same events, and the guest lists that were printed in the local papers frequently included, along with Vanderbilt and Chalif, the names of Mr. and Mrs. Harold Adamson, Mr. Jimmy McHugh, and Miss A. Lhoest. Later in the year, just as had happened with Lhoest's earlier engagement to Robert O. Lynch, a wartime navy veteran who was a mature student at Los Angeles City College, her attachment to McHugh gently fizzled out. Furthermore, although McHugh was now legally free to remarry, it seems that his Catholic scruples still prevented him from taking the final steps back to the altar. Nevertheless, Louella Parsons was grateful to McHugh for the scoop, and when he needed some press help for his biggest swimming event since the wartime aquacade, his contacts with her helped him get first-rate coverage from the *Examiner*'s sports columnist, Vincent X. Flaherty.

In August 1949, McHugh expected to stage the National AAU Men's Swimming and Diving Championships at the Los Angeles Olympic Swimming Stadium. McHugh's influential show business contacts meant that since the days of Owney Madden and the Harlem hoodlums, he had seldom had much trouble with unions or the closed-shop agreements that dogged much of the entertainment industry, but the sporting world was a different matter. The combination of local government bureaucracy and unionism that prevailed at the Los Angeles stadium threatened to kill McHugh's event before it got off the ground.

McHugh decided to tough it out, taking the view that the loss of face for the city of Los Angeles in allowing the meet to collapse—after he had personally intervened with President Truman to persuade a military aircraft to fly in as special guests the Japanese national swimming team (making their first appearance on American soil since the end of the war)—would eventually win the day. But he needed help, and his old talents as a master of publicity and spin, plus Louella's new contacts, came to his aid.

Flaherty brilliantly expounded on McHugh's track record as the "man who has done more for swimming in Southern California than any other individual" and cited many of the events that McHugh had sponsored out of his own pocket. Then, in meticulous detail he listed the dozens of costs and charges imposed by the stadium that were threatening to undermine the economic viability of the meet. Explaining that 10 percent of the takings went to the stadium for rent, Flaherty said McHugh "didn't wince at that," but then he went on to itemize the "extra" costs that were being sought: "fence removal, $250; bleachers, $500; electrical installation $150; electrical labor $357; clean up $250; locker attendants $60; life guards $85; direction and management, $35; extra chairs $520; towels, $45; watchmen, $21."

Flaherty pointed out that McHugh normally met such peripheral costs himself, but on this occasion he was being denied the catering franchise but nevertheless was expected to pay for clearing up after it; in addition, McHugh was being charged for jobs that would be done anyway if the building were open, as well as for installations such as electrical equipment and bleachers that were already in place.

The result of this exposé in the city's most widely syndicated newspaper was twofold: first, the stadium authorities rapidly reduced their list of fees to a single cost of less than $1,000, including stadium hire; and second, McHugh was given a special award by Paul Helms, founder of one of the country's largest athletic foundations, for "making Los Angeles the swim center of the United States."[5]

Prior to the meet, McHugh was photographed selling tickets for the first block of reserved seating to actress Rhonda Fleming, the star of that year's big movie musical, *A Connecticut Yankee at King Arthur's Court*, and he also hired two hundred billboards across the city to advertise the event. It was, naturally, a great success, featuring not only the United States amateur team but men from Mexico and Canada, plus the Japanese, whose outstanding performer Hironoshia Furuhashi was nicknamed the "flying fish of Fujiyami." McHugh recalled: "The Japanese boys broke every American and World's record, and established new ones. The stadium was absolutely packed all three nights, and we were forced to turn away thousands of people. It was one of the most exciting and thrilling meets ever held."[6]

From the end of the war onward, McHugh had donated the financial surpluses made at his swimming events to a youth center that he had founded in Beverly Hills to provide a meeting place for the young. However, after negative comments made to him by some of the young men and women who ran the canteen at the center, McHugh decided to withdraw his interest in it and to begin what was to become the main thrust of his charity work for the two decades that followed, namely, acquiring hospital respirators for child polio patients. Although he began work on the fundraising immediately after the 1949 swimming meet, it took two years, almost to the day, for the fruits of his efforts to be seen. He later wrote:

The first respirator that I donated to the County Hospital, I did in memory of my mother. This was a special iron lung which was invented by Dr. Al-bert C. Bower, Head of the Communicable Diseases section of the County Hospital, and it took two years to complete. He learned through experience that by putting a youngster in an adult machine 89% of their lives were lost, due to the fact that a child respirates 50 times per minute, whereas an adult [breathes] only 25 times. So, with long hours and hard work, he invented this miracle machine which can save up to 89% of the children's lives. The first one cost me $5,000. . . . With the presentation of the first respirator, I formed the Jimmy McHugh Polio Foundation Inc., gathered several of the important women in town, and have formed a very excellent committee. We have staged various affairs, and the proceeds go for the purchase of more of these iron lungs.[7]

The presentation of the first respirator was marked by a party at the Vaga-bond's House attended by numerous swimming stars, at which McHugh announced his foundation's work, saying, "They tell me the hospital needs at least six more, urgently." Interestingly, McHugh was now being described in the papers as "sportsman-songwriter."[8]

By August 1951, when the iron lungs were presented, it might have been more accurate to describe McHugh as "songwriter-pianist." Over the previous year, he had increasingly turned himself into a performer, albeit one who lived at what *Examiner* columnist Flaherty referred to as "a swimming pool surrounded by a house," where an increasing number of international sporting stars from all disciplines could be found alongside big names from the musical and movie worlds at the regular poolside parties.[9] In late November 1950, McHugh threw a party at his home for orchestral conductor Frank DeVol, who had made a Capitol album of symphonic arrangements of his songs, and he accompanied Jeanne McLaren himself as she sang selections from the disc. Two weeks later he appeared with singer Jane Wyman—with whom he was frequently seen around town—at the Shrine Auditorium, on a bill that also included the Andrews Sisters, Donald O'Connor, Red Skelton, and Ann Sheridan, for the *Examiner* Christmas benefit. A few days after that, at a benefit for Marine veterans of the Korean conflict, he premiered new verses that he and Harold Adamson had written for the "Marines' Hymn."

In the first weeks of January 1951, McHugh was filmed at the keyboard for Louis Sanders's Telescriptions, in a program called *Jimmy McHugh's Song Shop*. He played his old hits, including "On the Sunny Side of the Street" and "Exactly like You," with Harry Zimmerman's Orchestra, plus a selection of singers including Carol Richards, Gloria Stewart, Jeanne McLaren, and Joy Lane.[10]

He had appeared as a performing musician very infrequently since the days of the Hotsy Totsy Boys back in the Roaring Twenties (apart from an occasional duet with Dorothy Fields), but as 1950 turned into 1951, McHugh managed more public performances in the space of a month than he had in the previous twenty-five years. No sooner was the excitement of the filming over than Louella Parsons announced that McHugh and Adamson would set off on a twenty-thousand-mile goodwill tour of Mexico and Central and South America, "getting ideas for Matty Kemp's *Pan-American Way* musical."[11] Before the songwriting team left town, apparently to work on half a dozen songs for this movie that was to be shot on location but appears never to have been made, there was another widely reported poolside party at McHugh's home that featured not only his own playing but the up-and-coming group the Four Freshmen, jamming alongside pianists Buddy Cole and Les Baxter with Dottie O'Brien singing.

Clearly McHugh was repositioning himself as a performing artist, as a way to exploit his back catalog. With movie songwriting work increasingly hard to come by, he was aiming to consolidate the celebrity status that his swim meets and charity activities had helped him achieve, by becoming a musical star in his own right. In late 1950 he had also been elected chairman of the Beverly Hills Chamber of Commerce, and this led to an extraordinary variety of photo opportunities, of which McHugh took full advantage. In 1951 he was pictured doing everything from making awards to tennis stars to taking a trial ride in the new observation car on the Santa Fe Chief. His role as chairman put him in a very privileged position in what was, as Associated Press entertainment writer Jim Bacon described, already a very privileged part of town: "Beverly Hills has always had an image of being a very rich community, which it is. And half a century ago, it was very much the same as it is today, with the best shops and the best restaurants. All the area's leading citizens lived there, especially the movie crowd. It was the country club set of the Los Angeles area."[12]

Toward the end of 1951, McHugh was able to combine his charitable work and his new persona as a performer in spectacular fashion. Through the contacts of his chamber of commerce colleague, real-estate agent John Haskell, he became one of a select group of Hollywood entertainers invited to take part in a Royal Command Performance in London during the conclusion of the Festival of Britain year.

Although this evening was nominally under the patronage of King George VI and Queen Elizabeth, it was in fact the first full-scale charitable event to be organized by Philip, Duke of Edinburgh, the husband of Princess Elizabeth, heir to the throne. Consequently, the young royals were to stand in for the King and Queen at the "Midnight Matinee" concert that was expected to raise $70,000. The show was to be staged on December 10 in the vast auditorium of the London Coliseum on St. Martin's Lane (later the home of the English National Opera), and Frank Sinatra, Dorothy Kirsten, Tony Curtis, Rhonda Fleming, Janet Leigh, Orson Welles, Noël Coward, and a host of other stars were scheduled to take part. The idea was to raise funds for the National Playing Fields Association, a pet charity of both the Duke and the Variety Club of Great Britain, and one which was very much in keeping with the Festival of Britain theme of rebuilding a country shattered by war. The U.S. press reported: "Because of the community called Hollywood, and one of its citizens named John Haskell, British kids for many generations to come will have playing fields—American style—they never would have had otherwise. The fields will be constructed on some of the still bare spots leveled by Nazi bombers during the time when England, and especially the people of London, won the respect even of Anglophobes by taking it uncomplainingly on the chin."[13]

Although the British climate in December is not particularly welcoming, especially to those used to the warmth of Hollywood, McHugh was struck on his return to England after twenty-four years by "the pageantry, the pomp, the sheer majesty of London during one of her great festivals." Although he would receive no fee for the concert, all expenses were taken care of, and on his arrival, in common with all the other stars who were to appear, he was "assigned a Rolls Royce and chauffeur, which remained at our disposal throughout our stay. Each car was equipped with warm blankets—a major point of luxury in heatless England."[14]

Safely checked in at his hotel, McHugh mused that in contrast to his first visit, when he had been dashing about the city's nightspots plugging songs to earn his living, he was now required to keep a number of volatile artistic temperaments in line for his twenty-five-minute segment of the show. Elsewhere on the program, to be hosted by the British comedian Tommy Trinder, Orson Welles was to do a recitation, Coward was to sing a selection of his own songs, and the Sadler's Wells Ballet would dance a short classical selection by William Walton, just before McHugh was to present several of the visiting Hollywood names in a medley of his compositions. These would be sung to a full orchestra and backed on stage by fifty Tiller girls, high-kicking their legs while twirling their top hats and canes in perfect synchronization. "As the day of the performance approached, our nerves tightened. To make matters worse, around six o'clock Monday afternoon, the Sinatras decided that Ava [Gardner]'s jewels had been stolen. As a result we were surrounded by nothing but Scotland Yard men, an unnerving distraction to the problem of shaping a show of too many acts into too little time."[15]

As it was originally planned, McHugh's act had three main elements. Janet Leigh would perform "When My Sugar Walks Down the Street" and "On the Sunny Side of the Street," Rhonda Fleming would sing "I Can't Give You Anything but Love, Baby" and "Comin' In on a Wing and a Prayer," and Sinatra would perform "I Couldn't Sleep a Wink Last Night."

McHugh worked hard on coaching the two actresses, neither of whom had sung regularly on stage before—Fleming complained at one point that all they were doing was "plugging Jimmy McHugh," which was not too far from the truth—and amending the arrangements to give them the best possible support. But Sinatra was a different problem entirely. He and Ava Gardner had been married just over a month before, on November 7, but their marriage, like their preceding affair, was a clash of titanic and volatile temperaments, fueled in Sinatra's case by the fact he was nearing the end of his Columbia recording contract and his movie career was in the doldrums, whereas his new wife was enjoying considerable critical and commercial success. His tempers and tantrums of the period became legendary.[16] McHugh remembered: "Frank had arrived from Paris in one of his difficult moods. During the rehearsal he sat with his feet dangling over the footlights, talking to the band while they ran through 'I Couldn't Sleep a Wink Last Night,' which Frank had introduced on film. But when the musicians were through playing it, Frank enquired, 'What was that, boys?' In the end he dismissed the orchestra and sang 'Soliloquy,' with Jimmy Van Heusen accompanying him at the piano."[17] As a result, Sinatra, singing a song by Rodgers and Hammerstein and accompanied by yet another prominent songwriter, was lifted out of the McHugh section of the show and fitted into the program as a stand-alone act.

To help Fleming relax after her strenuous rehearsal, and in an attempt to give her a treat to remember, McHugh took her on a sightseeing trip to the top of the tower of London's major Roman Catholic church, Westminster Cathedral. Despite the mist and general gloom of a December afternoon, the wintry sun cast a romantic glow over the Houses of Parliament, Westminster Bridge, and the sweeping curve of the Thames, and Fleming was charmed by the sight. It was unfortunate that the elevator attendant was slightly deaf and did not hear their frantic signals for him to return. When he finally showed up as the sun went down, Fleming was not only as fraught as she had been at rehearsal but chilled to the bone and no longer on speaking terms with McHugh.

At the Duke of Edinburgh's reception for the visitors at the Embassy Club that evening, the night before the Command Performance, McHugh spotted a familiar figure in the crowd. It was Adelaide Hall, wearing a brilliantly colored red satin dress. At that time she was appearing as Hattie, singing the show-stopping "Another Op'nin, Another Show" in the West End run of Cole Porter's *Kiss Me Kate*.[18] McHugh immediately cajoled her into singing with him at the piano, and she performed "I Can't Give You Anything but Love, Baby," which she had introduced to London in *Blackbirds of 1928*, and "Diga Diga Doo." After introducing her to the Duke, McHugh talked her into repeating the performance at the Command show, which she duly did.

By McHugh's own account, the show itself passed in something of a blur. Noël Coward—who shared the dressing room—expressed admiration for McHugh's satin cuffs, a feature of his Hollywood tuxedo, and mentioned in his clipped tones that he would have to order some for himself. By contrast, McHugh was not prompted to follow Coward's example in covering himself with pancake make-up before going on stage.

The royal protocol of not applauding before the Princess and the Duke started to clap made for a slightly chilly start to the show, but after Trinder and the Weire Brothers had gone down well, McHugh's section began, with Adelaide Hall winning over the crowd as effectively as she had in the 1920s, Janet Leigh (reappearing after a cowboy sketch in which she had starred with Tony Curtis) singing and dancing along with the Tiller Girls, and finally Rhonda Fleming performing "Comin' In on a Wing and a Prayer." McHugh recalled: "There was a moment of dead silence, then the house simply came down. It was as though God had opened up the heavens and let loose a volley of celestial praise. . . . Rhonda took bows for a full minute. Then I joined her. The continuing thunder of the applause was the sweetest music I ever heard."[19] At the end of the show, Princess Elizabeth moved down the line of performers, finding a word or two to say to each of them as they were formally introduced. When McHugh bowed to her, she told him, "Mr. McHugh, not only do I love your songs, but I sing them as well."

The next day, the principal performers, McHugh among them, left for Germany to play a series of concerts at U.S. bases, as morale-boosting events for the troops who had been stationed there after the war. Everyone in the party was shocked at the widespread evidence of destruction caused by the Allied bombing of Germany. In McHugh's case this was not helped by the heavy cold that he had caught after his drafty trip up the cathedral tower. In an effort to shake off the fever, he went to the public baths in Wiesbaden. After five minutes soaking in the warm mineral waters, the attendant instructed McHugh to pull on a ring in the wall. Instantly he was deluged with freezing water, beginning a chill that was ultimately to turn to pneumonia and a spell in the hospital after his return to the United States.

His health was not helped by the decision to travel to Paris for a few days after the shows had finished. The only transport available at short notice was a troop train, and McHugh undertook the journey squeezed into a carriage full of soldiers, with standing room only. Maybe this explains why he momentarily lost his judgment and once again ended up featured in Louella Parsons's column: "From Paris," she wrote, "comes a cable from Jimmy McHugh announcing his engagement to Polly Aaron. She's an American girl living in Paris."[20]

Despite his fever, it appears he met this young New Englander, who was visiting mutual friends, soon after his arrival in Paris He proceeded to show her the sights. "Every evening we ended up at Maxim's, where I played the piano until my fingers were numb," he recalled.[21] They were given a table by the dance floor to watch Perry Como's cabaret. The rumors spread when they were photographed together there, but according to McHugh, when Louella Parsons contacted him, his cable denied, rather than confirmed, a forthcoming engagement.

For Christmas, having disentangled himself from this "fiancée," he went to Rome to stay with Mary Pickford's niece Gwen Ornstein and her husband Doug, the Italian representative for Universal Pictures. The couple lived in some style. Once again, McHugh's habit of playing the piano late at night and surrounding himself with female company led to yet more rumors of an "engagement," this time to a young Swedish woman, but this relationship did not make it into the Parsons column.

He rounded off his visit with an audience with Pope Pius XII. In the tranquility of the preceding confessional, he was able to begin to sort out the complexities of his love life and convince himself that for the time being, at least, he would remain single, since, strictly speaking, in the church's eyes he was still married to Bess. He wrote: "Confession is a rigorous experience. The priest delved into my life like a surgeon probing with forceps without anesthetic. In many ways it was as painful."[22]

McHugh had first encountered Pius XII before his election to the Holy See, when as Cardinal Eugenio Pacelli he was the diplomatic envoy of the Vatican to New York in 1936. The pontiff remembered that visit well, and after they shared reminiscences he told McHugh, "I bless you and your work." Obviously not one to be drawn into the political controversy surrounding Pius XII and what have (in many quarters) been seen as actions of appeasement before and during the war, McHugh wrote admiringly: "My little problems and conflicts melted away in the presence of the serene being in whose eyes and face were written the knowledge of all suffering."[23]

Back in Beverly Hills, McHugh took some time to get over his illness, but by the late spring of 1952, he had returned to action. He was once more furthering his plans to become a performer, an enterprise which would culminate at the end of the year in a residency at Ciro's nightclub, playing his songs at the piano for "five luscious dolls who sing as well as they look."[24]

Before that, however, his personal life was to undergo a major change, as he acquired the social companion who would be his consort at openings, parties, dinners, and nightclubs for the rest of his life: Louella Parsons. Since her twenty-fifth anniversary testimonial featuring the song he had written for her, they had been good friends, but in 1951–52 events conspired to bring them closer.

In June 1951, Parsons's husband, Dr. Harry Martin, a consultant urologist who had specialized for many years in treating venereal disease in the Hollywood community, died from leukemia. Parsons was devastated, and this plus the subsequent death of her mentor, Randolph Hearst, had temporarily driven her to drink. She somehow maintained her working regime and filed the columns written at her home on Maple Drive, where stars visited and where she watched movie previews with her own specially installed projector. Like McHugh, she believed in hard work as the way out of a problem, and like him she was—despite being born into a Jewish family—an ardent Roman Catholic, to the extent that one of her most prized possessions became an illuminated statue of the Virgin Mary that McHugh gave to her for her back garden. As he sympathized with her over the loss of her husband—a fellow Irish-American, once described by Parsons as "the most Irish face" she had ever seen[25]—he realized that by offering her companionship he would also have constant and immediate access to her publicity machine, and because he was concurrently reinventing himself as a performing musician, this ought to prove invaluable. So, for some months after his audience with the Pope and his subsequent illness, there were no further rumors of new engagements. None, that is, until his relationship with Parsons herself began to fill other writers' gossip columns.

Despite his highly active social life, McHugh had been practically teetotal ever since the 1920s debauchery with Al Dubin. When he and Parsons began to be seen regularly about town together in the summer of 1952, one of his personal missions was to limit her alcohol intake, and with typical McHugh devotion, he applied himself to the task. Debbie Reynolds, who was under contract to MGM and at the time making what was to be one of her most successful movies, *Singin' in the Rain*, remembers his diligence: "Jimmy took her everywhere. I got along with them both very well. But Jimmy didn't like her to drink. He thought she ought to drink just plain water, so he was always relieved to see me, because I used to fix her a 'glass of water.' In fact, I used to give her straight vodka over ice, but he never found out and she was very happy. As far as he was concerned, she didn't get to drink when they were together!"[26]

This aspect of their relationship did not go unnoticed in the press, and the *Rambling Reporter* column jumped to the natural conclusion: "Jimmy tastes Louella's cocktails first to see they're just right. It's LOVE!"[27] Within weeks, this harmless mention had fanned the flames of rumor into yet another McHugh engagement: "Hollywood lowdown is that Louella Parsons will wed Jimmy McHugh as soon as her period of mourning is over. His dating a starlet is just a blind. . . ."[28]

Parsons was not amused, despite one report suggesting she became "all flustered and schoolgirlish" when the romance was mentioned, and she took pains to ensure that further marriage rumors were strangled at birth, including insisting to Walter Winchell that he amend one of his columns at the last moment to remove such a reference.[29] As time passed, Hollywood got used to the idea that Parsons and McHugh functioned in public as a platonic couple, having in effect a nonmarriage of convenience, although many observers believed that Parsons was more than fond of him, even if her feelings were not reciprocated. Indeed, McHugh conveniently allowed his religious scruples concerning marriage for life to stand in the way of getting more involved with a fellow Catholic, despite the fact that Bess had legally divorced him. Columnist Jim Bacon of the Associated Press, who attended the same round of social events, recalled: "Louella was madly in love with Jimmy. She used to say to me, 'I'd marry that man in a minute, but he's got a wife. I just love that man!' But Jimmy was not about to go marrying some old bag like Louella."[30]

Others who were close to them speculated further. For example, the "ice-blond bombshell" Mamie Van Doren, whose career McHugh took in hand after hearing her sing with Ted Fiorito's Orchestra in Las Vegas, wrote many years later: "Did they do any more than show up at parties and premiers [*sic*]? Did they fuck? Thinking back on Jimmy's bald head and Louella's pinched face and raptor eyes, it's a frightening thought."[31]

McHugh would have been outraged by such a suggestion from his protégée, not least because of his continuing penchant for forming attachments to much younger women. Despite what their respective press agents told the public about their ages, when they started appearing around Hollywood together he was fifty-nine, and Parsons was a carefully preserved seventy-one. His stage act featured him accompanying a selection of young female singers, and as a working musician he wished still to be seen regularly in such company in the press. As Debbie Reynolds said: "He was usually with Louella, but he escorted a lot of single ladies. He seemed to me to be 'single' at the time—I don't know about his wife—but he certainly chaperoned a lot of ladies. He seemed to chaperone them all."[32]

McHugh was precise about how his relationship with Parsons should go down for posterity. In his own draft memoir he wrote: "On my piano is a picture of a woman. It bears the inscription: 'To dear Jimmy, whose thoughtfulness, gaiety and companionship has helped so much. Love, Louella.' There are many people in Hollywood, and I suppose elsewhere, who can't grasp the meaning of friendship. To them, it is inconceivable that a man and a woman can enjoy a mutually beautiful companionship, in the full meaning of that word, without sex creeping into the picture."[33]

Others who knew both of them well saw the relationship not so much as a matter of mutual companionship but as entirely expedient. For McHugh it offered a convenient passport to every major Hollywood social event amid boundless free publicity, and for Parsons it provided an enthusiastic, reliable escort who was something of a star in his own right. Certainly that was the view of *Daily Variety*'s Army Archerd, who used to call McHugh "Mister First-Nighter," because, he recalled: "Louella was always there, and so was he, escorting her. He was ageless and looked the same for years and years. Often he would play when he and Louella were guests somewhere." Despite McHugh's lifelong habit of playing his own songs wherever he appeared, Archerd did not see these "spontaneous" invitations to play as shameless self-promotion. "I don't think this was a question of him plugging his songs, because in some ways Hollywood people took advantage of him. If he played at their event, they had a *star* present."[34]

On the other hand, Jim Bacon felt that McHugh's commercial instincts were too strong for him to suppress: "Jimmy was always plugging his songs. I've never known a songwriter plug more than Jimmy. Every time we went to a party, Jimmy always played, and naturally, he played his own music. Of course the other songwriters did it, too, people like Jimmy Van Heusen and Sammy Cahn, but Jimmy was always out playing his songs. But it's true he was a star, and furthermore, he knew every star in town, and they knew him."[35]

By the end of 1952, McHugh and Parsons had slipped into a partnership that remained constant for most of the next sixteen years. Her rival, Hedda Hopper, pointed out that in 1952 alone, the Parsons column had mentioned him twenty times; this was to be the pattern for the future, with Parsons slipping in mentions of McHugh whenever she could—for example, when Tony Martin opened at the Cocoanut Grove: "Tony called on Jimmy McHugh to come to the piano while he sang several McHugh tunes"; or when a television company decided to make a McHugh special: "A very nice New Year's gift for Jimmy McHugh is Hal Roach's deal with him to put all the McHugh songs into a TV cavalcade."[36] Early in their partnership, Parsons took over the place formerly occupied by McHugh's mother at the Sunday brunches at the Beverly Hills Hotel, although now there was a telephone installed in their booth in the Polo Lounge, and Louella was able to call in her last-minute copy before the two o'clock deadline for the early evening paper.[37]

From mid-1952, when he had been working on the idea of writing inspirational songs for the U.S. Army, until about halfway through 1955, McHugh broke the pattern of the previous thirty years and allowed songwriting to take second place to his other activities. As well as continuing his swimming promotions, charitable work, and promoting the chamber of commerce in Beverly Hills, his main professional energies went into his stage act with his "Singing Starlets" and into finding and independently promoting the careers of young singers or actresses. For some of these performers he was an agent or manager, as he became for Mamie Van Doren; for others he was more of an adviser, urging the teenage heartthrob Tommy Sands to record a selection of McHugh songs, helping to produce discs by the three Paris Sisters, or throwing an elaborate poolside party at his home to introduce the teenage-opera-singer-turned-actress Anna Maria Alberghetti to Hollywood. For the latter event, the young singer was photographed sitting on one of McHugh's knees, while Natalie Wood adorned the other.[38]

One singing group he took to his heart was the four Ames Brothers, and although he never had any formal role in their management, he was consistently supportive, as the most famous of the brothers, Ed Ames, recalls:

> When he found out we were from Boston, he took us under his wing. He became "Uncle Jimmy" to us, and he was so kind. He let us hang around his house and swim in his pool, like we were his favorite nephews. So naturally, we never made an album that didn't have a couple of Jimmy McHugh songs on it. He would take us around town with Louella to show us off and get us up to sing. Because Louella knew how fond he was of us, we were always in her column. We could never have paid for that kind of publicity, and it went on for a long time.[39]

In general, Parsons was very supportive of McHugh's young charges and took every opportunity to mention them in her column, but the platinum blonde Marilyn Monroe–look-alike Mamie Van Doren, described by Parsons's rivals as "the glamour find of the decade,"[40] received very much the opposite treatment when Parsons became convinced that McHugh was taking more than professional interest in her. As it turned out, this was not the case, and Van Doren confirms that McHugh never made any romantic advances to her. Nevertheless, many of his efforts on Van Doren's behalf were thwarted by Parsons. He enrolled his protégée in Ben Bard's Hollywood acting school, and Parsons exerted her influence behind the scenes to have her expelled. He got her a screen test at Paramount, which she passed, only to have Parsons make some phone calls to the head of the studio to ensure that Van Doren would not be taken on.

When Van Doren found out what had happened, she understandably became angry at McHugh for not standing up for her, but she finally got her chance when he enrolled her in another acting school, the Bliss-Hayden Theater, where Paramount's Phil Benjamin saw her in a play by William Inge and cast her as a singer in the Tony Curtis movie *Forbidden*. Van Doren passed her screen test on a Friday and was on the set to shoot her scene on the following Monday. Within a day or two, Universal opened negotiations with McHugh and signed Van Doren to a seven-year contract with two-year options, under which her next picture was billed to be *Stand at Apache River*. Parsons was out of town that week, and when she returned, Van Doren's contract was a done deal. The young actress and singer went on to make a number of movies, all of them promoted in similar breathless style to the feature *Black Stockings:* "Mamie Van Doren stirs up more electricity at U-I than all the studio generators put together."[41]

In many ways, McHugh's own act, initially with a bevy of five young girls singing his songs but later with just two singers, was simply an extension of his managerial ambitions. The first group, with which he opened at Ciro's, featured Eve Marley, who, after a much publicized affair with the Hollywood bandleader Matty Malneck, to whom she was allegedly "closer than bread and butter," went on to marry Billy Fox. The later groups were built around the former *Our Gang* child star Darla Hood, billed as "a vivacious personality-type singer," and the "coloratura soprano Judy Collins."[42] What started out as a single short-term engagement in a Hollywood nightclub soon became something of a way of life for McHugh. He played house parties for movie stars, including Bing Crosby, who wrote: "One of the nicest things that happened to me at Christmastide was your acceptance of my invitation to you to bring your show out to the house to entertain the boys and their fraternity friends, during Christmas week. . . . I sent the girls each a little bottle of perfume in lieu of cash. I thought possibly they'd like this although money is nice, too."[43]

Undoubtedly, since his show had begun as something of a personal indulgence, McHugh also compensated his singers out of his own pocket when they performed the homes of the biggest stars in town, but for the most part, the act was a thoroughly professional endeavor. He played for Beverly Hills clubs and associations and at his own poolside parties, but above all he liked playing in nightclubs. In December 1954 he was resident at the Copa Room at the Sands, Las Vegas, opposite Danny Thomas, before returning for a series of holiday engagements in and around Los Angeles; then, when entertainer Charlie Morrison was unexpectedly taken ill in late January, McHugh brought his show at short notice into the Mocambo nightclub in Hollywood. A few weeks into the new year, he was off again to play for a club audience in Washington, D.C. Wherever he and the Starlets went, the effect was the same. "The young ladies took turns in a continuous *pot-pourri* of McHugh songs. The first medley included 'I'm in the Mood for Love,' ending on 'Comin' In on a Wing and a Prayer.' Hearty applause interspersed the singing as the audience recognized the various songs."[44]

However, even though McHugh had composed at the piano for years and would happily hop onto the stage in the clubs he visited to perform a medley of his favorite tunes, his new nightly task of playing from his "bellows of a score, specially arranged for the girls," took its toll. Today we would diagnose his condition as repetitive strain injury, or R.S.I. The following summer, his act was forced into abeyance when he was hospitalized for "restorative surgery" on his right hand.[45] Nevertheless, becoming a nightclub entertainer in his own right worked to his advantage: before his surgery he was invited to appear in a number of television episodes and later in several movies in which he played himself, including *A Star Is Born* and *The Great Al Jolson*. When he had recovered from surgery, he appeared—again as himself—in *The Helen Morgan Story*, with Ann Blyth (dubbed on the soundtrack by Gogi Grant) in the role of the actress who had starred in the Ziegfeld *Midnite Frolic* and whom he had befriended during his 1927 trip to London.

Despite the success of his starlets, McHugh's illness brought home to him that he was fortunate not to have to rely on live appearances to make a living. The early 1950s had seen a big revival of interest in his older songs, with many of them soon among the most-played tunes on radio and used in the soundtracks to movies of all kinds. However, the McHugh revival stirred up controversy when jazz saxophonist James Moody released a disc called "Moody's Mood for Love," an instrumental improvisation on the melody and chords of "I'm in the Mood for Love." Actually recorded in Europe at the end of the 1940s, the disc was released by Prestige on Moody's return to America in the early 1950s and became a hit. Unfortunately, McHugh and Fields were not credited on the label, and so *Down Beat* sent reporter Hal Holly to meet "the veteran songwriter . . . who is relaxing comfortably on his royalties and amassing a collection of great modern paintings." Holly pointed out the omission, and "the ordinarily genial Jimmy became downright grim. 'That kind of thing,' he stated, 'is simply disgusting.'"[46]

McHugh's publishers took action to assert his rights and to win a royalty settlement, but McHugh—who had always been close to the jazz community—voiced his concerns about "jazz solos where the casual listener might not be able to recognize the original melody and chord structure on which the improvisation is based"; and when he heard a recording of the song by King Pleasure that departed even further from the original, he "just sat back . . . in shocked amazement." He was outraged that Fields's carefully crafted lyrics had been altered, just as his melody line had been. But once the legal dust had settled, McHugh was able to collect his usual fees and was, perhaps, less troubled by the liberties taken with his work.

He was certainly far from troubled by the decision of the producers of the 1954 blockbuster movie *The Caine Mutiny* to use "I Can't Believe That You're in Love with Me" as a featured song on the soundtrack, which was the most high-profile appearance of one of his earlier tunes. As the decade went on, more McHugh numbers popped up in pictures such as *So This Is Paris?*, *The Benny Goodman Story*, *Never Say Goodbye*, and *The Naked and the Dead.*

Maybe buoyed by the publicity that these songs had created, McHugh unexpectedly announced in the summer of 1955 that he and Harold Adamson would be reuniting to write the score for a Broadway musical called *Strip for Action*. The plot was a flimsy one, adapted from a successful wartime revue by Howard Lindsay and Russel Crouse, that looked at the backstage life of a burlesque troupe. Maybe if its backers, Howard Hoyt and Igor Cassini, had read the reviews of the 1942 run of the original stage play they would have thought twice about whether what had been a successful morale booster during the war could be as effective in peacetime. *Time* had observed that it was "a ramshackle play . . . a plot too complicated to explain and too silly to bother about. . . . The show is built like a house of cards but somehow stays up."[47] Rumors first surfaced about the new musical version of the show in August, and it finally began previews in New Haven the following March.

For those in it, the show was a memorable experience. Hoofer Don Emmons was in the cast and recalled: "I loved it. It had a fine score by Jimmy McHugh, elaborate costumes, good choreography by Jimmy Starbuck, funny burlesque sketches, and beautiful girls. Of course, I loved it!" The idea was to see how titillating the show could be, within the bounds of acceptability, and some of its sketches came close to a complete striptease. Emmons continued:

> There was a number called "Monkey on My Back." Showgirls paraded around in flesh colored tights, which made them look nude except for the Ziegfeld-type showgirl hats and the monkeys built into their costumes on their back. The idea was quite clever and the costumes were incredible. One had a monkey looking over a shoulder with its hands covering the breasts and its tail curled up between the legs and covering the crotch. Another with the tail over one breast, a hand over the other, and one hand covers the crotch. Each costume, a variation on this idea.[48]

Unfortunately, despite such visual ingenuity, the critics hated the show. After a few tweaks, it moved on for its second preview in Philadelphia, where the verdict was still damning: "despite good-looking femmes and a catchy score, the lack of book and any kind of material killed this from the start."[49] When it finally came to Boston, *Strip for Action* fell off the rails completely. The city authorities tried to ban it for gratuitous nudity, because of a scene involving two girls in flesh-colored body stockings who posed discreetly upstage. The show closed early and never made it to Broadway. Walter Winchell, despite his long friendship with the composer, wrote: "Jimmy McHugh in tears over fate of *Strip for Action*."[50]

The best thing to come out of this last attempt at a return to Broadway was that McHugh and Adamson had actually written some rather good songs. The finest of them, "Too Young to Go Steady," became a big hit for Nat King Cole, who also recorded three other songs from the show. The same song was subsequently heavily plugged by McHugh's teenage star in the making, Tommy Sands.[51] But briefly successful as this return to the charts was for McHugh, it was completely eclipsed in 1957 by Fats Domino's version of "I'm in the Mood for Love," which gratified McHugh firstly by being far closer to the original than James Moody's or King Pleasure's version had been, and secondly when its sales soared beyond a million copies. With Domino's recordings of his songs, and a beat-inflected version of "Louella" released the same year by Pat Boone, McHugh's songwriting career genuinely had stretched from ragtime to rock and roll.

Such successes kept McHugh in the public eye as a songwriter, just as his Singing Starlets had established him as a working musician, but overall the 1950s was the decade when McHugh consolidated his transformation from songwriter to Hollywood personality. A significant indication of his status in the community occurred when July 10, 1954, was proclaimed "Jimmy McHugh Day" in Beverly Hills by Mayor Harold L. George, in honor of the composer's fifty-ninth birthday. (It was in fact his sixty-first, but in all his publicity McHugh had skillfully shaved yet another year off his age, despite correspondence that survives from this period in which the Massachusetts registrar for births sent McHugh two duplicate birth certificates that confirm 1893 as the year he was born.) The mayor hailed McHugh as "a useful citizen, a civic worker, a philanthropist and a humanitarian of considerable stature." The following March he was elected "Beverly Hills Businessman of the Year" by the chamber of commerce. He and his Singing Starlets appeared at the celebration, and "the glamor girls took the audience through the best of Jimmy's hit tunes."[52]

Socially, McHugh was now part of the Hollywood "in crowd" of celebrities, as Debbie Reynolds remembered:

> I recall him playing at everybody's house. It might be at Gary Cooper's home, his own place or Louella's, at Humphrey Bogart's. Basically, at any of the houses of the people he ran around with. Maybe Dean Martin, Mike Todd's house in Hollywood, or Elizabeth Taylor's in Beverly Hills. Often we all had dinner together, and then after dinner, we'd not stay on at the restaurant or go to a club. Instead we'd make our way to somebody's house. We'd visit and talk, and then Jimmy'd get up to play and we'd all sing. I saw Judy Garland and Mickey Rooney singing with him, in fact whoever was there and who wanted to would get up and sing.[53]

Each year, he and Louella Parsons threw ever more magnificent parties for one another's birthdays, culminating in 1957 with a "birthday blowout" reception for McHugh at Parsons's home. Dozens of stars turned out, and those who could not make it sent congratulatory telegrams, including one from Nat King Cole, who promised to dedicate the closing number on his radio show that evening to McHugh. For Parsons, three weeks later, there was an even more lavish event at McHugh's poolside, during which Arthur Godfrey's private plane flew low over the city and buzzed the house with birthday congratulations.

"Reach for Tomorrow"

ALTHOUGH McHUGH'S POOLSIDE parties and Louella's garden receptions were among the most significant events on the calendars of those luminaries who inhabited Hollywood's rarified social atmosphere, the general public only participated in them by way of press reports and occasional telecasts. But that state of affairs was to change on September 5, 1959, when the Hollywood Bowl scheduled a special concert entitled "The Songs of Jimmy McHugh." For this event, a glittering array of stars would pay tribute not just to McHugh's talent as a songwriter but, by virtue of the venue and its significance, to his place in the pantheon of local personalities; and thousands of "ordinary people" would also be present to witness performances by McHugh himself, as well as by Anna Maria Alberghetti, Vic Damone, and Bobby Darin, with the Hollywood Bowl Pops Orchestra conducted by the young arranger and bandleader, Buddy Bregman.

Press reports that appeared during the buildup to the show suggested that the stars who appeared would be "fulfilling a reciprocal treaty that has been in effect for 40 years between Jimmy McHugh and the top vocalists of America. Under the terms of this pact, McHugh writes good songs for them and they sing his songs well. Everybody wins."[1] Although this evening at the Bowl was to consist entirely of McHugh compositions, the publicity—no doubt employing statistics supplied by McHugh's own press office—pointed out that in almost any contemporary show consisting of a medley of popular songs, as many as 20 percent of those compositions would be his work: "With the exception of Irving Berlin, it is not likely that any composer has as many titles among the so-called 'standards.'"[2]

Twenty-nine-year-old Buddy Bregman was the musical director of the Bowl concert. He had a family pedigree in popular music—his mother's brother was the songwriter Jule Styne—and during his childhood in Chicago, he had encountered many of the greatest names in show business at first hand. Bregman started to write arrangements while he was still in high school, playing clarinet and saxophone in the school band, and he was fortunate enough that the composer Bill Russo, who was slightly older, acted as an informal mentor for him there and helped develop his skills. While studying at UCLA, he arranged Chuck Meyer and Bill Jones's "Suddenly There's a Valley" for the young singer Gogi Grant, who was then working in the Santa Monica branch of Woolworth's. Grant's recording of this arrangement made the pop charts and effectively launched her musical career. With a handful of other comparably successful pop arrangements under his belt, Bregman left UCLA to try his hand as a full-time arranger and band director.

The flipside of one of Bregman's early arrangements was a rock-and-roll version of Lieber and Stoller's "Bernie's Tune," and by chance, shortly after its release, he was teamed up for a game at his local tennis club with the impresario Norman Granz, who had just caught this cut on the radio. Granz was impressed by what he had heard, and during their post-match conversation he offered Bregman a job. For much of the three years leading up to the Hollywood Bowl concert, Bregman was head of artists and repertoire for Verve Records, in which capacity he had not only launched the Ella Fitzgerald *Songbook* series of recordings but also conducted the orchestra on Bing Crosby's most contemporary jazz album of the time, *Bing Sings Whilst Bregman Swings*.

Working at Verve with such a galaxy of stars (others with whom he recorded included Anita O'Day, Fred Astaire, and Sammy Davis Jr.) naturally brought Bregman into the orbit of Louella Parsons. He recalled:

> She took a liking to me, and consequently so did Jimmy McHugh. The Alberghetti family had hired me when they first came over from Italy, to do the orchestrations for their act in Las Vegas, and not only was Louella in love with their whole family, but Jimmy adored Anna Maria's operatic voice, so initially through the Alberghettis in Vegas, but subsequently through our general social

orbit, I got to know Louella and Jimmy real well. At one time, I think we would meet three or four times a week at the big social events around the city.

Like my uncle Jule, Jimmy was very active in ASCAP, but he was also—despite the fact that he had his technical limitations as a pianist—the best demonstrator of his own songs there ever was. He had that rolling left-hand bass, like they had in New York in the 1920s, and so he never needed a drummer. He could play that catchy Broadway rhythm at the same time as putting across the lyric, so he was a really great demonstrator of a song, as well as being the best possible enthusiast for his own work.

I think the biggest influence on my life as a musician was one time when I was going somewhere in my parents' car, and the Tommy Dorsey Orchestra came on the radio, playing Sy Oliver's arrangement of "On the Sunny Side of the Street." I didn't even really know what an arrangement was at that age, but I knew I loved the sounds and the textures in that chart, particularly the muted trumpets. But one of the reasons it worked so well is that the song itself can't be beat. I remember at one of our first meetings telling Jimmy how much I loved that arrangement, and particularly the harmonies of the song itself, not just the way the first two bars move from C to E7, but the passing chords he introduced, including a thirteenth. Nowadays, in fact ever since the era of bebop chording, you can figure that kind of thing out, but back in the 1930s and early 1940s nobody could figure it out. I remember buying a stock arrangement of the song when I was at high school in Chicago just to help me understand the chords.

Normally, however, we never talked music. We talked social. Which premieres, which parties, which receptions, which movie openings we were going to. If I wasn't going to something or other, then they'd invite me, and we wound up spending a lot of time together. I think at one point I raised the idea of doing an album of Jimmy's songs, but it was Louella who transformed it into a plan for a concert, and her power was still such at that stage that with one phone call from her, things could be made to happen.[3]

The choice of artists came down to mutual friends or colleagues of Bregman's, Parsons's, and McHugh's. At the time, Anna Maria Alberghetti was close to all three of them, so she was a natural choice. The young arranger had recently rewritten several charts for Bobby Darin's current act, so they were actively working together at the time, and Bregman had also been hired by Nick Sarano, Vic Damone's manager, to work on some songs for him. The balance between these three singers, their personalities and their voices, was ideal for showing off the variety of styles and content in McHugh's catalog of work.

The concert was announced to the public in June 1959: McHugh night was to be one of three "songwriter" special evenings in the venue's July-to-September program, the others being Lerner and Loewe (starring Johnny

Green, Jane Powell, and Carl Olsen) and Rodgers and Hammerstein (with Alfred Newman, Gloria Kreiger, and Katherine Hilsenberg). As soon as the program was announced, Louella's column began plugging McHugh night. She wrote: "Last year our Hollywood Bowl had its most successful season, and after looking over the program that Wynn Rocamora has lined up, indications are this will be an even greater success."[4]

The season sold well, and the concert attracted a full house for what the *Los Angeles Examiner* called "Jimmy McHugh's finest hour." McHugh himself, described by the paper as "pink and white and looking more like a banker or a diplomat than a graduate of Broadway's rough and ready Tin Pan Alley," admitted backstage before the show began that he was as nervous as a debutante.[5] He was also moved close to tears while reading the dozens of telegrams from music business associates, politicians, chamber of commerce colleagues, and friends, particularly when among them he found a goodwill message from a small boy whose life had been saved by one of the iron lungs provided by the McHugh Polio Foundation. Anna Maria Alberghetti recalled:

> By this time, his days of writing music for the movies were nearly over, and I think that's why he was so anxious to hear his catalog of songs being performed. When it came to the Hollywood Bowl concert, we were really good friends. I'd known him a long time, almost since I'd first arrived in L.A. and he'd thrown that welcome party for me. His interest in me began when I was really young, and it continued through to the end of his life. He was a big fan of mine, and anything he could do for me, he did. He was charming and fun to be around, although he would also make sure that he promoted his own music whenever he could, encouraging me to sing his songs in absolutely every show—although I liked his songs so much I would probably have sung one or two of them in each performance anyway! That night at the Hollywood Bowl turned out to be a wonderful concert, a great evening.[6]

Her enthusiasm was shared by Bobby Darin, who sent McHugh a cable that read: "THE OPPORTUNITY TO SING SO MANY GREAT SONGS IN ONE EVENING COMES ONLY ONCE IN A LIFETIME. THANK YOU FOR THE ONE."[7]

Of the participants, only Buddy Bregman came close to disaster that night, although he was fortunately rescued by the calm professionalism of his orchestra. He had produced a rip-roaring arrangement of "Diga Diga Doo" to kick off the evening, but he described what actually happened as follows:

> The orchestra take their places, the lights dim, there are no announcements. I'm thinking about the tempo of that first arrangement, and I raise my baton. And we hit. Only I'm conducting in four, and they're calmly playing "The Star-

Spangled Banner" in three. It was the gaffe of the century in front of 17,000 people. Nobody'd told me the concerts always begin with "The Star-Spangled Banner," but once I'd given the downbeat, as far as the orchestra was concerned I might as well not have been there. They just carried on and played it the way they always did. I'm not too sure how many people in the crowd watched me slowing down my arm movements and changing tempo to get in time with the orchestra, but I looked up and saw Jimmy. He knew![8]

Bregman had time as the anthem continued to recover his composure, and the evening went on to become a triumph. "Cheer after cheer, wave after wave of applause greeted his patriotic and sentimental numbers entwined with the nation's history of peace and war," ran one review, which went on to praise the "youthful stars of the present [who] probed the past with the melody and lyrics of yesteryear."[9]

Anna Maria Alberghetti sang "the song that America took to her heart in the war years," "Say a Prayer for the Boys over There," and reports praised her "exquisite technique and beautiful voice" as she sang "This Is a Lovely Way to Spend an Evening." Performing "I'm Shooting High," Vic Damone was hailed for "one of his greatest nights—his nonchalant air, smooth voice and superb technique," while Darin was feted for his talents as a "winsome, sparkling entertainer," notably with "On the Sunny Side of the Street." Despite the plaudits for these young talents and Bregman, all the reviews agreed that the most enthusiastic applause was reserved for McHugh himself, who came out and ran through a medley of his hits at the piano.[10]

The concert was the culmination of the presentation of numerous awards to McHugh, including Certificates of Recognition from the cities of Los Angeles and Beverly Hills and the naming of September 4 as "Jimmy McHugh Day."[11] This kind of public acknowledgment meant a lot to McHugh, particularly after he had opted in the 1940s to throw more of his energies into civic and charity work than into songwriting. The inescapable conclusion is that the concert reaffirmed to him that whatever he had done in the civic field, his real lifetime achievement was as a composer.

By the time of the concert, his eldest grandchild, Judy McHugh, was nineteen and had been working for him for some months. Reflecting on the event, she said: "I don't think he realized the full extent of his talent. That's why he was always plugging his songs. He didn't feel that he was considered one of the elite, and he thought that he was a notch below Rodgers, Porter, Gershwin, Kern, Berlin, and so on. I think that throughout his whole life he strived to become one of their number in the world of music."[12] Certainly the training that Judy herself received at McHugh's side never had anything to do with songwriting or composing but was exclusively concerned with plugging and promoting his catalog of songs.

Judy found her paternal grandfather's outgoing, hustling, publicity-seeking influence a direct contrast to her experience of her other grandfather, Eddie Cantor, and the sheltered atmosphere of his home at 1012 North Roxbury Drive, where she had grown up after her mother moved back following her divorce from Jimmy McHugh Jr. This large mansion, with its bevy of staff—maids, laundresses, handymen, publicists, masseuses, and chauffeurs—was the pampered and privileged environment in which she lived until her mid-teens; she knew little of the world south of Sunset Strip and assumed that everyone must live in similar style. Although she visited McHugh regularly—he had taught her to swim in his pool from the age of five and encouraged her to be an athlete, until she rebelled against the tough training regime as a teenager—it was not until she began working in the McHugh office at age seventeen that she really saw another side of life. She relates:

> From the day I started there, he put a huge amount of time and effort into grooming me to be a song plugger. He sent me out into the streets, armed with a box of records. In the block around Sunset and Vine there were four or five radio stations, and it was my job to go to each of them with the new Andy Williams recording of a McHugh song, or the latest Johnny Mathis recording of McHugh, or Bobby Darin's new McHugh disc. I was basically peddling records to DJs, and I had a ball.
>
> He made a lot of money as a songwriter, but every penny he made he put back into the business of promoting his repertoire. He spent most of his afternoons at the jeweler, buying baubles and gifts. For example, I remember him getting gold money clips and having them engraved to Nat Cole, to Dean Martin, and to Bobby Darin. He'd send bracelets with his own selection of charms to women singers. When he died, he really didn't have any money, just his home, his silver collection, and some paintings. There was no cash, because as soon as it came in he would turn right around and spend it getting singers to record his songs. They were constantly being gifted.[13]

In McHugh's files and scrapbooks, there are copious letters of gratitude for his carefully targeted presents and notes from singers, agents, and record company executives reporting their successes in recording his songs. Not everybody succumbed to his charm, however, and George Shearing firmly resisted McHugh's attempts to suggest the repertoire for his quintet. He wrote to McHugh: "As you probably know, I pick all my own tunes purely on the basis of how musical they sound when played by our group. Jimmy, this is the only way I can work in this business. I think that if I had to have songs picked for me there would no longer be the degree of sincerity in what is referred to as the Shearing Sound."[14]

Shearing was one of the very few artists at any level to resist the barrage of gifts, flowers, cables, and publicity suggestions. More typical was the way McHugh worked with MGM Records to promote Joni James's 1960 recording of "I'm in the Mood for Love," from her album *100 Strings and Joni*. He ordered five hundred copies of the disc direct from Sidney Brandt, vice president of the record company, and immediately set about getting them distributed to his personal contacts among DJs and record stations. Simultaneously, McHugh organized a poolside cocktail party for the Italian-American singer, after receiving a discreet subsidy from MGM, and within days, the promotion office was back in touch to inform McHugh that "YOUR EFFORTS HAS [*sic*] NOT BEEN IN VAIN. THE ALBUM IS DEFINITELY A WINNER." Brandt congratulated him, making clear that "it is always the intention of MGM Records to give the finest co-operation possible, especially to people like yourself who are anxious to help in so many ways." As a direct result of McHugh's efforts, James went on to sing the song as part of the entertainment at that year's Academy Awards ceremony.[15]

The professional habits that McHugh had adopted in the 1920s remained his modus operandi, with the promotion of his back catalog now taking precedence over writing, although he never forsook composition entirely. He "leads a well-organized almost formalized life," ran one report, which continued: "He lives alone and when he arises and comes down the stairs in the morning, two secretaries, two housekeepers and one gardener are already on the job. He has a rigorously well-organized mind. After a tomato juice breakfast, during which he dictates correspondence, he goes to the piano and tries out some musical ideas already in his mind."[16]

Jimmy McHugh III confirms that in the 1960s, when he spent considerable amounts of time with his grandfather, seldom a day went by when McHugh did not sketch out some outline for a song, but by then comparatively few of his efforts ended up being published. One briefly famous example was "It's Me Remember?," which McHugh and lyricist Dotty Smith turned out for Keely Smith's solo debut at the Cocoanut Grove in November 1962; the song was a topical allusion to the fact that Smith had just divorced her longtime performing partner Louis Prima and was setting about creating a new solo career. The most notable song from the period, a piece both widely performed and written about, was the "First Lady Waltz," which McHugh wrote with Ned Washington and dedicated to Jacqueline Kennedy, wife of President John F. Kennedy, in 1961.

His last significant piece of movie writing was for the American version of Joseph E. Levine's film *Jack the Ripper*. The original English music, written by Stanley Black, was replaced for the U.S. market with a completely new, much jazzier symphonic score that McHugh co-composed with the big-band arranger Pete Rugulo. It was recorded in Hollywood during October 1959, and the film had its U.S. release in February 1960. Levine blew part of his $1,250,000 promotion budget (five times the cost of shooting the movie) on a gala reception at the Plaza Hotel in New York, at which the Meyer Davis orchestra gave a concert performance of the new music to over five hundred film executives and press representatives.[17]

As the 1960s went on, rather than spending time composing, McHugh focused each morning on reading *Daily Variety* or the *Hollywood Reporter* from cover to cover and then planning his self-promoting correspondence for the day. Jimmy McHugh III witnessed this in action:

> He'd finish his breakfast and then sit there immaculate in a cashmere sweater and slacks—never jeans—and start calling the papers. One day I heard him telling the columnists, "Jimmy McHugh is writing a book." A couple of weeks later I asked him, "How's that book coming on?" He hadn't a clue what I was talking about, and when I reminded him, he said, "Oh, I'm not actually writing a book." It was all about placing copy, getting his name in the papers. He'd check to see if he was in the gossip columns from the night before when he'd done his round of the clubs, because he was just built to seek publicity. Then he'd start lining up his social evening for that night, before going to lunch. Usually that'd be a fancy lunch, at a Beverly Hills restaurant, and then he'd come back and prepare for the evening. Sometimes a singer, or one of his young protégés, would come over and run through some songs while he played for them. Then that night he'd stop by the Cocoanut Grove or Ciro's with Louella, before setting off to the round of parties. Wherever he went he'd work the room.[18]

Jimmy III's perception of 709 North Sierra Drive, where his grandfather lived and worked, was that it was "a playpen." In other words, with the exception of McHugh's bachelor quarters upstairs, his den on the same floor that held the Gershwin piano on which he preferred to compose, and a small office downstairs, the entire place was designed for him to live his life among invited guests. It was built for entertaining, with a huge ground-floor living room, complete with grand piano, famous paintings, and floor-to-ceiling windows looking out over the Olympic-sized pool, trim lawns, and cabana. The room also paid testament to another of McHugh's abiding interests, as his granddaughter Adele recalls: "It was adorned with scores of silver-framed photos of

Grandpa with various priests and nuns. I'm sure there were celebrities, too, but I noticed the religious pictures."

On Saturday afternoons he invited the great and the good to come and sit by the pool. The mayor and other Beverly Hills dignitaries would rub shoulders with local police chiefs, and they, in turn, would hobnob with a selection of A-list stars. As Jimmy III observed: "If you got pulled over, or parked in the wrong place, it was good to have had the police chief at your house on Saturday afternoon and for him to have passed the time of day with Dean Martin or Frank Sinatra. Because from that moment on, he's forever your pal."[19]

The other thing his grandson remembered about McHugh's house was that the office always seemed to contain a spectacularly good-looking "assistant secretary." She might be a talented swimmer, or a singer, or a would-be actress, and almost always, when he returned for his next visit a week or two later, that particular "assistant" would have left, to be replaced by another equally striking young woman, several decades younger than McHugh himself. The one constant, who had been with him ever since the 1940s, was his principal secretary, Lucille Meyers.

She diligently filed away every press clipping, every manuscript song, and every half-formed idea and kept immaculate records of his contracts, publishing deals, and civic events. Singer Michael Feinstein remembered: "The first time I went to visit the Jimmy McHugh office, his longtime assistant Lucille Meyers showed me stacks of hundreds of manuscripts containing treasures of wonderful melodies patiently waiting for a little love, attention, and a lyric."[20]

Meyers was in every respect the stereotype of a middle-aged, efficient secretary. She came from the Midwest and had an accountancy background but no prior experience of show business until she began working for McHugh in the early 1940s. He trained her, and she responded by running everything with an efficiency and devotion that—according to Judy McHugh—went beyond sheer professionalism:

My impression was, that Lucille was madly in love with him from the time I was a child. He was not, I must emphasize, madly in love with her. She was, in his eyes, just his secretary. He was off dating all these fabulous stars or going to events with Louella, and at night, Lucille would be there to tuck him into bed. She was totally devoted to him. She called him Mr. McHugh until the day he died. Never Jimmy. And he never called her Lucille, always Miss Meyers. Towards the end of his life he started to take her with him on his trips to New York. On one of those occasions he bought her a mink coat, and I think from that moment she finally felt she was a part of his life. But you only had to spend the shortest time in his office to realize that she ran his world. When I was working there, I felt it was kind of sad. There she was, head-over-heels in love, and he wouldn't give her the time of day in terms of romance.[21]

Partly because she was family, and partly because she was not in any romantic sense a rival for McHugh's affection, Judy McHugh got on well with Lucille Meyers. They conspired together to make everything run smoothly at his house. One typical example concerned the silver photograph frame on McHugh's grand piano, mentioned in the previous chapter. Normally, as he wrote in his memoir, it contained a signed photograph of Louella Parsons. But hidden behind that was a selection of other key photographs. One was a signed portrait of John F. Kennedy and his family, and whenever one of the Kennedys or a prominent local Democrat came calling, Louella's picture was hidden behind the Kennedy photo. Another was inscribed to McHugh by Frank Sinatra, and so on.

From time to time, Parsons's chauffeur, a distinguished African American known simply as Collins, would arrive unexpectedly at the house on some mission from Louella. If the wrong picture happened to be on display, Lucille Meyers, in a conspiratorial whisper, would send Judy to engage Collins in conversation at the front door while she unclipped the silver frame and switched Louella's photograph back into pride of place.

Both Lucille Meyers and Judy McHugh also observed on a day-to-day basis the almost proprietorial way McHugh behaved toward other women. Judy recalled:

He was very keen on women. Not in a kinky way, but he loved to be in female company. He didn't want the women in his life to have husbands or boyfriends. He felt he had to control them, and he was both possessive and obsessive. There were many beautiful girl singers who used to hang about the house. But if they happened to mention another man in their lives, he didn't want to hear about it. They belonged to him.

While I was working for him, he was up in bed scanning the papers before coming downstairs one morning, and he saw a blurb in the *Hollywood Reporter* that said, "Judy McHugh to wed Eddie Kafafian," indicating that I had become engaged to the man who did, eventually, become my husband. My grandfather buzzed downstairs to the office completely frantic, saying agitatedly, "What's this? Why didn't you tell me?" I had to say, "I didn't realize we were engaged, but you know what the press is like!"

That afternoon he went to his favorite jeweler in Beverly Hills and came back with a big box, inside which was one of those gaudy cocktail rings, covered in diamonds, pearls, and rubies. He presented it to me, saying, "Now you're engaged to me!" I knew he didn't mean anything malicious, but it was very indicative of how protective he was, and how he didn't want any of the women he knew to have a life outside of their life with him. He never made any kind of sexual advance to me, but he was definitely possessive. Fortunately, as time went on he became very close with Eddie, and they became friends. After that we often went out to the same functions and clubs with McHugh and Louella.[22]

Many of the women whom McHugh accompanied around town in between his social obligations with Louella found themselves the object of the same possessive obsession. Yet, few of McHugh's female protégées were controlled with quite the same vigor as Mamie Van Doren, whose career he oversaw for three years in the early 1950s, leading up to the Universal Pictures contract mentioned in the previous chapter. She had started out singing in Las Vegas with Ted Fiorito and then moved to New York, where she attempted to launch her singing career and also became engaged (briefly) to former world heavyweight boxing champion Jack Dempsey. When Van Doren decided to leave New York to seek her fortune in Los Angeles, her stunning looks and nascent talent as a vocalist had already brought her to the attention of various songwriters, including Sammy Fain, who furnished her with an introduction to McHugh. She recalled:

Jimmy considered himself my Svengali. He wanted me to learn acting and singing, and I remember him saying, "Listen to what I have to tell you and you will become a star." He took me and molded me into being capable of achieving something I didn't think I could do. Every day I'd go over to his home and sing and sing and sing. When he thought it was time for me to start getting into the theater, he gave me tickets for shows, made sure that I was groomed for the stage, and paid for me to attend drama school. After I'd played the lead in a couple of drama school shows, each time he sent me roses and then took me to nightclubs like Ciro's or the Mocambo. He said that to become a good singer I also had to become a good actress, and he had me learning Shakespeare speeches like Portia's "the quality of mercy" soliloquy from *The Merchant of Venice* so I could recite them for him. He'd say, "Do this, do that," and at times it got to the point that I hated him. But looking back, I think that in two years with him I learned things that it takes a normal person as long as fifteen years to learn.

He had very sparkling blue eyes, a very kissable mouth and lips, and a George Clooney–type Irish face. I could see why Dorothy Fields must have fallen madly in love with him. But we never had any kind of love affair, and except when Louella interfered, he did his best for my career. Unfortunately he was starting to suffer from high cholesterol during the time he was promoting me, and just as my career was taking off, he got ill with heart trouble. I needed to speak to him about a role, and his doctor wouldn't let him take calls, so in the end I had to break my contract with him. But he did a lot for me—he loved to play the piano for me, and he loved me to sing his songs.[23]

McHugh's heart problems were quickly overcome in the 1950s, but even with his teetotal habits, his regular swimming regime, and a careful diet, he became increasingly prone to carrying a little too much weight, and he was to suffer again from cardiac difficulties in the 1960s. Anna Maria Alberghetti recalls that in his final decade he often had trouble catching his breath and had to take particular care of his health, although he did not let up on his regular rounds of nightclubs, parties, and premieres. Nor did he ever let up on his interest in politics, and Democratic politics in particular.

It is true that in January 1960 he accompanied Jeanette MacDonald as she sang the national anthem at a Republican fundraiser for President Eisenhower held at the Pan Pacific Auditorium, but McHugh was quick to tell Hollywood gossip columnist Mike Connolly that "I played the right hand for the Democrats and the left for the Republicans."[24] For the most part, ever since his childhood association with the Curley brothers, McHugh had been a staunch Democrat, and like many of those active in Boston's Irish politics, he retained particular connections with Joe Kennedy and his clan.

Joseph Patrick Kennedy, a banker, businessman, and entrepreneur, and ultimately one of the richest men in the United States, was a Bostonian five years McHugh's senior. Their paths crossed many times during the years, not only in Massachusetts politics but also because for a time Kennedy invested heavily in the entertainment industry, becoming the owner of RKO and also of the Pantages Theatre circuit. In 1930, when McHugh's parents first visited Hollywood, he borrowed Joe Kennedy's Cadillac and chauffeur to drive them around in style. (He also rented Harold Lloyd's house for them, as Lloyd was another longtime friend who later served with McHugh in the Beverly Hills Chamber of Commerce.)

McHugh would often send gifts or flowers to Rose Kennedy, Joe's wife and mother of the future president, and there are plentiful examples of their affable correspondence in the McHugh files. Equally, McHugh used every visit to the East Coast to develop his political contacts. His first official tour of the U.S. Senate was in May 1934, when Massachusetts Senator Marcus A. Coolidge was his host. Thereafter, with his own brother heavily involved in Democratic politics, first in Massachusetts and later in California (where Lawrence ran for the judiciary), and McHugh himself taking a leading role in Beverly Hills civic life, his political contacts grew. Few songwriters would be able to cajole a president into providing transport for the Japanese swimming team, as McHugh did with Harry S. Truman, but by producing a slow but steady sequence of official (if largely unmemorable) songs for the army, navy, and marines, McHugh managed to maintain his high profile with the Washington elite, who remembered the Presidential Certificate of Merit he had received for wartime fundraising.

The election of John F. Kennedy in 1961 brought McHugh closer to the center of American political life than he had ever been. He assiduously sent cables to the White House to celebrate birthdays, Thanksgiving, and New Year's Day, and these were invariably answered by personal communications from the president or his family. In addition, the barefaced flattery of the "First Lady Waltz," published in 1961 and dedicated to the president's wife Jacqueline on the occasion of her thirty-second birthday—with such lines (by Ned Washington) as "No melody could ever be / as beautiful, as beautiful, as she"—had an effect on the Kennedy clan equivalent to the success of "Louella" with Miss Parsons.

Whenever the president came to California, McHugh made the effort to meet him. Judy McHugh recalls a time when Kennedy was coming to Palm Springs on a semiprivate visit. McHugh took her, Louella, and Eddie Kafafian to the airstrip where the official plane was to land. About twenty people were waiting to greet the president at the perimeter fence, and he made a point of coming over and embracing McHugh, who introduced Kennedy to his granddaughter and her husband. Judy said: "He was the most gorgeous human being, with red hair, blue eyes, a tan, and that famous smile. There was to be a round of parties for him, and I remember attending the first one where I danced with his press secretary, Pierre Salinger. We had a glorious night, but at some point I noticed that Kennedy himself had not shown up for this party, and apparently he didn't show at the other receptions either. Rumor had it that after greeting us all at the airfield, he had hidden away with the actress Angie Dickinson for the weekend."[25]

In May 1962 McHugh was a guest at the White House for the annual Correspondents' Dinner, and, according to Louella Parsons's column: "He had the thrill of his life when the U.S. Navy Band played his and Ned Washington's tribute to Jacqueline Kennedy, the 'First Lady Waltz.' The president later complimented Jimmy and Ned on the lovely tune."[26]

Having seen at firsthand the flattering effect of his composition on Kennedy and his retinue, McHugh wasted no time in composing a sequel—this time written specifically with military bands in mind. By the end of the month, the press was announcing: "Jimmy McHugh has a new march in release, 'Massachusetts: Home of JFK,' a swinger dedicated to the president. Also getting a strong play around the country are McHugh's school dance and marching band arrangements of the 'First Lady Waltz,' and 'The Navy Swings.'" McHugh was subsequently commended in the *Congressional Record* by Representative Philip J. Philbin for bringing "great luster to our great Commonwealth and its historical capital City of Boston." Republican opponents of Philbin complained at his use of this official publication to promote a songwriter, but all the resulting publicity was beneficial to McHugh's overall standing within the political community.[27]

Although the "First Lady Waltz" had been well and truly launched in 1962, McHugh extracted more publicity mileage from it the following July, when he released an autographed copy of the song to the press for reproduction, accompanied by a release that read: "Jacqueline Bouvier Kennedy will be 34 tomorrow. As she rests at Hyannis on Cape Cod, she will receive many gifts. One of the most lasting will be a delightful song, the 'First Lady Waltz,' composed by Jimmy McHugh with lyrics by Ned Washington. The words and music are reproduced here by special permission of McHugh, the all-time hit composer."[28] Yet McHugh's earnest attempts at ingratiation were taken with a grain of salt by the president and his retinue, who were not above teasing the starstruck composer with an occasional practical joke, a good example occurring in August 1962, when Kennedy was visiting Beverly Hills. While there, he attended Mass at the Church of the Good Shepherd. On that occasion McHugh and his brother Larry helped take up the collection. "The President put in a $100 bill," Larry McHugh told the press, saying, "Even in Beverly Hills that is noticed."[29]

In fact, the McHugh brothers had been neatly duped by one of Kennedy's staffers, Jimmy Powers, who spotted Associated Press writer Jim Bacon sitting just behind the Kennedy entourage. Bacon recalled:

> Jimmy wanted me to see him put the bill on the collection plate for the McHughs. So I wrote a story about it, and believe it or not, it got front page coverage around the country. It really was unusual in the early 1960s for somebody to put as much as $100 in a church collection, even in as rich an area as Beverly Hills. Apparently, when Kennedy got back to Washington he asked Powers if he really had put in $100 on the President's behalf. "No," said Powers, "I was fooling Jim Bacon. I took a $10 bill and folded it so it could be mistaken for $100!" Kennedy laughed and said he was going to rib me about that, and whenever I saw him after that he did. But he not only fooled me at the time, but McHugh as well.[30]

As 1962 gave way to 1963, friendly contact between McHugh and the White House continued. On June 1, a couple of days after his forty-sixth birthday, Kennedy replied to McHugh's usual birthday greetings with a personal cable that thanked him for his thoughtfulness, saying, "IT WAS KIND OF YOU TO REMEMBER ME ON THIS OCCASION. I AM MOST APPRECIATIVE." It was the last message McHugh received from the president.

After the shocking event of John F. Kennedy's assassination on November 22, 1963, McHugh—after sending the appropriate condolences—nevertheless remained on good terms with the family for the rest of his life. "There were many lunches, meetings, visits," recalled Judy McHugh. There was also, characteristically, a steady flow of correspondence that was always reciprocated, with Senator Edward Kennedy, for example, writing in August 1968 to say "how much my entire family appreciates your continuing interest and friendship."[31]

As the decade progressed, McHugh's own family featured ever more prominently in his life as a man about Beverly Hills. In addition to his and Louella Parsons's regular Sunday gatherings at the Polo Lounge, at which a grandchild or two would normally be present, he would invite the entire family for somewhat more public celebrations of special holidays or events. His granddaughter Adele recalls:

> My favorite memories of Grandpa are of the times he and Louella would take my parents, Jim, Judy and I, and later, pregnant Judy with husband Eddie, for Easter or another special occasion to either the Polo Lounge or the Beverly Wilshire Hotel for lunch. Those meetings were wonderful family gatherings. Grandpa would always generously give me a dollar at Louella's suggestion, which was a thrilling gift to me in those early years. Grandpa and Louella were favorite guests. Of course all of the people at the restaurant, beautifully decorated for the season, would fuss over him and over us and everyone would have a good time asking after one another and catching up on family news.[32]

Yet beneath the outwardly calm surface, new tensions had arisen in the family and in particular in the relationship between McHugh and his son and namesake. After running the London office of MCA and becoming a vice-president of that corporation, Jimmy McHugh II had returned to the United States, where he suffered a nervous breakdown. He divorced his second wife, Shirley, and after his recovery, he married his third wife, Irene. (Adele was the daughter of this third relationship.) When his health returned, he decided to rebuild himself as an agent, setting up his own Artists' Management Corporation, and expanding on the most successful part of his previous career. But when he approached his father for financial help, he was turned down. Jimmy II's daughter Judy observes:

My father had had this major mental breakdown at a pretty young age. He'd achieved too much too soon, and he ended up going into a psychiatric hospital and came out a different man. His character was pretty severe, and he didn't come out of the hospital anything like the gregarious man who had gone in. When my grandfather turned down his requests for money to start his own agency, he went ahead on his own and built up a business that did really well. He had [the cast of] *The Beverly Hillbillies* on his books, along with a number of other major stars. But the setting up of the agency highlighted the strained relationship between my father and my grandfather. In the end, my father was written out of McHugh's will. Obviously, disinheriting his only son led to a lot of stories within the family, and I think it probably goes back to the way he left Bess back at the start of the 1920s, abandoning her and Jimmy Jr. in Boston. According to my father, although he always provided for them, he didn't look after Bess's interests very well, and although technically she was entitled to a share of the copyright in his big hits from the 1920s, she received nothing. Apart from being sent enough to live on, she was left completely outside McHugh's life, and I think my father had the feeling when it came to both setting up his agency and being left out of my grandfather's will that in some way it harked back to the way that he and his mother had been abandoned when he was a child.[33]

Although McHugh had denied his son financial help with the agency, and late in his life, while staying at the Waldorf Astoria on a visit to New York on ASCAP business, signed a series of codicils to his will that cut off Jimmy II from his estate, as far as their everyday lives were concerned, the two men retained an uneasy truce. Indeed—albeit at arms' length—despite his refusal of funds, McHugh was officially "partnered in the Armstrong-Denser-McHugh Jr. Agency," a part of the Artists' Management Corporation that his son founded.[34] Actually, as Jimmy II built up his firm, not only handling the stars of *The Beverly Hillbillies* but other television casts from top-rated shows such as *Family Affairs*, and becoming a self-made millionaire in the process, the older man contributed little. However, his role, distant as it may have been from the core of the business, did afford him the opportunity to sound off to the press from time to time with his views on agents and their work. Given his own involvement with the likes of Mamie Van Doren, he spoke from a position of some experience when he said in an interview that agents were "professionals who down the years have rendered personal management services to their clients, with the hope and expectation of contributing to their best interests."[35]

It is perhaps no surprise, as the 1960s went on, and agencies became ever bigger and more detached from the day-to-day lives of their clients, that McHugh should be arguing consistently for a return to smaller, more personal businesses, built on long-term trust and familiarity. That was very much the way he had operated himself within the Hollywood system and now saw his son doing as well. But even though they shared a common view of managing a small personal agency for their clients, their methods were extremely different. As Judy put it, "whereas my grandfather was a hustler and relied on being highly intuitive, my father was calculating, thoughtful, and careful, the epitome of the shrewd businessman."[36]

Yet, despite the emotional distance between McHugh and his son, there were no such barriers to the next generation of McHughs, and he became extremely close to his grandchildren. With the arrival of Judy's son, Lee Newman, in January 1964, he was to establish a good relationship with his infant great-grandson as well, relishing the role of being patriarch of the McHugh family. As Jimmy III recalled:

After my parents divorced, my grandfather became the father figure. When I was a child he paid for my schools, and when we were living in Los Angeles, I would see him every weekend. I'd have brunch on Sundays with him and Louella at the Beverly Hills Hotel, and I grew up around the pair of them. When I was sent to military school, I'd come home and McHugh would remind me to sit up straight, but it would be Louella, whom I'd christened the "lollipop woman" because of her generosity on Christmas and birthdays, who stepped in and said to my grandfather, "Come on Jimmy, leave the boy alone." It was a fascinating relationship between him and Louella. He liked to go out, he liked the press and particularly the enormous coverage that her column gave him. What he gave her in return was a well-connected man-about-town with whom she could attend all her functions. I know my sister Judy and I can both recall a time when he tried to break it off, and Louella told him that if he did, he'd never be in a newspaper again. The partnership was back on again immediately because he was hard-wired for the kind of press attention she gave him.[37]

During the years that Jimmy III was at military school, McHugh would take Judy and her husband Eddie Kafafian to watch the parades held each term. Kafafian remembered: "We would watch Judy's brother marching, and McHugh would sit up there in the bleachers as these uniformed kids marched by, and he'd point and say proudly, 'That's my grandson!' So McHugh was really very close to him and totally financially supportive after his mother Shirley remarried."

In the Hollywood society to which Judy belonged, namely the circles of McHugh and Eddie Cantor, Kafafian was an outsider, a New Yorker who was just starting to make his way in Hollywood as a journalist. He had first met Judy McHugh when she was listening to her grandfather address an ASCAP branch meeting that Kafafian had been sent to cover for his paper. One reason that McHugh swiftly overcame his possessive nature and was eventually enthusiastic about Eddie Kafafian becoming his grandson-in-law was that the paper in question was *Daily Variety*, and getting on good terms with his granddaughter's potential husband would thereby ensure McHugh yet more access to the press attention he craved. Kafafian observed: "He got more press than any of the other top composers in Hollywood. And there were a lot of other top composers in this town at the time. In the beginning I probably didn't live up to his ideal of who his granddaughter should marry ... but I had a name because of *Variety* and he could see my byline there, and so he couldn't openly object to me."[38]

Despite reaching an age when many of his surviving contemporaries in songwriting were turning their minds toward retirement, McHugh seems to have been unable to switch off his desire for publicity and the chance to keep plugging at his catalog in any way he could. One of the lyricists with whom McHugh occasionally wrote in the late 1950s and early 1960s was Jay Livingston, who produced the words for such songs as "Warm and Willing" and "36-26-36." Before his death in 2001, Livingston spoke to Jimmy McHugh III about his grandfather's skills at manipulating the press well into his final years: "When we wrote a song, by the time it was ready to go in whatever show or movie we were working on, it was being sung in every club in the city. Even before it was published, Jimmy would have upward of twenty singers all over town singing it. By nature, McHugh was, and remained, an instinctive song-plugger."[39]

His main interests in the 1960s, apart from continuing to write what were by now predominantly patriotic songs and sending out press releases about himself, had to do with Beverly Hills and ASCAP. For the former, he composed an official song, "The Wonderful World of Beverly Hills," to celebrate the city's fiftieth anniversary in 1964. For the latter, he took up the cudgels as enthusiastically toward the government as he had once done against ASCAP itself, in order to protest against the U.S. copyright law for songs. He fulminated over what he called the government's "bread and butter ruling," namely, the practice of avoiding full reform of the 1909 copyright bill by simply extending its provisions on an annual basis. Songwriters were aggrieved, because under that antiquated law, which predated the mass media of recording and broadcasting, their work was only protected for a maximum of fifty-six years from the date of first publication. McHugh lobbied for something better than those prevailing conditions (a statutory first period of twenty-eight years, followed by a single option to renew for a further twenty-eight years) and proposed a system of protection similar to that enjoyed by novelists and poets, which continued well beyond their lifetimes.

After almost a decade of wrangling and continual amendments and counter-amendments between the House of Representatives and the Senate, the law was finally changed in the Copyright Act signed by President Gerald Ford in October 1976. This protected the rights of composers for life plus fifty years and was in no small measure due to McHugh's sustained ASCAP campaign of the 1960s. He was equally emphatic about the parallel campaign to levy an ASCAP royalty from jukebox operators, following Representative Emanuel Celler's 1963 report to the House Judiciary Committee that "juke boxes alone, of all media of entertainment, remain exempt from obligation to compensate the Copyright owner." In the course of campaigning, McHugh wrote personally to every member of Congress urging them to vote for the bill. Again, despite the 1967 passage of a bill approving a levy of $8 per jukebox, it took almost a further decade, until the passing of the 1976 Copyright Act, finally to enshrine in law the principle of jukebox owners paying a portion of their profits to songwriters.[40]

Early in the decade, recovered from his wrist problems, and helped by the producer James Fitzgerald, McHugh made a limited return to the stage with his Singing Stars, this time a mixed-sex group, notably at the Seattle World's Fair in the fall of 1962. That same September he also made guest appearances in a touring package show called the *Wonderful World of Music*, starring with Stan Kenton's Orchestra, Jane Powell, and Vic Damone, and playing a selection of his hit songs.[41] As the 1960s went on, he gradually made fewer such live concert appearances, but he continued to be a frequent guest on a range of Hollywood television shows, playing one or two of his old hits and telling tales of the Cotton Club or of early days in the movie studios. One of his last public appearances was in May 1968, when he chaired, introduced, and played at the Hollywood composers/ASCAP gala in aid of muscular dystrophy charities. However, in spite of McHugh's sterling efforts, the majority of the press coverage for that event went to his old songwriting colleague Johnny Mercer, who limped to the microphone to sing despite having his leg in a plaster cast.[42]

Although Jimmy McHugh III recalled his grandfather still composing well into that decade, fewer and fewer of his new songs ever saw the light of day. Despite his degree of popularity with contemporary singers such as Pat

Boone and Fats Domino in the 1950s, the new decade saw an irrevocable shift of taste in popular music. Jimmy III recalls: "My grandfather would listen to pop radio, and the moment the Beatles came along, suddenly he and his songs weren't on the air any more. That was just crushing to him. Times had changed."[43] Outwardly, he put up a display of enthusiasm for the new sounds emerging from Britain, and when the Fab Four came to Los Angeles, he made sure that he was introduced to them. His granddaughter Adele, who was very much of the generation to take Beatlemania to heart, recalls: "We visited him the day after he met the Beatles and he was so excited to have met them."[44]

Inwardly, McHugh must have felt, just as Louella Parsons did as the 1960s progressed, that the world had changed, and for the first time he had been left behind. For a man who had reinvented himself time and again—moving from classical music to ragtime, from Tin Pan Alley to Harlem and thence to Broadway, writing for movies from the close of the silent-film era to the age of the great Hollywood musicals, and seeing some of the first rock-and-roll stars sell millions of recordings of his songs—this must have been not only crushing but confusing.

The meeting with the Beatles came at a garden party held in Beverly Hills in August 1965, at the home of a Capitol Records executive, where Brian Epstein, their manager, realized the huge publicity value of inviting everyone who was anyone in Hollywood to meet his young stars. McHugh was one of a long line of celebrities to be ushered past the four Liverpudlians as they sat side by side on stools, "amused but not especially thrilled," as their business manager Pete Brown put it, to meet the likes of Tony Bennett, Groucho Marx, Dean Martin, James Stewart, Gregory Peck, and Kirk Douglas. If the Beatles were largely unimpressed, some stars were apparently so charmed that they got in line a second time to have another chance to shake hands with John, George, Paul, and Ringo.[45]

The year 1965 was not only the time that the Beatles firmly ousted McHugh and his generation of songwriters from everyday airplay on the popular music stations, it was also the end of Louella Parsons's long run as a journalist for the Hearst Corporation. She had increasingly shared the writing of her column with her assistant Dorothy Manners, who took over completely for periods in 1962 when Parsons was incapacitated, first by getting parts of a lobster stuck in her throat and then by shingles and pneumonia. Although during the latter of these illnesses she received the last rites, she eventually returned to more or less full health and was back to writing her column and undertaking her social rounds with McHugh in 1963. However, her physical decline was apparent to those who spent any time with her. Judy McHugh recalled:

Eddie Kafafian, Jimmy, Louella, and I went up to see Frank Sinatra in Las Vegas that year. We set out for the show from Louella's bungalow in the grounds of the Sands Hotel. My grandfather and Eddie were walking a little ahead of us, when Louella suddenly grabbed my arm and said, "I have to pee."

I said, "OK, shall I take you back to your room?"

She said, "No, don't bother, I'll pee right here." She spread her legs and peed right there on the ground. She apparently wore no underpants because of her bladder problem, and when she had to go, she just peed where she stood. Once she had finished, she just said, "OK, let's go!" and walked off to hear Frank as if nothing had happened.[46]

Despite such increasing physical frailties, which her censorious younger self would never have countenanced, Parsons somehow survived not only indisposition but the merging of the *Los Angeles Examiner* with the *Herald-Express*, being one of the relatively small number of columnists from the old morning paper to be retained by the new title, the *Herald-Examiner*.

Midway through 1964, Parsons fell and broke a hip, again taking her out of circulation for some weeks, but this time Dorothy Manners took over the reins for good. Despite the fact that her byline still appeared every day, Louella Parsons was a presence in Hollywood in name only. She no longer wielded any journalistic power, and although she and McHugh still carried on their visits to openings, clubs, and movie receptions, this was on the strength of her reputation and his star quality, not her commercial currency as a writer. In December 1965 she bowed to the inevitable, and her name finally disappeared from the masthead of her famous column. She was eighty-four years old.

Thereafter, her decline was quite swift. She moved from her Maple Drive residence of many years to the Brentwood Convalescent Home, and in the spring of 1966, her house and its contents—a remarkable collection of antiques, porcelain, and silver—were auctioned. Personable when she first arrived at Brentwood, she gradually slid into a silent decline, sitting alone in her room. She died, isolated from the outside world, in December 1972.

McHugh—twelve years younger, and despite his cholesterol problems, largely in good health—continued his social rounds with his granddaughter Judy or with one or another of his current collection of aspirant singers, movie stars, or swimmers. He served as vice president of ASCAP and continued to be active in the organization even when he stepped down from that office. He appeared on television to reminisce about his early days, seizing the opportunity to play (or hear being played) his most famous songs.

His correspondence continued as well, with Lucille Meyers still sending off a daily round of reminders to sing this song or that song, packing discreet presents for those who had recorded or broadcast McHugh pieces, and—characteristically—sending flowers, gifts, and cables of congratulations to actresses, singers, and now, fellow songwriters. He was increasingly anxious to cement his place in the pantheon of popular song composers. Richard Rodgers, for example, wrote from New York thanking McHugh for a sizable donation to the charity launch of the movie *The Sound of Music*, mentioning in passing that the "picture is, I think quite wonderful" but mainly praising his "kindness and generosity."[47]

In May 1969 McHugh flew to New York for an ASCAP meeting, where he not only caught up with many of his songwriting colleagues but was reelected to the board and set out the next steps in his campaign for composers' rights. He had barely returned home when he was taken ill, and at three o'clock in the morning of May 23, he died from the effects of a heart attack. He was in his own bed, at home, with Jimmy McHugh II, Judy McHugh, Lucille Meyers, and his family physician, Dr. Rex Kennamer, at his bedside. Although the death certificate and the press notices gave his age as seventy-four, he was in reality a year older.

There was a requiem Mass at the Church of the Good Shepherd and memorial services in Boston as well, together with a raft of affectionate obituaries that not only summarized his remarkable achievements as a musician and composer but as a charity fundraiser and civic dignitary. Jim Bacon, writing in the *Herald-Examiner*, lamented that "we no longer will see the Boston Irishman's face around Beverly Hills any more. Jimmy McHugh gave the world much happiness with some of the best songs ever written." *Variety* praised him as "one of the best-known songwriters of the century," going on to applaud his ASCAP work as well as his compositions, while the *New York Times* totted up his "scores for 55 films" and "numerous pop hits."[48]

Overall, the statistics are extraordinary. There may not have been a blockbuster book musical such as *Guys and Dolls* or *South Pacific*. But there were over five hundred songs, five Oscar nominations, numerous anthems and patriotic pieces (including the "Crusade for Freedom," commissioned by President Eisenhower), as well as the wartime hits and Kennedy tunes, a sizable number of contributions to Broadway and Harlem stage shows, plus the movies.

The most remarkable thing about McHugh was his longevity as a composer. He wrote music from the First World War to the Cold War, and until the final four years of his professional life, he managed to take the popular pulse with unerring skill. Of course, there were lapses, and some of his minor movie scores are best forgotten, but there were major hits in every decade from the 1920s to the 1960s, a feat managed by few other composers in the field. The principal songwriters who did stay the course over the same years, Irving Berlin and Richard Rodgers, were both active in several charities, but they were evenly matched in this area by McHugh, who saved lives through his Polio Foundation and turned swimming in California from a pastime into a serious competitive sport at an international level.

The real mark of McHugh's achievement as a songwriter, however, is the enduring quality of his best songs. Years before his death, the first tribute album came out from Capitol Records at the start of the 1960s, when the McHugh and Parsons partnership was in full swing. On the liner notes to Capitol's *I Feel a Song Coming On*, which contains songs performed by June Christy, Nat King Cole, Judy Garland, Jackie Gleason, Peggy Lee, Dean Martin, Frank Sinatra, and Keely Smith, among others, Louella wrote, "you were born with a song in your heart, and your life has been dedicated to making the world happy with your great love songs."[49] This album contained Judy Garland's cover of "I Can't Give You Anything but Love," which was McHugh's favorite version of the song, and her timeless rendition demonstrates just how well one of his pieces written in the 1920s could still be current in the 1960s (and remains so today).

Nothing shows McHugh's durability and longevity as a composer better than the long-running Broadway show *Sugar Babies*, which was built around his music and ran for over twelve hundred performances between October 1979 and August 1982, pulling in a weekly profit of over $70,000. It starred Ann Miller and Mickey Rooney, who was making his Broadway debut. Although many of the reviews focused on Rooney's comic talent and his unpredictable stunts, designed to make a long run less boring for the cast and keep them on their toes, it was the solid core of McHugh songs that allowed different bits of comic business to be added or subtracted without affecting the overall feel and style of the show. At various times there were dog acts, pigeon teams, and veteran comedians, all slotted into a loose revue structure, but the show was anchored by Rooney's comic talent and Miller's tap-dancing, and the audience went home singing "I Feel a Song Coming On," "I'm Shooting High," or another of the dozen or so McHugh pieces that comprised the score.[50]

There has not been a comparably large-scale McHugh musical since, although the 2007 Tony-winning show *Jersey Boys*, which had lengthy runs in New York, Los Angeles, London, and other cities, included three McHugh songs. Nevertheless, with every year that passes, his songs remain in the public consciousness, not least because of the revival of interest in the "Great American Songbook" and a variety of performers—from rock veterans such as Rod Stewart to up-and-coming jazz singers such as Michael Bublé and Jane Monheit—recording McHugh's compositions.

If there is one performer who has been dedicated to bringing McHugh's work into the public eye, it is the singer and pianist Michael Feinstein. His show *A Lovely Way to Spend an Evening*, presented in 2007 at the Mark Taper Forum in Los Angeles, was (at the time of this writing) the latest in a line of McHugh projects that he has devised to show the depth and variety in McHugh's work. Of his efforts in this direction, Feinstein says:

> Time has a peculiar way of winnowing down the catalog of any given song-writer. In the 21st Century even the number of hits by Kern, Gershwin and Berlin are diminished in number to an essential handful and the rest seem to drift away. Jimmy McHugh is no exception to this situation and his catalog is filled with great works laying in wait for rebirth.
>
> Although McHugh's songs maybe do not carry the patina of a Gershwin or the legend of Berlin, at their best they boast inspired works that were indeed admired by both Gershwin and Berlin among countless others. McHugh was extremely gifted and might have become a lasting household name had he continued to collaborate with Dorothy Fields or worked with more sophisticated lyricists on Broadway. But he just wanted to work, and work he did, through passing fancies and tremendous changes in the world.
>
> Anyone willing to investigate his stacks of scores will find among them songs of unique character, structure and quality. While they are not all gems, McHugh can rest peacefully in the satisfaction of a job well done. He deserves to be remembered, celebrated and appreciated.[51]

These would be good words with which to end this survey of McHugh's life and career. Feinstein makes the acute observation that McHugh's relentless work ethic—that ferocious energy he brought to continuous creation in order to allay his Depression debts, and which became a way of life for him—perhaps steered him away from seeking lasting fame in favor of transitory rewards. Yet what has struck me about McHugh is his extraordinary staying power, his lifelong ability to create melodies that are anything but transitory. The handful of his greatest hits that are still played and sung regularly today are as well if not better known than the songs of many of his contemporaries who did write full-length book musicals. "I Can't Give You Anything but Love, Baby," "On the Sunny Side of the Street," "I'm in the Mood for Love," "Don't Blame Me," and "Let's Get Lost," in particular, have all acquired that universal quality that marks them out as timeless, as applicable now as they were to the audiences for whom they were written.

Whether they were created in the drafty Mills offices at three in the morning, quickly scribbled in response to an unexpected scene change on a movie set, or written at leisure in Beverly Hills, almost all McHugh's songs are superbly crafted, and most have that touch of originality that has made them last. That originality might be the creative way that McHugh keeps the vocal range within quite a narrow compass—as in the octave and a fifth range of "Exactly like You," which was singled out by Alec Wilder in his survey of popular songs for this very ingenuity. Or it might be the startling C to E7 chords that open "On the Sunny Side of the Street," which Buddy Bregman so admired, or the harmonic contrary motion at the start of "Don't Blame Me," which was pointed out earlier. Equally, it might be McHugh's chameleon-like ability to inhabit a variety of styles with total conviction, whether he was writing convincing rumbas for Carmen Miranda or equally brilliantly parodying Stephen Foster in the unusual twenty-measure structure of "Dixie-Anna" for Shirley Temple.

McHugh's legacy is a subtle mixture of all those ingredients, a remarkable catalog of songs that together reflect all the passing moods of twentieth-century life from 1910 to the 1960s. His mother's gift of music helped him to become a great Irish-American, using every opportunity he was given to rise from the poverty of his background to the heights of fame and Hollywood fortune, the kind of journey through life that was only possible in the United States of his time. McHugh once said that the knocks of early life made him reluctant to wear his heart on his sleeve, and that a smile and a joke were the way out of trouble, and yet his music is remarkably open, his melodies and choice of harmonies revealing a soul far more sensitive than his public persona and relentless plugging contrived to suggest. Funny or heartbreaking, whimsical or profound, as Michael Feinstein has observed, all the songs McHugh left to us were created on what he once said was his guiding principle: "Never let a suggestion or an idea fly out of the window. Get it down somewhere, even if on the tablecloth while you eat, or on the bedsheet. All ideas have merit and the more of them you possess, the more chance you have of succeeding. . . . Of course, inspiration helps, but nothing in the world can take the place of hard work."[52]

Notes and Abbreviations

BIBLIOGRAPHICAL ABBREVIATIONS

The following items are in the McHugh family archive and are unpublished manuscripts. They are referred to in the notes that follow in abbreviated form. (Throughout this book, the capitalization of song titles mentioned in extracts from these materials has been amended to be consistent with standard "headline" style.)

McHugh (1948)	Jimmy McHugh, "McHugh—Maker of Musical History" (autobiographical typescript), July 1948.
McHugh (1967)	Jimmy McHugh, "Pals and Personalities" (unpublished memoir), circa 1967.
McHugh (n.d.)	Jimmy McHugh, "The Story behind . . . 'I Can't Give You Anything but Love, Baby,'" (unpublished manuscript).
McHugh/St. John (c. 1967)	Jimmy McHugh, with Anne St. John, "Bring Him Along—He Plays!" (typescript of unpublished autobiography), circa 1967.

| Meyers (1955) | Lucille Meyers, "Notes on the Life of Jimmy McHugh" (manuscript in Jimmy McHugh Music offices), circa 1955. |
| Turley (1952) | George Turley, "Interview with Mr. Jimmy McHugh, Sr.," Beverly Hills, July 23, 1952. |

All of the McHugh scrapbooks mentioned in the notes and letters or cables to or from McHugh and not otherwise attributed are located in the McHugh family archive in Los Angeles.

CHAPTER 1. "HOME BEFORE DARK"

1. "The Best-Equipped Temple of Music in America," *Boston Globe*, November 9, 1909.
2. McHugh/St. John (c. 1967).
3. Ibid.
4. Ibid.
5. George W. Clarke, "The Story behind a Song Hit," *Green Magazine* (Boston), April 28, 1940.
6. McHugh/St. John (c. 1967).
7. Jack Burton, "Jimmy McHugh—The Honor Roll of Popular Songwriters, No. 62," *Billboard*, May 27, 1950.
8. Elliott Norton, "Big Song Hits Due to Jamaica Plain Woman," *Boston Sunday Post*, September 2, 1945.
9. Turley (1952).
10. McHugh/St. John (c. 1967).
11. Jerome Power, "John L. Sullivan, the Boston Strong Boy," *American Life Histories 1936–1940* (WPA oral history program).
12. McHugh/St. John (c. 1967).
13. Power, "John L. Sullivan."
14. Ticket stubs in McHugh scrapbook, 1924–26.
15. McHugh/St. John (c. 1967). A few of McHugh's statements are not entirely accurate. Curley, born in 1874, was not elected as alderman until 1904, at the age of thirty. He also returned to the office of mayor of Boston in 1946, serving until 1950, some years after his governorship of the Commonwealth of Massachusetts, which lasted from 1935 to 1937. See Jack Beatty, *The Life and Times of James Michael Curley* (Reading, Mass.: Addison Wesley, 1993).
16. Ernest Jones, "1910 Proved Banner Year in History of Early Birds," *Chirp* (Detroit), August 17, 1935.
17. McHugh/St. John (c. 1967).
18. Turley (1952).
19. McHugh/St. John (c. 1967).

20. Details from the brief biography by Patricia Browne, amended by Giacinta Bradley Koontz, of the Harriet Quimby Research Conference. The paper and my account draw also on Henry M. Holden, *Her Mentor Was an Albatross* (Mt. Freedom, N.J.: Black Hawk Publishing, 1993); and Terry Gwynn Jones, *For a Brief Moment, the World Seemed Wild about Harriet* (Washington, D.C.: Smithsonian, January 1984).

21. McHugh/St. John (c. 1967).

22. Ibid.

23. Ibid.

24. Ibid.

25. Turley (1952).

26. McHugh/St. John (c. 1967).

27. Ibid.

28. Ibid.

29. Ibid.

30. Ibid. I have referred to Madame Leblanc as Maeterlinck's "wife," though in reality this was a common-law arrangement, as her first husband never divorced her. However, newspapers and journals of the time generally referred to her as his wife, and I have followed that practice.

31. "Notes of the Stage," *Washington Post*, October 15, 1911; "Maiterlinck [*sic*] Coming Over," *Coshocton (Ohio) Morning Tribune*, October 19, 1911. Interestingly, the fact that these stories, particularly the one concerning the wager, were planted in these and numerous other papers some two and a half months before the premiere suggests that Bauer had been working on his little scam for some time, and almost certainly before the *Elijah* tour. However, Cahill and McHugh seem to have been so involved in trying to rescue the tour that they were unaware of the Maeterlinck scheme until they returned to Boston after their chilly Thanksgiving.

32. McHugh/St. John (c. 1967).

33. Northeastern University Libraries Archives and Special Collections Department: Boston Opera House records, 1908–58.

34. Turley (1952).

35. McHugh/St. John (c. 1967).

36. Ibid.

37. McHugh's comments about Bess from McHugh/St. John (c. 1967). Undated press clipping in McHugh scrapbook for 1923: "Entering the music publishing business in 1913 [*sic*], Jimmy was successively Boston manager for several of the New York publishers, at one time representing, in the Hub, the same firm that Jack Mills represented at the same time in Philadelphia." Waterson, Berlin, and Snyder was formed in 1913 out of Snyder's previous company and lasted until 1919, when Irving Berlin Inc. was incorporated to take over the Berlin catalog. Waterson was also a pioneer of recorded music,

and his separate business ventures included a number of fledgling record companies.

38. Turley (1952).

39. "Inspiration at Boston [Opera for] career as songwriter" (damaged clipping in McHugh file, published to promote "Flying High," 1931).

40. McHugh/St. John (c. 1967).

41. Date of Jimmy McHugh Jr.'s birth confirmed by his grandson, Lee Newman, in a letter to the author, June 10, 2005.

42. McHugh always referred to his regiment as a "cavalry" regiment, but in effect it was a quartermaster supply corps. The 101st was originally organized on August 22, 1917, as the 101st Supply Train, an element of the 26th Division, Massachusetts National Guard, then in federal service at Camp Barlett, Massachusetts. It drew its personnel from both cavalry and infantry elements of the Guard, and consequently its coat of arms combines the blue of the U.S. infantry with the gold of the cavalry. Its successful World War I actions are commemorated by a gold fleur-de-lys on its shield. The unit was demobilized on April 29, 1919, at Camp Devens, Massachusetts.

43. "Inspiration at Boston [Opera for] career as songwriter," damaged clipping, as above.

44. Meyers (1955); Turley (1952).

45. Press advertisement, "Geo. Friedman Inc. Music Publishers, 165, W 47th Street, New York: 'I am now connected with the above firm in the capacity of professional manager,' James McHugh," December 1, 1919. (Unknown source: McHugh scrapbook for 1919.) From his own account, McHugh actually made the move to New York after the start of the new year.

CHAPTER 2. "WHEN MY SUGAR WALKS DOWN THE STREET"

1. Singer, *Black and Blue*, 78.

2. McHugh/St. John (c. 1967). A "yeggman" was a burglar or safecracker, named after one "Yegg" who was a notorious exponent of the craft.

3. Shipton, *New History of Jazz*; further information from Gronow and Saunio, *International History of the Recording Industry*.

4. Krummel and Sadie, *New Grove Handbook*.

5. A letter to McHugh from ASCAP dated January 23, 1922, addresses him as professional manager at Jack Mills, 152 West Forty-fifth Street.

6. E. M. Wickes, "Along Melody Lane—Pretty Evelyn Hoey Pulls a New Act in Melody Lane," *New York Morning Telegraph*, hand dated 1925 in McHugh scrapbook.

7. McHugh/St. John (c. 1967).

8. Wickes, "Along Melody Lane."

9. "Evelyn Hoey Starred with Miss Compton," *Syracuse Herald*, September 12, 1935.

10. Rogers was a familiar name in the headlines for quite different reasons from his businessman father. His "adventurous bent," as one paper put it, his fondness for weaponry and attractive women, and his attempts to become a film cameraman and producer, the former with no union card and the latter featuring a comedy about nudism, all landed him on the front pages. His father considered him a bad lot, and in the older man's will, he was cut out of the family trust, leaving him with a mere $500,000 of capital investment rather than the billions he might have inherited. Despite this limitation of his means, by the time of his father's death in July 1935, Rogers had become a notorious playboy. His six-year marriage to a respectable doctor's daughter and former society girl, Virginia Lincoln, had been on the rocks for some time, and she had returned to her family in Cleveland.

11. "Open Verdict Returned by Jury in Hoey Death Inquest," *Sheboygan (Wisconsin) Press*, September 25, 1935; "Story of Stage Star Is Told at Inquest," *Reno Evening Gazette*, September 20, 1935; "Hoey Death Is Held to Be Suicide," *Frederick (Maryland) Post*, November 19, 1935.

12. "New York and Paris Torch Singer Dies during Farm Party," *Clearfield (Pennsylvania) Progress*, September 12, 1935.

13. McHugh (1967); McHugh/St. John (c. 1967).

14. "That for You Irving! Highbrows Tell Ragtime Composer What 'Wicky Wicky' Means," *Washington Post*, January 29, 1917.

15. "Midnight Plugging," *New York Morning Telegraph* (undated, on same page of McHugh scrapbook as handbill for November 15, 1921, National Vaudeville Artists' "Clown Night").

16. Unattributed clipping in McHugh's scrapbook for May 1923. However, *Out Where the Blue Begins* was copyrighted in 1923, confirming the dating of the scrapbook.

17. McHugh/St. John (c. 1967).

18. "Clown Night Pianist," unattributed clipping in McHugh scrapbook for 1923.

19. McHugh/St. John (c. 1967).

20. "Overnight Song Sensation," *New York Clipper*, c. July 1923.

21. Undated clipping in McHugh scrapbook for 1923.

22. Ibid.

23. Ibid. Also *Billboard*, November 17, 1923, announces McHugh getting a "generous block of stock" in Jack Mills Inc. A clipping concerning the Bermuda trip mentioned in this paragraph is in the 1923 pages of the scrapbook, but the McHugh family archive also contains a passenger list for the S.S. *Fort Hamilton* sailing from New York to Bermuda on February 27, 1926, and it is possible the picture dates from this voyage, as both McHugh and Mills are listed as passengers.

24. McHugh/St. John (c. 1967).

25. "Mixup over Song Royalties," unattributed clipping in McHugh scrapbook for 1930.

26. George A. Little (w), Jimmie [*sic*] McHugh (m), *Emaline* (New York: Jerome H. Remick, 1921). Recorded by Isham Jones, July 1921, Brunswick 25005.

27. McHugh/St. John (c. 1967).

28. "Death of Rudolph Valentino: Hero of American Girls; Emotional Scenes in New York," *Manchester Guardian*, August 24, 1926.

29. Ibid.

30. McHugh/St. John (c. 1967).

31. Ibid.

32. "Fred Fisher Inc. Claims Itself Damaged $25,000 by Jack Mills Inc.," unattributed clipping in McHugh scrapbook for 1923.

33. McHugh/St. John (c. 1967); mortgage deed for 41 Westbourne Terrace, Boston, dated April 1, 1924, in the names of James F. McHugh and Thomas J. McHugh, in McHugh family archive. Judy Kashalena (daughter of McHugh's sister Helen), telephone interview with author, January 2005: "He was devoted to my mother and always sent her a monthly check for twenty-seven years."

34. McHugh/St. John (c. 1967).

35. Ibid.

36. Ibid.

37. Ibid.

38. Unattributed advertisement in McHugh scrapbook for 1924, which continues: "This song was suggested by the official 'army anthem' of four million doughboys. They taught it to their friends, and it's [*sic*] memory will always be cherished."

39. McHugh/St. John (c. 1967).

40. "Mrs. Gallagher Angry: Wife of Comedian Grows Excited When She Sees Him with Follies Beauty," *Zit's Weekly Newspaper* [aka *Zit's Theatrical Newspaper*], New York, May 11, 1923.

41. E. M. Wickes, "Along Melody Lane—Willie Raskin Takes away Spotlight from Al Dubin," *New York Morning Telegraph* (in McHugh scrapbook for 1925).

42. "How a Popular Song Is Born and Reaches the Public," *Midweek Pictorial*, March 11, 1926.

43. Barrett, *Irving Berlin*.

44. E. M. Wickes, "Along Melody Lane—Al Dubin's New Song Is Expected to Make Some Quick Coin," *New York Morning Telegraph* (in McHugh scrapbook for January 1926).

45. Ibid.

46. McHugh/St. John (c. 1967).

47. Ibid.

48. Ibid.

49. Ibid.

50. Cable to McHugh dated July 2, 1925.
51. McHugh/St. John (c. 1967).
52. Cable to McHugh dated September 17, 1925.
53. McHugh/St. John (c. 1967).

CHAPTER 3. "EVERYTHING IS HOTSY TOTSY NOW"

1. Bob Mills, "Irving Mills 1894–1985," memoir by his son, http://www.redhotjazz
    .com/irvingmills.html (accessed August 19, 2008).
2. Letter from Frank Roberts to Jack Mills, August 10, 1925.
3. *Billboard*, May 2, 1925.
4. "McHugh Accompanies Mlle Fifi," January 24, 1926, unattributed clipping
    in McHugh scrapbook that reports on a "Franco-American interpretation
    of *Hotsy Totsy*" at the Theatre Club Dinner at the Astor.
5. *Variety*, March 4, 1925.
6. McHugh/St. John (c. 1967); unaccredited clipping in McHugh scrapbook
    dated June 1925.
7. Tucker, *Ellington: The Early Years*, 175–76. The author is clearly under the
    impression that the recording is by Ellington. But the Gennett files and re-
    search by Ellington expert Stephen Lasker suggest otherwise. Lasker wrote:
    "Lucille Meyers of Jimmy McHugh Music, who worked for McHugh the last
    twenty years of his life, told me on 10 March 1994 that McHugh had been
    a very competent pianist. When I played *Everything Is Hotsy Totsy Now* for
    her, she 'swore' it had to be McHugh. Musicologist Larry Gushee is of the
    opinion that the pianist isn't Ellington; Mark Tucker believed it is" (*DEMS
    [Duke Ellington Music Society] Bulletin*, January 2005).
8. McHugh/St. John (c. 1967).
9. Bob Mills, "Irving Mills."
10. Receipt for 1925 annual policy in McHugh family archive.
11. "Last Night on WAAM," November 5, 1925, unaccredited clipping in McHugh
    scrapbook.
12. *New York Morning Telegraph*, November 8, 1925.
13. McHugh/St. John (c. 1967).
14. *Metronome*, September 1, 1926.
15. Unattributed clipping in McHugh scrapbook for 1926, beginning "When
    Jim McCue [*sic*] who wrote *Big Parade* song hit. . . ."
16. Unattributed clipping in McHugh scrapbook dated September 15, 1926.
17. For a concise summary of the "Black Bottom" fad, see Shipton, *New History
    of Jazz*.
18. Rose Felswick, "Gilda Gray Creates Sensation at Devil Dancer Premiere,"
    New York Morning Telegraph, undated clipping in McHugh scrapbook for
    1927.
19. Letter in McHugh family archive dated April 17, 1927.

20. A letter in the McHugh family archive, dated January 4, 1927, is from St. Paul's Friary in Garrison, New York; it thanks McHugh for his recent donation of $25 for the friary's building fund. This letter is one of the first of many such acknowledgments that show McHugh became an energetic and active donor to various branches and activities of the Roman Catholic Church for the rest of his life.

21. Letter from Jimmy McHugh Jr., 1923.

22. McHugh/St. John (c. 1967).

23. Ibid.

24. Letter to McHugh from Wright (undated).

25. Milton Broxner, "2 Colored Girls Take Europe by Storm," *Reno Evening Gazette*, July 4, 1927.

26. McHugh/St. John (c. 1967).

27. Ibid.; Karl K. Kitchen, "A Broadwayite Abroad," *Syracuse Herald*, July 29, 1927: "Miss Helen Morgan is the star of the supper show at the Café Anglaise."

28. "A New Phase in Ballroom Dancing," *Westminster Gazette*, December 10, 1927.

29. Broxner, "2 Colored Girls."

30. McHugh/St. John (c. 1967).

31. Ibid.

32. Penciled telegram from *Leviathan*, with confirmation that McHugh's message had been sent, July 1927; telegram from Paris, October 8, 1927.

33. "Transatlantic Fliers Honored On Board Ship," *The Havre News Promoter*, July 1927.

CHAPTER 4. "I CAN'T GIVE YOU ANYTHING BUT LOVE (BABY)"

1. Opening night flier for *Breezy Moments in Harlem*, July 13, 1927.

2. McHugh/St. John (c. 1967).

3. Ibid.

4. Program for *Dan Healy's Blushing Browns* (undated) from McHugh scrapbooks, with "Special restricted music by Jimmy McHugh." The show included Aida Ward and Eddie Burks singing "I Can't Believe That You're in Love with Me" and Aida Ward and the entire company singing "Baltimore." Also on the program were Leitha Hill, Leonard Ruffin, Brown and McGraw, and Shirley Jordan. I date this program prior to McHugh's involvement with either Fields or Ellington, as there are no Fields–McHugh songs included, and the band is listed as the "Cotton Club Orchestra, starting their third year here," which is consistent with Andy Preer and the Missourians having arrived at the club under that name in 1925.

5. McHugh/St. John (c. 1967); Turley (1952).

6. McHugh/St. John (c. 1967); Turley (1952).

7. D. J. Kennally, "Owney Madden" (Leeds: privately published, 1991); Kennally's

research (at the University of Bradford) into Leeds local history has established the essential dates and places in the Madden family's connection with Kirkgate, which he describes in a letter to the author as "a terrible insanitary overcrowded slum of alleys and courtyards."

8. McHugh/St. John (c. 1967).

9. Ibid.

10. "Cotton Club, Harlem, Bars Colored Couple, Accompanied by White Friends," *New York Age*, July 9, 1927.

11. "McHugh's View," *Down Beat*, April 14, 1960.

12. Ellington, *Music Is My Mistress*, 72.

13. Tucker, *Ellington: The Early Years*, 268ff.

14. Collier, *Duke Ellington*, 69.

15. McHugh/St. John (c. 1967).

16. Ned E. Williams quoted in Shapiro and Hentoff, *Hear Me Talkin' to Ya*, 231; Block quoted in Haskins, *The Cotton Club*, 46. Williams overcame his initial dislike and subsequently became Ellington's press agent. The Duffy anecdote is from McHugh/St. John (c. 1967). Additional information in this section of the chapter comes from Lasker, *A Cotton Club Miscellany*.

17. *Variety*, December 7, 1927.

18. From the original program in McHugh's scrapbook. This is at odds with the information in Winer, *On the Sunny Side of the Street*, which suggests the program included "Hottentot Tot," "Freeze 'n' Melt," and "Harlemania" (all of which I date slightly later), and in Williams, *Underneath a Harlem Moon*, which titles the show *Rhythmania*. According to Lasker in *Cotton Club Miscellany*, and reproductions of the programs therein, *Rhythmania* was the title of the revue that opened on February 5, 1932.

19. Review from *Variety*, quoted in Lasker: "Duke Ellington, Jungle Nights in Harlem 1927–1932" (liner note to Bluebird 2499-2-RB, 1991). This Bluebird CD by Ellington contains the majority of the Fields and McHugh compositions featured in the Cotton Club shows. The reference to Annapolis is a thinly disguised racist remark: it concerns the Maryland city named for Queen Anne of England, which was one of the principal centers of the slave trade.

20. Turley (1952); Winer, *On the Sunny Side of the Street*, 28.

21. Mitchell Parish, "Meet Dorothy Fields and Jimmy McHugh," *Metronome*, March 1929.

22. "Ruth Elder Rescued after Plane Falls in Sea," *Detroit Free Press*, October 14, 1927; Fields comments quoted in Winer, *On the Sunny Side of the Street*, 22.

23. McHugh/St. John (c. 1967).

24. Ibid.

25. McHugh (n.d.).

26. McHugh's own account (see note above) says the song lasted "two weeks,"

but Winer says it lasted one night before being withdrawn. So did Dorothy Fields in her recorded performance *An Evening with Dorothy Fields*, DRG Records 5167.

27. *New York Post*, June 8, 1929, quoted in Singer, *Black and Blue*, 209–11. "I Can't Give You Anything but Love, Baby" was copyrighted by Fields and McHugh on March 6, 1928 (E687442). In his study of Fats Waller transcriptions, Paul Machlin, who has also published papers on Waller's compositional methods and working drafts, suggests that the song might be the work of Waller and Razaf but is unable to go further than the speculation offered by Singer. See Machlin, *Fats Waller*.

28. "About Broadway," *Sunday News*, March 24, 1929. See also Andy Razaf, "Fats Waller," *Metronome*, January 1944. The Fats Waller claim is discussed in Waller and Calabrese, *Fats Waller*. It is also the subject of scrutiny in Sheed, *The House That George Built*, but after weighing up the evidence Sheed comes down on the side of McHugh/Fields authorship.

29. "50,000 Negroes Wail Last Tribute to 'Florence' in 4-Hour Funeral Rites," United Press report in *Syracuse Herald*, November 7, 1927.

30. McHugh/St. John (c. 1967).

31. "Young Kahn," *Time*, August 16, 1926; "Able Mr. Kahn," *Time*, September 19, 1927.

32. McHugh/St. John (c. 1967).

33. Ibid.; McHugh (1967).

34. Gilbert Swan, "See-sawing on Broadway," *Appleton (Wisconsin) Post-Crescent*, January 28, 1928.

35. "Lew Leslie's All-Colored Revue Provides Good Diversion," undated fragment in McHugh scrapbook, reviewing the April 1928 production of *Blackbirds* in Atlantic City; Ogren, *The Jazz Revolution*.

36. "Jimmy McHugh's New Darktown Production," unattributed clipping in McHugh scrapbook for 1928, citing Winchell's review in the *New York Evening Graphic*, May 1928.

37. Gilbert Swan, "In New York," *Warren (Pennsylvania) Morning Mirror*, March 1, 1928.

38. Burns Mantle, "Blackbirds a Lively Flock: New Colored Revue the Best of Its Kind on Broadway," *New York Daily News*, May 10, 1928.

39. Ibid.; Alexander Woollcott, "A Harlem Revue," *World*, May 10, 1928; Percy Hammond, "'The Blackbirds of 1928,' a Slow Revel in which Many Talented Harlemites Eagerly Desport Themselves," *New York Herald Tribune* (same date); "Raising the Curtain—Black Birds of 1928," *Broadway Official Guide*, May 1928; other reviews quoted in Williams, *Underneath a Harlem Moon*.

40. "Song Takes Blackbirds from Cut-Rates to Capacity," unattributed clipping in McHugh scrapbook for 1928.

41. Ibid.

42. Williams, *Underneath a Harlem Moon;* "Second Place," *Chicago Defender,* December 29, 1928.

43. Figures from Williams, *Underneath a Harlem Moon,* and weekly count-up statements in the McHugh family archive.

CHAPTER 5. "LIVIN' IN A GREAT BIG WAY"

1. Titles and dates from Lasker, *Cotton Club Miscellany.*

2. Charles Weller, "Night Club Buzz," October 1928, unattributed press clipping in McHugh scrapbook.

3. Kelcey Allen, "Lew Fields in 'Hello Daddy' Wins Ovation," December 1928, unattributed press clipping in McHugh scrapbook.

4. Robert Coleman, "'Hello Daddy'—Lew Presents and Plays in Musical Comedy Written by Son and Daughter," December 1928, unattributed press clipping in McHugh scrapbook.

5. McHugh/St. John (c. 1967).

6. "Ziegfeld Midnight Frolic," *New York Magazine Program,* February 18, 1929.

7. McHugh (1967).

8. McHugh/St. John (c. 1967); Turley (1952).

9. McHugh/St. John (c. 1967).

10. Ibid.

11. Ibid.

12. Ibid.

13. Insurance revaluation in McHugh family archive. McHugh's account with the Longacre Bank, no. 4420, held a balance of $3,062 at the time of the crash and accrued interest throughout 1930 until December 16, when he withdrew $2,500, taking out a further $700 a week later.

14. McHugh/St. John (c. 1967).

15. Winer, *On the Sunny Side of the Street.*

16. "50 Metros for 30–31 with Stars—Stories," unattributed clipping in McHugh scrapbook for 1930. It continues: "Metro will make fifty talkers for next season."

17. *The Film Mercury,* April 1, 1930.

18. "$2,000 for McHugh-Fields," unattributed clipping in McHugh scrapbook for 1929, also reported in the *Chicago Defender,* December 21, 1929.

19. "*Zit's Weekly* Lists the Ten Best-Selling Songs of the Week . . . ," in "Up and down the Rialtos," *Syracuse Herald,* May 16, 1930.

20. Unattributed clipping in McHugh scrapbook for 1930; *New Yorker,* April 12, 1930.

21. McHugh (1967).

22. "Lew Leslie Broke," *Variety,* August 13, 1930; "Dorothy Fields after $1000 Unpaid Royalties Alleged Owing from Blackbirds," clipping in McHugh scrapbook dated October 1930.

23. McHugh (1967).

24. Mamie Van Doren, telephone interview with author, September 6, 2007.

25. W. B., "New Dress for Talkie at Capital: 'Love in the Rough' Revival of Old Picture," undated clipping in McHugh scrapbook for September 1930.

26. F. E. Pelton, "Organization Chart of Music Department," September 2, 1933, McHugh family archive.

27. Memos from Louis K. Sidney in McHugh family archive.

28. Telegram in McHugh scrapbook for 1930.

29. Alison Such, "Vanderbilt Revue," unattributed clipping in McHugh scrapbook for November 1930.

30. "Team Ahead of Time," Press Association wire, Los Angeles, October 28, 1930.

31. Winer, *On the Sunny Side of the Street*.

32. McHugh (1967).

33. "Faint at Love Song: Six Baltimore Women Drop When Tibbett Sings," United Press wire, December 12, 1931, from McHugh scrapbook.

34. Letter to Fields and McHugh, October 20, 1931.

35. "New Music Will Be Heard," *Los Angeles Times*, n.d., clipping from McHugh scrapbook for 1931.

36. Cable from Bregman, April 8, 1931.

37. Rowland Field, "Singin' the Blues Wins Its Audience at Brooklyn Debut," *Brooklyn Daily Times*; Edwin C. Stein, "Singin' the Blues," unattributed clipping; both from McHugh scrapbook for April 1931.

38. "New Plays in Manhattan," *Time*, May 18, 1931.

39. Robert Garland, "Cast and Miscast," unattributed clipping from McHugh scrapbook for June 1932.

40. Russell McLaughlin, "Leslie Revue Has Premiere," *Detroit News*, June 20, 1932.

41. Ray Bill, "Broadcasting from the Editor's Chair," unattributed clipping in McHugh scrapbook for December 1932.

42. "Fields, McHugh Broadcasting Weekly on WJZ, NY," unattributed clipping, May 21, 1933; "OK" column, unattributed source, June 2, 1933; both from McHugh scrapbook.

43. McHugh (1967).

44. Ibid.

45. Ibid. (The French Hospital was in New York City.)

46. Dorothy Fields, "Meet the Baron: Musical Opening," draft script, Hollywood, 1933; Harry Poppe, interoffice memo, August 29, 1933; both from McHugh family archive.

47. "Orient Opera to Be Staged," undated clipping in McHugh scrapbook for July 1933; Dorothy Fields and Jimmy McHugh, "Hopper's Entrance," manuscript score, July 1933; both from McHugh family archive.

1. Margaret Ford, "Composes Nation's Song Hits on His Bedsheet," *Boston Herald*, June 4, 1939; Jimmy McHugh "How to Write a Song Hit," unpublished manuscript in McHugh family archive.

2. "Writer of Popular Songs Lets You into Secrets," *New York Enquirer*, February 18, 1934.

3. Ibid.

4. McHugh (1948). A typical report in McHugh's scrapbook runs: "For the novel supper party at the Walter Kings . . . their guests included Jimmy McHugh and Dorothy Fields, the Harry Joe Browns, the Pandro Bermans, the Mervyn Leroys, the Casey Robinsons, the Stanley Berermans and the Walter Marxes."

5. Paragraph in unattributed report on *The Prize Fighter and the Lady*, in McHugh scrapbook for 1933.

6. McHugh (1967).

7. "Whether Writing Songs or Toting a Revolver . . . ," *Marksman*, from McHugh scrapbook for 1934.

8. Mary Margaret McBride, "With 'Love' Appearing at Least 5000 Times in Her 500 Songs, Dorothy Fields Is Too Busy to Celebrate the Lyric Landmark," *New York World-Telegram*, March [unknown day], 1934.

9. McHugh/St. John (c. 1967).

10. Receipt dated March 10, 1930, in McHugh family archive.

11. Letter from Robbins, March 31, 1939.

12. "No Chance for Early Revision as Committee Extends Copyr't Hearings til April: Duffy Slaps ASCAP," *Variety*, March 11, 1936. This is a summary of the bill's progress through Congress and the House Patents Committee hearings. Duffy's draft legislation meandered through the House, finally getting close to enactment in early 1936. The proposed legislation would have diminished the rights of composers over their work in the interests of bringing music as cheaply as possible to the consuming public. At the public hearings, Duffy argued that "Congress should give more consideration to the users than to creators," thereby threatening the very means by which ASCAP acquired much of the revenue that it distributed. Had his bill gone through, the $250 minimum levy that restaurants, clubs, and dance halls paid to be licensed to present music would have been repealed as "antiquated legislation." Duffy presented evidence to suggest that ASCAP had intimidated club and bar owners into paying this "minimum damage" levy, to which the society answered that it was only doing what it had to do to protect the rights of its members. "Tunesmiths only want what's coming to us," said one aggrieved composer, George M. Cohan. In return, Duffy, backed by the powerful broadcasting lobby, branded ASCAP as "racketeers."

13. Letter from Hubbell, April 13, 1931.

14. Letter from Gene Buck, president of ASCAP, September 13, 1935.
15. McHugh/St. John (c. 1967).
16. Palais-Royal "News Telegram," February 19, 1934.
17. Cast and sequence details from original programs in McHugh files; review in the *New York Times*, March 6, 1934.
18. It is included in Frankie Ortega's October 1956 McHugh album for Imperial and forms part of a McHugh medley played by the trombonist Urbie Green and recorded for Victor in May 1958 during a concert at Webster Hall, New York City.
19. Unattributed clipping in McHugh scrapbook.
20. Unattributed clipping in McHugh scrapbook.
21. "Harry Richman Back at Riviera Tonight" (undated) and "'Lost in a Fog' New Song Hit" (undated), unattributed clippings from McHugh scrapbook. The latter clipping implies that the show was still running in 1935.
22. Ford, "Composes Nation's Song Hits on His Bedsheet."
23. Interoffice memo from Jack Robbins, March 9, 1934.
24. Robbins panel advertisement from *Variety*, in McHugh scrapbook for late 1934.
25. "'In a Fog' Author wins right to sue for $25,000. Juanne Arliss [real name Judiah Wattenberg] widow of a prominent New York builder and composer of several song hits yesterday won the right to sue Metro-Goldwyn-Mayer for infringement of her song *I'm In A Fog . . .*," undated clipping in McHugh scrapbook for 1934.
26. "Tuning Titles," *Variety*, McHugh scrapbook for 1935.
27. Hollywood Reporter, "Radio's Hooray for Love: Dull Backstage Musical, Weak on Story but Excellent Music," *Variety*, May 16, 1935.
28. "Every Night at Eight," *Variety*, July 24, 1935.
29. McHugh (1967).
30. *Variety*, May 5, 1935.
31. "Fields–McHugh East," *Variety*, in McHugh scrapbook for 1935.
32. "An Evening with Dorothy Fields," April 9, 1972 (issued on CD as DRG 5187).
33. McHugh scrapbook for May 1935.
34. Gary Stevens, "An Evening with Dorothy Fields," liner note to DRG 5187, April 1998.
35. "An Evening with Dorothy Fields," April 9, 1972.
36. McHugh (1967).
37. George C. MacKinnon, "The Wisdom Box," from McHugh scrapbook for 1935.
38. McHugh/St. John (c. 1967).
39. Ibid.

40. Shipton, *Fats Waller*; Vance, *Fats Waller*.

41. Furia, *Poets of Tin Pan Alley*.

42. "Fields–M'Hugh Team Courted by Metro," *Variety*, from McHugh scrapbook for 1936.

43. Unattributed clipping advertising the songs in McHugh scrapbook.

44. Telegram from Leslie, April 4, 1936.

45. Telegram from Robbins, April 5, 1936.

CHAPTER 7. "DIMPLES"

1. William Boehnel, "Shirley Temple Is up to Her Old Tricks: Child Marvel Charms Audience in Sentimental Film at the Roxy," *New York World-Telegram*, October 10, 1936.

2. "Preview: Dimples," *Variety*, undated clipping in McHugh scrapbook for October 1936.

3. "Jimmy McHugh Writing Tunes for Shirley Temple's New Movie Has Raft of Successes," *Boston Post*, May 29, 1936.

4. Geoff Milne, "Shirley Temple—Oh, My Goodness!" liner note to Jasmine JASCD 111, January 1999.

5. Temple Black, *Child Star*.

6. Unattributed clipping in McHugh scrapbook for May 1936.

7. "113,262 (All Time Record) Attend *Dimples*," *Variety*, October 14, 1936.

8. Boehnel, "Shirley Temple Is up to Her Old Tricks."

9. "Preview: Dimples."

10. "Let's Sing Again," *Variety*, undated clipping in McHugh scrapbook for late 1936.

11. "Jimmy McHugh and Harold Adamson Have Been Granted Another Year's Contract by the New Universal," *Progress*, October 2, 1937.

12. Details of staff contracts from Loesser, *A Most Remarkable Fella*.

13. Paul Harrison, "'Ja Da, Diga Do' New Music to You," syndicated Hollywood news column, December 7, 1937.

14. Letter from Gus Kahn to McHugh, October 11, 1937.

15. Letter from Jack Robbins to McHugh, April 23, 1937.

16. Letter from Jack Kapp to McHugh, confirming assignment of song to Ethel Waters, January 4, 1938.

17. Card from Dorothy Fields in McHugh scrapbook for 1938.

18. McHugh/St. John (c. 1967).

19. Included in the documentary film *Judy Garland: By Myself*, directed by Susan Lacy, originally presented on the PBS program *American Masters*, 2004.

20. Frank S. Nugent, "The Screen in Review: Score Another for Deanna Durbin in 'Mad about Music' at the Roxy," *New York Times*, undated clipping in McHugh scrapbook for March 1938.

21. "'Mad about Music' Another Comedy Smash for Durbin," *Hollywood Reporter*, March 5, 1938.

22. "L. A. Legalists to Whistle in Court," unattributed clipping in McHugh scrapbook for 1938.

23. "McHugh, Adamson Sweep," *Hollywood Reporter*, October 17, 1938.

24. "That Certain Age," *Variety*, September 29, 1938.

25. The standing invitation to send him songs is in Dorsey's letter to McHugh of March 22, 1936. "Tommy Dorsey Previews McHugh–Adamson Songs," *Variety*, undated clipping in McHugh scrapbook for September 1938; band dates in letter from Bobby Dorsey to McHugh, August 15, 1938: "Thanks for your swell wire which came tonight. . . . We start to work Wed. with the program. . . . We open at the Paramount Theatre in N.Y. on Sept. 28th, and we'll go from there to the [New Yorker] hotel."

26. "Robbins World Sell-Out," *Variety*, October 6, 1937.

27. "Inheritor Last January of $51 Million . . . ," *Time*, November 22, 1937.

28. "Singers to Have Chance in Operas at Beverly Hills," Associated Press report, August 12, 1937.

29. "Debutante Plans Film Career," *Los Angeles Examiner*, undated clipping from McHugh scrapbook for 1937.

30. "Newlyweds on Northern Journey," Associated Press clipping in McHugh scrapbook for September 1938.

31. McHugh (1967).

32. Ibid.; McHugh/St. John (c. 1967).

33. McHugh (1967); McHugh/St. John (c. 1967).

34. George Holland, "Boston after Dark," unattributed clipping in McHugh scrapbook for May 1939.

35. McHugh/St. John (c. 1967).

36. Elinor Hughes, "Streets of Paris," *Boston Herald*, May 30, 1939.

37. "The New York Play: Streets of Paris," *Variety*, June 20, 1939.

38. "Harms, Inc. Presents 'Streets of Paris,'" *New York Enquirer*, June 26, 1939.

39. Unattributed clipping in McHugh scrapbook for June 1939.

40. "Newest Cantor before Camera," *Los Angeles Examiner*, June 20, 1940.

41. McHugh/St. John (c. 1967).

42. McHugh (1967).

43. Ibid.

44. Eliott Norton, "Musical Opens at Shubert: Keep Off the Grass First in Many Months," *Boston Post*, annotated in McHugh scrapbook as "May 1940."

45. John Anderson, "Keep Off the Grass Opens at Broadhurst," unattributed clipping in McHugh scrapbook for May 1940.

46. Duplicate of telegram sent by Dubin, August 6, 1943, in McHugh files.

47. McHugh (1967).

1. Furia, *Skylark*.
2. Ibid.
3. "'You'll Find Out' Sure Hit: All Elements Good in New Kyser Film," *Hollywood Reporter*, November 14, 1940.
4. Cameron Shipp, "You Keep His Songs Alive," *Coronet*, September 1945; "Attorney Lawrence P. McHugh" (obituary), *Daily News*, July 18, 1966, Huntingdon and Mount Union, Pennsylvania, edition.
5. "Music: How to Stay Contemporary," *Time*, May 31, 1948.
6. Loesser, *A Most Remarkable Fella*.
7. Ibid.
8. "Lester Jacobs Column," *Weekly Variety*, December 20, 1943.
9. Letter from McHugh to Loesser, December 1942.
10. Turley (1952).
11. "Bill Stern Uncovers Unique Story behind Song Hit 'Comin' In on a Wing and a Prayer,'" undated transcript from Bill Stern's "Sports Newsreel" program for NBC Radio, in McHugh scrapbook for early 1943.
12. "How to Write a Song Hit," undated clipping in McHugh scrapbook for 1943.
13. "Precisely how much does a hit tune earn, and where does the money come from? Take *Comin' In On A Wing and a Prayer*, written in 1943. It sold 800 thousand copies in the United States and 700 thousand in England, which fetched thirty thousand dollars. It brought in at least ten thousand dollars from 'mechanicals' that is to say records and transcriptions, and 7500 dollars from motion pictures. The total is 47,500 dollars" (Shipp, "You Keep His Songs Alive").
14. Ibid.
15. Original poster for *Higher and Higher*.
16. Zeke Zarchy, interview with author, Los Angeles, February 14, 2005.
17. Original poster for *Higher and Higher*. Details of the Rodgers and Hart rift can be found in Nolan, *Lorenz Hart*.
18. Original poster for *Higher and Higher*.
19. "I'd give anything to be back on the road again with Harry James and making onion sandwiches." Nancy Sinatra, speaking to McHugh during the Sinatra family Christmas dinner in the late 1940s, quoted in Summers and Swan, *Sinatra: The Life*.
20. "How to Write a Song Hit."
21. Ibid.
22. "Hollywood Friends of Songwriter Insist Boston Man Making Plans for New Marriage," *Boston Post*, undated clipping in McHugh scrapbook for 1941.
23. McHugh (1967).

24. Ibid.
25. Ibid.
26. *Time*, September 16, 1946.
27. "Phyllis Pablos . . . ," undated clipping in McHugh scrapbook for spring 1947.
28. "Doesn't Expect M'Hugh to Wed: Divorced Wife of Songwriter Scoffs at Reports He'll Marry Girl of 17," *Boston Post*, in McHugh scrapbook for April 1949, includes the following: "Mrs. Bessie McHugh of Allston . . . divorced him on grounds of desertion in 1945 after 31 years of marriage." Further information from Judy McHugh, interview with author, Los Angeles, February 12, 2005.
29. "Lester Jacobs Column," *Weekly Variety*, December 20, 1943.
30. Letter from Louis Armstrong, March 25, 1943.
31. Letter from Joe Glaser, February 2, 1944.
32. Letter of thanks from B. D. Russell, program director at Victory House, March 11, 1942.
33. Original poster for *All-Star Bond Rally*.
34. McHugh/St. John (c. 1967).
35. Ibid.
36. "$26,000,000 in Bonds Raised at Colorful Swim Show," *Los Angeles Times*, July 3, 1945, sports section; "War Bond Aquacade Raises 26 Millions," *Evening Herald-Express*, July 3, 1945.
37. Letter from Justice Murphy, February 12, 1947; cable from Senator Johnstone, January 7, 1947; War Department press release, February 10, 1947.
38. Debbie Reynolds, interview with author, Los Angeles, November 8, 2006.
39. Judy Kashalena, telephone interview with author, October 2005.
40. Dorothy Brooks, telephone interview with author, October 2005.
41. Ruth Fasken, "Jimmy McHugh, Oral Submission," January 11, 1948 [*sic*]. The events described mean that this transcription of a recorded interview must actually have been deposited in the McHugh archives during January 1949.
42. Elinor Hughes, "Opera House: As the Girls Go," *Boston Herald*, October 14, 1948.
43. Fasken, "Jimmy McHugh, Oral Submission."
44. "New Musical In Manhattan," *Time*, November 22, 1948.
45. "1948–1949 Broadway Season," *Variety*, May 25, 1949.

CHAPTER 9. "A LOVELY WAY TO SPEND AN EVENING"

1. Barbas, *First Lady of Hollywood*.
2. Dwight Whitney, "We Love You, Louella," *Time*, March 15, 1948.
3. Associated Press report, April 5, 1949.

4. Louella O. Parsons, "Jimmy McHugh Plans to Marry Anita Lhoest," undated clipping from McHugh scrapbook for April 1949.
5. "The Vincent X. Flaherty Column," *Los Angeles Examiner*, June 20, 1949; Al Franklin, "Board OKs Swim Meet," *Los Angeles Mirror*, July 7, 1949; "Honored—Jimmy McHugh," *Los Angeles Times*, July 29, 1949.
6. Meyers (1955).
7. Ibid.
8. "McHugh Gift: Iron Lung for Hospital," *Los Angeles Evening Herald and Express*, August 4, 1951.
9. Vincent X. Flaherty, "McHugh Has Habit of Booking Distant People," *Los Angeles Examiner*, August 24, 1951.
10. *Citizen* [city unknown], December 1, 1950; "Andrews Trio Aids Yule Show," *Los Angeles Examiner*, December 2, 1950; "Big Show for Vet Marines," *Los Angeles Herald-Express*, December 28, 1950; Walter Ames, "Jimmy McHugh to Film Top Musical Choices," unattributed clipping, January 5, 1951. Telescriptions were filmed performances sold individually to visual jukeboxes, to movie theaters, or (syndicated as complete programs) to television companies.
11. Louella O. Parsons, "Tony Martin to Play Star Role in 'The Life of Harry Richman,'" *Los Angeles Examiner*, January 8, 1951.
12. Jim Bacon, interview with author, Los Angeles, November 8, 2006.
13. Bob Considine, "Charity of Filmland," syndicated column, *Galveston Daily News*, November 5, 1951.
14. McHugh/St. John (c. 1967).
15. Ibid.
16. Clarke, *All or Nothing at All*.
17. McHugh/St. John (c. 1967).
18. Bourne, *Sophisticated Lady*.
19. McHugh/St. John (c. 1967).
20. Louella O. Parsons, "Lana Goes into Lawrence Story," syndicated column, *Cedar Rapids (Iowa) Gazette*, December 24, 1951.
21. McHugh/St. John (c. 1967).
22. Ibid.
23. Ibid.
24. James Bacon, "In Hollywood," Associated Press report, *Fitchburg (Massachusetts) Sentinel*, January 16, 1953.
25. Barbas, *First Lady of Hollywood*.
26. Reynolds, interview with author.
27. *Hollywood Reporter*, November 6, 1952.
28. Hy Gardner, "Coast to Coast," *Long Beach Press-Telegraph*, January 3, 1953.
29. Barbas, *First Lady of Hollywood*.
30. Bacon, interview with author.

31. Quoted by permission of Mamie Van Doren from her autobiographical Web site: http://www.mamievandoren.com/louella (accessed September 6, 2007).

32. Reynolds, interview with author.

33. McHugh (1967).

34. Army Archerd, interview with author, Los Angeles, November 8, 2006.

35. Bacon, interview with author.

36. *Los Angeles Times,* January 2, 1953; Louella O. Parsons's syndicated column, "In Hollywood," *Haywood (California) Daily Review,* October 17, 1955, and January 5, 1956.

37. Jimmy McHugh III, interview with author, Los Angeles, November 11, 2006.

38. "Tommy Sands," *Billboard,* April 13, 1957; "I predict a hit for Bonjour Tristesse which the three Paris Sisters have recorded for Jimmy McHugh," in Louella O. Parsons's column, *Los Angeles Examiner,* July 13, 1957; Florabel Muir, "Behind Hollywood's Silken Curtain" (report of party for Alberghetti at McHugh's home), *Daily News* [city unknown], August 8, 1955.

39. Ed Ames, interview with author, Beverly Hills, November 11, 2006.

40. "Blond Bombshell Mamie in Movies," *Newark (New Jersey) Advocate,* September 30, 1953.

41. http://www.mamievandoren.com; original flier for *Black Stockings.*

42. "Eve Marley who toured with the Jimmy McHugh show . . . ," in Louella O. Parsons's column, *Los Angeles Examiner,* November 27, 1957; program for McHugh show at "The Men's Club, Beverly Hills," January 19, 1955.

43. Letter from Bing Crosby to McHugh, January 8, 1953.

44. McHugh dates are from *Fabulous Las Vegas Magazine,* December 18, 1954; *Newslife,* January 20, 1955 (including review quoted); Louella O. Parsons's column, *Los Angeles Examiner,* February 4, 1955.

45. "Songwriter Ill," *Hammond (Indiana) Times,* August 3, 1956.

46. Hal Holly, "McHugh in No Mood for Love with Moody Discs," *Down Beat,* September 24, 1952.

47. *Time,* October 11, 1942.

48. Quoted from Don Emmons's autobiography, http://emmonstapdance.com/autobiography.htm (accessed November 2007).

49. *Variety,* April 11, 1956.

50. *Daily Mirror,* April 25, 1956.

51. *Billboard,* April 13, 1957.

52. "Jimmy McHugh Day: Issue Proclamation to Honor Composer," *Los Angeles Daily News Life,* July 9, 1954; correspondence from McHugh's personal files; *Beverly Hills Business,* March 1955.

53. Reynolds, interview with author.

1. "McHugh Has Reciprocal Pact with Stars of Hollywood Bowl Concert," *Los Angeles Mirror News*, August 31, 1959.
2. Ibid.
3. Buddy Bregman, interview with author, Los Angeles, November 10, 2006.
4. Louella O. Parsons's column, *Los Angeles Examiner*, June 30, 1959.
5. Frank Lee Donoghue, "Thousands at Bowl Honor Songwriter Jimmy McHugh," *Los Angeles Examiner*, September 6, 1959.
6. Anna Maria Alberghetti, telephone interview with author, September 5, 2007.
7. Telegram to McHugh from Bobby Darin, September 5, 1959.
8. Bregman, interview with author. In this conversation, Bregman recalled the opening tune as "Diga Diga Doo," but contemporary reviews suggest the opening orchestral piece was "I Feel a Song Coming On."
9. Donoghue, "Thousands at Bowl Honor Songwriter."
10. Ibid.; "Bowl Tribute Tops for Jimmy McHugh," *Los Angeles Examiner*, September 7, 1959; Mimi Clar, "Jimmy McHugh Songs Presented in Bowl," *Los Angeles Times*, September 7, 1959.
11. *ASCAP News*, September 1959.
12. Judy McHugh, interview with author.
13. Ibid.
14. Letter from Shearing to McHugh, April 23, 1957.
15. Cable from Stu Weiner and Julie Rifkind in MGM Promotion Office, June 27, 1960; letter from Brandt to McHugh, June 24, 1960.
16. "McHugh Has Reciprocal Pact with Stars of Hollywood Bowl Concert," *Los Angeles Mirror News*, August 31, 1959.
17. Keely Smith, "Cocoanut Grove Smash Opening Night Song Hit," *Hollywood Reporter*, November 5, 1962; "Levine Using Ripper Rhythm to Plug Pic," *Hollywood Reporter*, November 19, 1959; "Movies: A Simple Guy," *Newsweek*, February 22, 1960. In November 1960, Louella O. Parsons's column announced that McHugh would supervise the music for the English-language versions of three further Levine films, coproduced in Italy and including *Morgan the Pirate* and *The Wonders of Aladdin*. It appears that the original Italian scores were retained and that McHugh did not work on these movies, although the formation of a music publishing business, Levine–McHugh International, with McHugh as president, was announced in *Variety*, February 8, 1961.
18. Jimmy McHugh III, interview with author.
19. Ibid. Letter from Adele (McHugh) Carter, September 6, 2007.
20. Michael Feinstein, "Jimmy McHugh," *The Jimmy McHugh Songbook* (Miami: Warner Bros., 2000).
21. Judy McHugh, interview with author.

22. Ibid.

23. Mamie Van Doren, interview with author.

24. Mike Connolly, "Mr. Hollywood," *Pasadena Independent*, February 2, 1960.

25. Judy McHugh, interview with author.

26. "Louella O. Parsons," *Los Angeles Examiner*, May 5, 1962.

27. *Hollywood Reporter*, May 22, 1962; "Jimmy McHugh, Extension of the Remarks of Hon. Philip J. Philbin," *Congressional Record*, March 26, 1965.

28. "It's the 'First Lady Waltz,'" *San Francisco News-Call Bulletin*, July 27, 1963.

29. *Pasadena Independent*, August 30, 1962.

30. Jim Bacon, interview with author.

31. Cable from John F. Kennedy, June 1, 1963; Judy McHugh, interview with author; letter to McHugh from Edward M. Kennedy, August 6, 1968.

32. Adele (McHugh) Carter, letter to author.

33. Judy McHugh, interview with author.

34. *Hollywood Reporter*, October 19, 1962.

35. Ibid.

36. Judy McHugh, interview with author.

37. Jimmy McHugh III, interview with author.

38. Eddie Kafafian, interview with author, Los Angeles, February 12, 2005.

39. Livingston quoted in Jimmy McHugh III, interview with author.

40. "Official Song for Anniversary," *Citizen-News* [city unknown], January 9, 1964; "Congress Aims Tax at the Jukeboxes," *Los Angeles Herald-Examiner*, September 5, 1963; "McHugh by the Way Is Leading the ASCAP Fight," *New York Mirror*, September 20, 1963; "Jimmy McHugh and ASCAP . . . ," *Lowell (Massachusetts) Sun*, February 6, 1968; William F. Patry, *Copyright Law and Practice* (Washington, D.C.: Bureau of National Affairs, 1994).

41. "An Evening with Jimmy McHugh," *Hollywood Reporter*, May 10, 1962; *Daily Sun* [city unknown], September 24, 1962.

42. *Van Nuys News*, May 21, 1968.

43. Jimmy McHugh III, interview with author.

44. Adele (McHugh) Carter, letter to author.

45. Brown and Gaines, *The Love You Make*.

46. Judy McHugh, interview with author.

47. Letter to McHugh from Richard Rodgers, April 5, 1965.

48. Jim Bacon, "It's Fun City . . . ," *Los Angeles Herald-Examiner*, May 27, 1969; "Jimmy McHugh Who Cleffed More Than 500 Songs," *Daily Variety*, May 26, 1969; *New York Times*, May 24, 1969.

49. Louella O. Parsons, liner notes for *I Feel a Song Coming On: A Tribute to Jimmy McHugh from Capitol Records*, c. 1961.

50. "To Spice Up a Long Run," *New York Times*, April 12, 1981.

51. Michael Feinstein, letter to author, January 26, 2008.

52. Clarke, "The Story behind a Song Hit."

Bibliography

Barbas, Samantha. *The First Lady of Hollywood: A Biography of Louella Parsons*. Berkeley: University of California Press, 2005.

Barrett, Mary Ellin. *Irving Berlin: A Daughter's Memoir*. London: Simon and Schuster, 1995.

Bourne, Stephen. *Sophisticated Lady: A Celebration of Adelaide Hall*. London: Ethnic Communities Oral History Project, 2001.

Brown, Peter, and Steven Gaines. *The Love You Make: An Insider's Story of the Beatles*. New York: McGraw Hill, 1983.

Clarke, Donald. *All or Nothing at All: A Life of Sinatra*. London: Macmillan, 1997.

Collier, James Lincoln. *Duke Ellington*. New York: Oxford University Press, 1987.

Ellington, Duke. *Music Is My Mistress*. Garden City, N.Y.: Doubleday, 1973.

Furia, Philip. *The Poets of Tin Pan Alley: A History of America's Great Lyricists*. New York: Oxford University Press, 1990.

———. *Skylark: The Life and Times of Johnny Mercer*. New York: St. Martin's Press, 2003.

Gronow, Pekka, and Ilpo Saunio. *An International History of the Recording Industry*. Translated by C. Moseley. London: Cassell, 1998.

Haskins, Jim. *The Cotton Club*. London: Robson Books, 1977.

Krummel, D. W., and Stanley Sadie, eds. *The New Grove Handbook of Music Printing and Publishing*. London: Macmillan, 1990.

Lasker, Steven. *A Cotton Club Miscellany*. Venice, Calif.: privately published, 2002.

Loesser, Susan. *A Most Remarkable Fella: Frank Loesser and the Guys and Dolls in His Life*. 2nd ed. New York: Hal Leonard, 2000.

Machlin, Paul S. *Fats Waller: Performance in Transcription*. Middleton, Wis.: A-R Editions, 2001.

Nolan, Frederick. *Lorenz Hart: A Poet on Broadway*. New York: Oxford University Press, 1994.

Ogren, Kathy J. *The Jazz Revolution: Twenties America and the Meaning of Jazz*. New York: Oxford University Press, 1989.

Shapiro, Nat, and Nat Hentoff. *Hear Me Talkin' to Ya*. Harmondsworth, U.K.: Penguin, 1962.

Sheed, Wilfred. *The House That George Built*. New York: Random House, 2007.

Shipton, Alyn. *Fats Waller: His Life and Times*. New York: Universe, 1988.

———. *A New History of Jazz*. 2nd ed. New York: Continuum, 2007.

Singer, Barry. *Black and Blue: The Life and Lyrics of Andy Razaf*. New York: Schirmer, 1992.

Summers, Anthony, and Robbyn Swan. *Sinatra: The Life*. New York: Knopf, 2005.

Temple Black, Shirley. *Child Star: An Autobiography*. New York: McGraw Hill, 1988.

Tucker, Mark. *Ellington: The Early Years*. Oxford, U.K.: Bayou Press, 1991.

Vance, Joel. *Fats Waller*. London: Robson Books, 1979.

Waller, Maurice, and Anthony Calabrese. *Fats Waller*. London: Cassell, 1977.

Williams, Iain Cameron. *Underneath a Harlem Moon: The Harlem to Paris Years of Adelaide Hall*. London: Continuum, 2002.

Winer, Deborah Grace. *On the Sunny Side of the Street: The Life and Lyrics of Dorothy Fields*. New York: Schirmer, 1997.

Index

Alyn Shipton is a writer and broadcaster on jazz whose work appears in the London *Times* and on BBC radio. His books include *Handful of Keys: Conversations with Thirty Jazz Pianists; Jazz Makers: Vanguards of Sound;* and *A New History of Jazz*, which won the 2001 Jazz Journalists' Award for Best Book of the Year. He has edited several oral histories, including the auto-biographies of Danny Barker, George Shearing, and Doc Cheatham. His previous biographies include those of Bud Powell, Fats Waller, Ian Carr, and Dizzy Gillespie; the latter received the Association of Recorded Sound Collections award for best research in recorded music. In 2003, Shipton won the Marian McPartland/Willis Conover Award for lifetime achievement in jazz broadcasting. He is currently a lecturer in jazz history at the Royal Academy of Music in London.

Music in American Life

The University of Illinois Press
is a founding member of the
Association of American University Presses.

Composed in 10/13.5 Janson Text
with Coronet display
by Celia Shapland
at the University of Illinois Press
Designed by Copenhaver Cumpston
Manufactured by Thomson-Shore, Inc.

University of Illinois Press
1325 South Oak Street
Champaign, IL 61820-6903
www.press.uillinois.edu